DISCRIMINATION
and
DISPARITIES

Revised and Enlarged Edition

Thomas Sowell

BASIC BOOKS
New York

Basic Books
Hachette Book Group
1290 Avenue of the Americas, New York, NY 10104
www.basicbooks.com

Printed in the United States of America

Originally published in hardcover and ebook by Basic Books in March 2018

First Revised Edition: March 2019

Published by Basic Books, an imprint of Perseus Books, LLC, a subsidiary of Hachette Book Group, Inc. The Basic Books name and logo is a trademark of the Hachette Book Group.

The publisher is not responsible for websites (or their content) that are not owned by the publisher.

Library of Congress Control Number: 2018967905

ISBNs: 978-1-5416-4563-9 (hardcover), 978-1-5416-1783-4 (ebook)

LSC-C

Printing 10, 2021

To Professor Walter E. Williams,

who has labored in the same vineyard.

CONTENTS

PREFACE

The first edition of this book addressed the seemingly invincible fallacy that statistical disparities in socioeconomic outcomes imply either biased treatment of the less fortunate or genetic deficiencies in the less fortunate. This edition takes on other widespread fallacies, including a non sequitur underlying the prevailing social vision of our time— namely, that if individual economic benefits are not due solely to individual merit, there is justification for having politicians redistribute those benefits.

Each fallacy seems plausible on the surface, but that is what makes it worthwhile to scrutinize both their premises and the underlying facts. Many other new issues are addressed in this edition— in an international context, as in the first edition— but these two fallacies seem to be at the heart of much, if not most, of the prevailing social vision, sometimes summarized as "social justice."

Disagreements about social issues in general seem to be not only inevitable but even beneficial, when opposing sides are forced to confront contrary arguments that might not have been considered before, and examine empirical evidence not confronted before. Neither side may have taken all the factors into consideration, but having to cope with each other's different views may bring out considerations that neither side gave much thought to at the outset.

Such searching re-examinations of opposing views have become all too rare in politics, in the media and even in academia, where the proud claim was once made that "We are here to teach you *how* to think, not *what* to think." Today, with whole academic departments devoted to promoting particular conclusions about social issues, it seems especially important that such re-examinations of conflicting views take place *somewhere*, lest we become a people easily stampeded by rhetoric, garnished with a few arbitrarily selected facts or numbers.

Those readers who are looking for policy "solutions" will not find them here. But there are ample, if not more than ample, sources of feel-good "solutions" available elsewhere. The goal of *Discrimination and Disparities* will be met if it can provide clarification on some major social issues that are too often mired in dogmas and obfuscation. Individuals can then decide what policies suit their own values and goals. As Daniel Patrick Moynihan once said: "You're entitled to your own opinion, but you're not entitled to your own facts."[1]

Thomas Sowell
The Hoover Institution
Stanford University

In no society have all regions and all parts of the population developed equally.

Fernand Braudel

Chapter 1

Disparities and Prerequisites

Large disparities in the economic and other outcomes of individuals, groups and nations have produced reactions ranging from puzzlement to outrage. Attempts to explain the causes of these disparities have likewise produced a wide range of responses. At one end of a spectrum of explanations offered is the belief that those who have been less fortunate in their outcomes are genetically less capable. At the other end of the spectrum is the belief that those less fortunate are victims of other people who are more fortunate.

In between, there are many other explanations offered. But, whatever the particular explanation offered, there seems to be general agreement that the disparities found in the real world differ greatly from what might be expected by random chance. Yet the disparities in outcomes found in economic and other endeavors need not be due to either comparable disparities in innate capabilities or comparable disparities in the way people are treated by other people.

The disparities can also reflect the plain fact that success in many kinds of endeavors depends on prerequisites peculiar to each endeavor— and a relatively small difference in meeting those prerequisites can mean a very large difference in outcomes.

PREREQUISITES AND PROBABILITIES

The effect of prerequisites on probabilities is very straightforward. When there is some endeavor with five prerequisites for success, then by definition the chances of success in that endeavor depend on the chances of having all five of those prerequisites simultaneously. These prerequisites need not be rare in order to produce skewed distributions

1

of outcomes. For example, if these prerequisites are all so common that chances are two out of three that any given person has any one of those five prerequisites, nevertheless the odds are against having all five of the prerequisites for success in that endeavor.

When the chances of having any one of the five prerequisites are two out of three, as in this example, the chance of having all five simultaneously is two-thirds multiplied by itself five times. That comes out to be 32/243 in this example,[1] or about one out of eight. In other words, the chances of failure are about seven out of eight. All those people with fewer than five prerequisites have the same outcome— failure. Only those with all five of those prerequisites succeed. This creates a very skewed distribution of success, and nothing like a normal bell curve of distribution of outcomes that we might expect otherwise.[2]

What does this little exercise in arithmetic mean in the real world? One conclusion is that we should not expect success to be evenly or randomly distributed among individuals, groups, institutions or nations in endeavors with multiple prerequisites— which is to say, most meaningful endeavors. And if these are indeed prerequisites, then having four out of five prerequisites means nothing, as far as successful outcomes are concerned. In other words, people with most of the prerequisites for success may nevertheless be utter failures.

Whether a prerequisite that is missing is complex or simple, its absence can negate the effect of all the other prerequisites that are present. If you are illiterate, for example, all the other good qualities that you may have in abundance count for nothing in many, if not most, careers today. As late as 1950, more than 40 percent of the world's adult population were still illiterate. That included more than half the adults in Asia and Africa.[3]

If you are not prepared to undergo the extended toil and sacrifice that some particular endeavor may require, then despite having all the native potential for great success in that endeavor, and with all the doors of opportunity wide open, you can nevertheless become an utter failure.

Not all the prerequisites are necessarily within the sole control of the individual who has them or does not have them. Even extraordinary capacities in one or some of the prerequisites can mean nothing in the ultimate outcome.

Back in the early twentieth century, for example, Professor Lewis M. Terman of Stanford University launched a research project that followed 1,470 people with IQs of 140 and above for more than half a century. Data on the careers of men in this group— from an era when full-time careers for women were less common[4]— showed serious disparities even within this rare group, all of whom had IQs within the top one percent.

Some of these men had highly successful careers, others had more modest achievements, and about 20 percent were clearly disappointments. Of 150 men in this least successful category, only 8 received a graduate degree, and dozens of them received only a high school diploma. A similar number of the most successful men in Terman's group received 98 graduate degrees[5]— more than a tenfold disparity among men who were all in the top one percent in IQ.

Meanwhile, two men who were tested in childhood, and who failed to make the 140 IQ cutoff level, later earned Nobel Prizes in physics— while none of those men with IQs of 140 and above received a Nobel Prize in any field.[6] Clearly, then, all the men in Terman's group had at least one prerequisite for that extraordinary achievement— namely, a high enough IQ. And, equally clearly, there must have been other prerequisites that none of the hundreds of these men with IQs in the top one percent had.

As for factors behind differences in educational and career outcomes within Terman's group, the biggest differentiating factor was in family backgrounds. Men with the most outstanding achievements came from middle-class and upper-class families, and were raised in homes where there were many books. Half of their fathers were college graduates, at a time when that was far more rare than today.[7]

Among those men who were least successful, nearly one-third had a parent who had dropped out of school before the eighth grade.[8] Even extraordinary IQs did not eliminate the need for other prerequisites.

Sometimes what is missing may be simply someone to point an individual with great potential in the right direction. An internationally renowned scholar once mentioned, at a social gathering, that when

he was a young man he had not thought about going to college—
until someone else urged him to do so. Nor was he the only person of
exceptional ability of whom that was true.[9]

Some other people, including people without his great abilities,
would automatically apply to college if they came from particular
social groups where that was a norm. But without that one person
who urged him to seek higher education, this particular internationally
renowned scholar might well have become a good worker in some line
of work requiring no college degree, but not a world-class scholar.

There may be more or less of an approximation of a normal bell
curve, as far as how many people have any particular prerequisite,
and yet a very skewed distribution of success, based on having all the
prerequisites simultaneously. This is not only true in theory, empirical
evidence suggests that it is true also in practice.

In golf, for example, there is something of an approximation of
a bell curve when it comes to the distribution of such examples of
individual skills as the number of putts per round of golf, or driving
distances off the tee. And yet there is a grossly skewed distribution
of outcomes requiring a whole range of golf skills— namely, winning
Professional Golfers' Association (PGA) tournaments.[10]

Most professional golfers have never won a single PGA tournament
in their entire lives,[11] while just three golfers— Arnold Palmer, Jack
Nicklaus and Tiger Woods— won more than 200 PGA tournaments
between them.[12] Moreover, there are similarly skewed distributions of
peak achievements in baseball and tennis, among other endeavors.[13]

Given multiple prerequisites for many human endeavors, we
should not be surprised if economic or social advances are not evenly
or randomly distributed among individuals, groups, institutions or
nations at any given time. Nor should we be surprised if the laggards
in one century forge ahead in some later century, or if world leaders
in one era become laggards in another era. When the gain or loss of
just one prerequisite can turn failure into success or turn success into
failure, it should not be surprising, in a changing world, if the leaders
and laggards of one century or millennium exchange places in some
later century or millennium.

If the prerequisites themselves change over time, with the development of new kinds of endeavors, or if advances in human knowledge revolutionize existing endeavors, the chance of a particular pattern of success and failure becoming permanent may be greatly reduced.

Perhaps the most revolutionary change in the evolution of human societies was the development of agriculture— within the last 10 percent of the existence of the human species. Agriculture made possible the feeding of concentrated populations in cities, which in turn have been (and remain) the sources of most of the landmark scientific, technological and other advances of the human race that we call civilization.[14]

The earliest known civilizations arose in geographic settings with strikingly similar characteristics. These included river valleys subject to annual floodings, whether in ancient Mesopotamia, in the valley of the Indus River on the Indian subcontinent in ancient times, along the Nile in ancient Egypt, or in the Yellow River valley in ancient China.[15]

Clearly there were other prerequisites, since these particular combinations of things had not produced agriculture, or civilizations dependent on agriculture, for most of the existence of the human species. Genetic characteristics peculiar to the races in these particular locations hardly seem likely to be the key factor, since the populations of these areas are by no means in the forefront of human achievements today.

Patterns of very skewed distributions of success have long been common in the real world— and such skewed outcomes contradict some fundamental assumptions on both the political left and right. People on opposite sides of many issues may both assume a background level of probabilities that is not realistic.

Yet that flawed perception of probabilities— and the failure of the real world to match expectations derived from that flawed perception— can drive ideological movements, political crusades and judicial decisions, up to and including decisions by the Supreme Court of the United States, where "disparate impact" statistics, showing different outcomes for different groups, have been enough to create a presumption of discrimination.

In the past, similar statistical disparities were enough to promote genetic determinism, from which came eugenics, laws forbidding inter-racial marriages and, where there were other prerequisites for monumental catastrophe, the Holocaust.

In short, gross disparities among peoples in their economic outcomes, scientific discoveries, technological advances and other achievements have inspired efforts at explanation that span the ideological spectrum. To subject these explanations to the test of facts, it may be useful to begin by examining some empirical evidence about disparities among individuals, social groups, institutions and nations.

EMPIRICAL EVIDENCE

Behind many attempts to explain, and change, glaring disparities in outcomes among human beings is the implicit assumption that such disparities would not exist without corresponding disparities in either people's genetic makeup or in the way they are treated by other people. These disparities exist both among individuals and among aggregations of people organized into institutions of various sorts, ranging from families to businesses to whole nations.

Skewed distributions of outcomes are also common in nature, in outcomes over which humans have no control, ranging from lightning to earthquakes and tornadoes.

People

While it might seem plausible that equal, or at least comparable, outcomes would exist among people in various social groups, in the absence of some biased human intervention, or some genetic differences affecting those people's outcomes, neither belief survives the test of empirical evidence.

A study of National Merit Scholarship finalists, for example, found that, among finalists from five-child families, the first-born was the finalist more often than the other four siblings combined.[16] First-borns were also a majority of the finalists in two-child, three-child, and four-child families.[17] If there is not equality of outcomes among people born to the same parents and raised under the same roof, why should equality of outcomes be expected— or assumed— when conditions are not nearly so comparable?

Such results are a challenge to believers in either heredity or environment, as those terms are conventionally used.

IQ data from Britain, Germany and the United States showed that the average IQ of first-born children was higher than the average IQ of their later-born siblings. Moreover, the average IQ of second-born children as a group was higher than the average IQ of third-born children.[18]

A similar pattern was found among young men given mental tests for military service in the Netherlands. The first-born averaged higher mental test scores than their siblings, and the other siblings likewise averaged higher scores than those born after them.[19] Similar results were found in mental test results for Norwegians.[20] The sample sizes in these studies ranged into the hundreds of thousands.[21]

These advantages of the first-born seem to carry over into later life in many fields. Data on male medical students at the University of Michigan, class of 1968, showed that the proportion of first-born men in that class was more than double the proportion of later-born men as a group, and more than ten times the proportion among men who were fourth-born or later.[22] A 1978 study of applicants to a medical school in New Jersey showed the first-born over-represented among the applicants, and still more so among the successful applicants.[23] Other studies, some going as far back as the nineteenth century, show similar results.[24]

Most other countries do not have as high a proportion of their young people go on to a college or university education as in the United States. But, whatever the proportion in a given country, the first-born tend to go on to higher education more often than do later siblings. A study of Britons in 2003 showed that 22 percent of those who were the eldest child went on to receive a degree, compared to 11 percent of those who were the fourth child and 3 percent of those who were the tenth child.[25]

A study of more than 20,000 young people in late twentieth-century France showed that 18 percent of those males who were an only child completed four years of college, compared to 16 percent of male first-born children— and just 7 percent of males who were fifth-born or later born. Among females the disparity was slightly larger. Twenty-three percent who were an only child completed four years of college, compared to 19 percent who were first-born, and just 5 percent of those who were fifth-born or later.[26]

Birth order differences persist as people move into their careers. A study of about 4,000 Americans concluded that "The decline in average earnings is even more pronounced" than the decline in education between those born earlier and those born later.[27] Other studies have shown the first-born to be over-represented among lawyers in the greater Boston area[28] and among Members of Congress.[29] Of the 29 original astronauts in the Apollo program that put a man on the moon, 22 were either first-born or an only child.[30] The first-born and the only child were also over-represented among leading composers of classical music.[31]

Consider how many things are the same for children born to the same parents and raised under the same roof— race, the family gene pool, economic level, cultural values, educational opportunities, parents' educational and intellectual levels, as well as the family's relatives, neighbors and friends— and yet the difference in birth order alone has made a demonstrable difference in outcomes.

Whatever the general advantages or disadvantages the children in a particular family may have, the only obvious advantage that applies only to the first-born, or to an only child, is the undivided attention of the parents during early childhood development.

The fact that twins tend to average several points lower IQs than people born singly[32] reinforces this inference. Conceivably, the lower average IQs of twins might have originated in the womb but, when one of the twins is stillborn or dies early, the surviving twin averages an IQ closer to that of people born singly.[33] This suggests that with twins, as with other children, the divided or undivided attention of the parents may be key.

In addition to quantitatively different amounts of parental attention available to children born earlier and later than their siblings, there are also qualitative differences in parental attention to children in general, from one social class to another.[34] Children of parents with professional occupations have been found to hear an average of 2,100 words per hour, while children from working-class families hear 1,200 words per hour, and children from families on welfare hear 600 words per hour.[35] Other studies suggest that there are also *qualitative* differences in the *manner* of parent-child interactions in different social classes.[36]

Against this background, expectations or assumptions of equal or comparable outcomes from children raised in such different ways have no basis. Nor can later different outcomes in schools, colleges or employment be automatically attributed to those who teach, grade or hire them, when empirical evidence shows that how people were raised can affect how they turn out as adults.

It is not simply that youngsters raised in different ways may have different levels of ability as adults. People from different social backgrounds may also have different goals and priorities— a possibility paid little or no attention in many studies that measure how much opportunity there is by how much upward movement takes place,[37] as if everyone is equally striving to move up, and only society's barriers produce different outcomes.

Most notable achievements involve multiple factors— beginning with a desire to succeed in the particular endeavor, and a willingness to do what it takes, without which all the native ability in an individual and all the opportunity in a society mean nothing, just as the desire and the opportunity mean nothing without the ability.

What this suggests, among other things, is that an individual, a people, or a nation may have some, many or most of the prerequisites for a given achievement without having any real success in producing that achievement. And yet that individual, that people or that nation may suddenly burst upon the scene with spectacular success when whatever the missing factor or factors are finally get added to the mix.

Poor and backward nations that suddenly moved to the forefront of human achievements include Scotland, beginning in the eighteenth century, and Japan beginning in the nineteenth century. Both had rapid rises, as time is measured in history.

Scotland was for centuries one of the poorest, most economically and educationally lagging nations on the outer fringes of European civilization. There was said to be no fourteenth-century Scottish baron who could write his own name.[38] And yet, in the eighteenth and nineteenth centuries, a disproportionate number of the leading intellectual figures in Britain were of Scottish ancestry— including James Watt in engineering, Adam Smith in economics, David Hume in philosophy, Joseph Black in chemistry, Sir Walter Scott in literature and John Stuart Mill in economics and philosophy.

Among the changes that had occurred among the Scots was their Protestant churches' crusade promoting the idea that everyone should learn to read, so as to be able to read the Bible personally, rather than have priests tell them what it says and means. Another change was a more secular, but still fervent, crusade to learn the English language, which replaced their native Gaelic among the Scottish lowlanders, and thereby opened up far more fields of written knowledge to the Scots.

In some of those fields, including medicine and engineering, the Scots eventually excelled the English, and became renowned internationally. These were mostly Scottish lowlanders, rather than highlanders, who continued to speak Gaelic for generations longer.

Japan was likewise a poor, poorly educated and technologically backward nation, as late as the middle of the nineteenth century. The Japanese were astonished to see a train for the first time, that train being presented to them by American Commodore Matthew Perry, whose ships visited Japan in 1853.[39] Yet, after later generations of extraordinary national efforts to catch up with the Western world technologically, these efforts led to Japan's being in the forefront of technology in a number of fields in the latter half of the twentieth century. Among other things, Japan produced a bullet train that exceeded anything produced in the United States.

Other extraordinary advances have been made by a particular people, rather than by a nation state. We have become so used to seeing numerous world-class performances by Jewish intellectual figures in the arts and sciences that it is necessary to note that this has been an achievement that burst upon the world as a widespread social phenomenon in the nineteenth and twentieth centuries, even though there had been isolated Jewish intellectual figures of international stature in some earlier centuries.

As a distinguished economic historian put it: "Despite their vast advantage in literacy and human capital for many centuries, Jews played an almost negligible role in the history of science and technology before and during the early Industrial Revolution." Moreover, "the great advances in science and mathematics between 1600 and 1750 do not include work associated with Jewish names."[40]

Whatever the potentialities of Jews during the era of the industrial revolution, and despite their literacy and other human capital, there was often little opportunity for them to gain access to the institutions of the wider society in Europe, where the industrial revolution began. Jews were not admitted to most universities in Europe prior to the nineteenth century.

Late in the eighteenth century, the United States became a pioneer in granting Jews the same legal rights as everyone else, as a result of the Constitution's general ban against federal laws that discriminate on the basis of religion. France followed suit after the revolution of 1789, and other nations began easing or eliminating various bans on Jews in various times and places during the nineteenth century.

In the wake of these developments, Jews began to flow, and then to flood, into universities. By the 1880s, for example, Jews were 30 percent of all the students at Vienna University.[41] The net result in the late nineteenth century, and in the twentieth century, was a relatively sudden proliferation of internationally renowned Jewish figures in many fields, including fields in which Jews were virtually non-existent among the leaders in earlier centuries.

From 1870 to 1950, Jews were greatly over-represented among prominent figures in the arts and sciences, relative to their proportion of the population in various European countries and in the United States. In the second half of the twentieth century, with Jews being less than one percent of the world's population, they received 22 percent of the Nobel Prizes in chemistry, 32 percent in medicine and 32 percent in physics.[42]

Here, as in other very different contexts, changes in the extent to which prerequisites are met *completely* can have dramatic effects on outcomes in a relatively short time, as history is measured. The fact that Jews rose dramatically in certain fields after various barriers were removed does not mean that other groups would automatically do the same, if barriers against them were removed, for the Jews *already* had various other prerequisites for such achievements— notably widespread literacy during centuries when illiteracy was the norm in the world at large— and Jews needed only to add whatever was needed to complete the required ensemble.

Conversely, China was for centuries the most technologically advanced nation in the world, especially during what were called the Middle Ages in Europe. The Chinese had cast iron a thousand years before the Europeans.[43] A Chinese admiral led a voyage of discovery that was longer than Columbus' voyage, generations before Columbus' voyage,[44] and in ships far larger and technologically more advanced than Columbus' ships.[45]

One crucial decision in fifteenth-century China, however, set in motion a radical change in the relative positions of the Chinese and the Europeans. Like other nations demonstrably more advanced than others, the Chinese regarded those others as innately inferior— as "barbarians," just as the Romans likewise regarded peoples beyond the domain of the Roman Empire.

Convinced by the exploratory voyages of its ships that there was nothing to be learned from other peoples in other places, the government of China decided in 1433 to not only discontinue such voyages, but to *forbid* such voyages, or the building of ships capable of making such voyages, and to greatly reduce the influence of the outside world on Chinese society.

Plausible as this decision might have seemed at the time, it came as Europe was emerging from its "dark ages" of retrogression in the wake of the decline and fall of the Roman Empire, and was now experiencing a Renaissance of progress in many ways— including progress based on developing things that had originated in China, such as printing and gunpowder. Columbus' ships, though not up to the standards of those once made in China, were sufficient to cross the Atlantic Ocean in search of a route to India— and to inadvertently make the world-changing discovery of a whole hemisphere.

In short, Europe had expanding opportunities for progress, both within itself and in the larger world opened up to it by its expansion into the other half of the planet, at a time when China's rulers had chosen the path of isolation— not total, but substantial, isolation. The strait jacket of isolation, inflicted on many parts of the world by geographic barriers that left whole peoples and nations both poor and backward,[46] was inflicted on China by its own rulers. The net result over the centuries that followed was that China fell behind in an era of great technological and economic progress elsewhere in the world.

In the pitiless international jungle, this meant that other countries not only surpassed China but imposed their will on a vulnerable China, which declined to the status of a Third World country, partly subordinated to other countries in various ways— including a loss of territory, as the Portuguese took over the port of Macao, the British took over the port of Hong Kong and eventually Japan seized much territory on the mainland of China.

What China lost were not the prerequisites represented by the qualities of its people, but the wisdom of its rulers who, with one crucial decision— the loss of just one prerequisite— forfeited the country's preeminence in the world.

That the qualities of the Chinese people endured was evidenced by the worldwide success of millions of "overseas Chinese" emigrants, who arrived in many countries in Southeast Asia and in the Western Hemisphere, often destitute and with little education— and yet rose over the generations to prosperity, and in many individual cases even great wealth. The contrast between the fate of China and the fate of the "overseas Chinese" was demonstrated when, as late as 1994, the 57 million "overseas Chinese" produced as much wealth as the billion people living in China.[47]

Among the more dire national projects that failed among other nations— fortunately, in this case— for lack of one prerequisite was the attempt by Nazi Germany to create a nuclear bomb. Hitler not only had such a program, he had it before the United States launched a similar program. Germany was, at that point, in the forefront of science in nuclear physics. However, it so happened that, at that particular juncture in history, many of the leading nuclear physicists in the world were Jewish— and Hitler's fanatical anti-Semitism not only precluded their participation in his nuclear bomb project, his threat to the survival of Jews in general led many of these physicists to leave Europe and immigrate to the United States.

It was expatriate Jewish nuclear physicists who brought the threat of a Nazi nuclear bomb to President Franklin D. Roosevelt's attention, and urged the creation of an American program to produce such a bomb before the Nazis got one. Moreover, Jewish scientists— both expatriate and American— played a major role in the development of the American nuclear bomb.[48]

These scientists were a key resource that the United States had and that Hitler could not have, as a result of his own racial fanaticism. The whole world escaped the prospect of mass annihilation and/or crushing subjugation to Nazi oppression and dehumanization because Hitler's nuclear program lacked one key factor. He had some leading nuclear physicists, but not enough.

Institutions

China was by no means the only nation to forfeit a superior position among the nations of the world. Ancient Greece and the Roman Empire were far more advanced than their British or Scandinavian contemporaries, who were largely illiterate at a time when Greeks and Romans had landmark intellectual giants, and were laying the intellectual and material foundations of Western civilization. As late as the tenth century, a Muslim scholar noted that Europeans grew more pale the farther north you go and also that the "farther they are to the north the more stupid, gross, and brutish they are."[49]

Such a correlation between complexion and ability would be taboo today, but there is little reason to doubt that a very real correlation existed among Europeans as of the time when this observation was made. The fact that Northern Europe and Western Europe would move ahead of Southern Europe economically and technologically many centuries later was a heartening sign that backwardness in a given era does not mean backwardness forever. But that does not deny that great economic and social disparities have existed among peoples and nations at given times and places.

Particular institutions, such as business enterprises, have likewise risen or fallen dramatically over time. Any number of leading American businesses began at the level of the lowly peddler (Macy's and Bloomingdale's, for example), or were started by men born in poverty (J.C. Penney; F.W. Woolworth) or began in a garage (Hewlett Packard). Conversely, there have been leading businesses that have declined from the pinnacles of profitable success, even into bankruptcy— sometimes with the loss of just one prerequisite.

For more than a hundred years, the Eastman Kodak company was the dominant firm in the photographic industry throughout the world. It was George Eastman who, in the late nineteenth century, first made photography accessible to great numbers of ordinary people, with his cameras and film that did not require the technical expertise of professional photographers. Before Kodak cameras and film appeared, professional photographers had to know how to apply light-sensitive emulsions to photographic plates that went into big, cumbersome cameras sitting on tripods, and know how to later chemically develop the images taken and then print pictures.

Small and simple, handheld Kodak cameras, and rolls of Kodak film in place of photographic plates, enabled people with no technical knowledge at all to take pictures and then leave the developing and printing of those pictures to others. Kodak cameras and film spread internationally. For decades, Eastman Kodak sold most of the film in the entire world. It continued to sell most of the film in the world market, even after film began to be produced in other countries and Fuji film from Japan made major inroads in the late twentieth century, gaining a 21 percent worldwide market share by 1993.[50]

Eastman Kodak also supplied both amateur and professional photographers with a wide range of photographic equipment and supplies, based on film technology. For more than a century, Eastman Kodak clearly had all the prerequisites for success. As of 1988, the company employed more than 145,000 workers around the world, and its annual revenues peaked at nearly $16 billion in 1996.[51] Yet its worldwide dominance came to a remarkably sudden end in the early twenty-first century, when its income plummeted and the company collapsed into bankruptcy.[52]

Just one key factor changed in the photographic industry— the substitution of digital cameras for film cameras. Worldwide sales of film cameras peaked in the year 2000, when their sales were more than four times the sales of digital cameras. But, three years later, digital camera sales in 2003 surpassed film camera sales for the first time. Then, just two years after that, digital camera sales exceeded the peak sales that film cameras had reached in 2000, and now digital camera sales were more than four times the sales of film cameras.[53]

Eastman Kodak, which had produced the world's first electronic image sensor,[54] was undone by its own invention, which other companies developed to higher levels in digital cameras. These included electronics companies not initially in the photographic industry, such as Sony, whose share of the digital camera market was more than double that of Eastman Kodak by the end of the twentieth century and in the early twenty-first century,[55] when digital camera sales skyrocketed.

With the sudden collapse of the market for film cameras, Kodak's vast array of photographic apparatus and supplies, based on film technology, suddenly lost most of their market, and the Eastman Kodak company disintegrated economically. Its mastery of existing prerequisites for success meant nothing when just one of those prerequisites changed. Nor was this collapse from overwhelming dominance in its field unique to Eastman Kodak.[56]

Nature

In nature, as in human endeavors, there can be multiple prerequisites for various natural phenomena, and these multiple prerequisites can likewise lead to very skewed distributions of outcomes.

Multiple factors have to come together in order to create tornadoes, and more than 90 percent of all the tornadoes in the entire world occur in just one country— the United States.[57] Yet there is nothing startlingly unique about either the general climate or the terrain of the United States that cannot be found, as individual features, in various other places around the world. But all the prerequisites for tornadoes do not come together as often, anywhere in the rest of the world, as in the United States.

Similarly, lightning occurs more often in Africa than in Europe and Asia put together, even though Asia alone is larger than Africa or any other continent.[58] Thunderstorms have prerequisites, and those prerequisites all come together more often in some geographic settings than in others. In the United States, thunderstorms are 20 times as frequent in southern Florida as in coastal California.[59]

Among many other skewed distributions in nature is the fact that earthquakes are as common around the rim of the Pacific Ocean, both in Asia and in the Western Hemisphere, as they are rare around the rim of the Atlantic.[60] Among other highly skewed outcomes in nature is that some geographic settings produce many times more species than others. The Amazon region of South America is one such setting:

> South America's Amazon Basin contains the world's largest expanse of tropical rainforest. Its diversity is renowned. On a single Peruvian tree, Wilson (1988) found 43 species of ants, comparable to the entire ant fauna of the British Isles.[61]

Similar gross disparities have also been found between the number of species of fish in the Amazon region of South America, compared to the number in Europe: "Eight times as many species of fish have been caught in an Amazonian pond the size of a tennis court as exist in all the rivers of Europe."[62]

Human beings are of course also part of nature. Genetic similarities between chimpanzees and human beings extend to well over 90 percent of their genetic makeup. But chimpanzees have obviously not produced 90 percent of what humans have produced, such as airplanes, computers and rockets that can reach the moon and go beyond, into outer space. There is even a microscopic, worm-like creature which also has most of its genetic make-up match that of human beings.[63] But having many or most prerequisites can count for nothing as far as producing the ultimate outcome.

IMPLICATIONS

What can we conclude from all these examples of highly skewed distributions of outcomes around the world? Neither in nature nor among human beings are either equal or randomly distributed outcomes automatic. On the contrary, grossly unequal distributions of outcomes are common, both in nature and among people, including in circumstances where neither genes nor discrimination are involved.

What seems a more tenable conclusion is that, as economic historian David S. Landes put it, "The world has never been a level playing field."[64] The idea that the world *would* be a level playing field, if it were not for either genes or discrimination, is a preconception in defiance of both logic and facts. Nothing is easier to find than sins among human beings, but to automatically make those sins the sole, or even primary, cause of different outcomes among different peoples is to ignore many other reasons for those disparities. Geography and demography, for example, are among the many factors that make equal or random outcomes among human beings very unlikely.

Geography

Geography is an intractable obstacle to the equal or random outcomes implicitly assumed to be the norm, in the absence of discrimination or genetic differences. The huge cost difference between water transportation and land transportation is just one aspect of geography that creates skewed distributions of outcomes.

Back in the days of the Roman Empire, the cost of shipping a cargo across the length of the Mediterranean Sea— more than 2,000 miles— was less than the cost of carting that same cargo 75 miles inland.[65] This meant that people living on the coast had a vastly larger universe of economic and cultural interactions with other people available to them. A geographic treatise pointed out that, in ancient times, the European hinterland was "lingering in a backward civilization as compared with the Mediterranean coastland."[66]

As late as the middle of the nineteenth century, San Francisco could be reached both faster and cheaper by water, across the Pacific Ocean from a port in China, than by land from the center of the United States.[67] Here again, what such huge cost differentials between land transportation and water transportation meant was that people living on coasts often had a vastly larger economic and cultural universe available to them than did those living inland.

People living on a coast have long been able to communicate and interact, economically and otherwise, over long distances with other people on that same coast, as well as more distant people elsewhere in many cases. There is no way that people located in more isolated areas, whether in distant mountain villages, tropical jungles or inaccessible deserts had comparable opportunities for economic and social development over the centuries.

Modern transportation revolutions in land, sea and air transport have eroded— but by no means eliminated— cost differences in access to a wider world by water than by land. Moreover, there is nothing that the modern transportation revolution can do to eliminate the continuing effects of past centuries of very different economic and social evolution by peoples living in very different geographic circumstances.

Coastal peoples around the world have long tended to be more prosperous and more advanced than people of the same race living farther inland, while people living in river valleys have likewise tended to be more prosperous and more advanced than people living up in the isolated hills and mountains around the world.[68]

Transportation costs to and from mountain communities have long been prohibitively expensive for all but goods with a very high value concentrated in products of a small size and weight. Exquisite handicrafts of various sorts, produced in many mountain communities around the world[69] have provided some economic relief from the poverty long common in such communities.

Climate and soil are likewise geographic obstacles to equal prospects or equal outcomes. Most of the most fertile land in the world is in the temperate zones and little or none in the tropics.[70] That affects not only agriculture, but also the timing and pace of urbanization, based on the productivity of food required to feed concentrated urban populations.

Areas that are located both near the sea and in the temperate zones have been found to have 8 percent of the world's inhabited land area, 23 percent of the world's population, and 53 percent of the world's Gross Domestic Product.[71]

Not all of this is due to the *current* significance of fertile land and agriculture. But even highly industrialized and commercial societies today arose only after centuries of civilization and urban development whose origins, scope and pace derived from an agriculture sufficiently productive to enable urban communities to be founded and grow, long before such societies could develop comparably in places with less fertile land.

Societies situated differently, as regards such geographic factors as fertile land, navigable waterways and the presence or absence of creatures capable of being used as draft animals or beasts of burden had— for centuries or millennia— very different prospects of developing into advanced societies at the same pace.[72]

Much of the Western Hemisphere is similar, geographically, to Europe, in terms of fertile soil, navigable waterways and climate, but was *utterly devoid* of heavy-duty draft animals and beasts of burden like horses and oxen before such animals, which played major roles in the economic development of Europe, were brought to the Western Hemisphere by Europeans. Even the smaller llamas, used as beasts of burden by the Incas before the Europeans arrived, were confined to a fraction of South America.

Factors with major influences on these societies' development in centuries past— such as the fertility of their land— may not be nearly so important today, when highly industrialized or commercial societies can readily import food and raw materials from a globalized world economy. Similarly, the once crucial socioeconomic role of draft animals and beasts of burden has now been largely replaced by automobiles, trucks, tractors, railroads and airplanes in most of the industrially and commercially developed countries. But draft animals and beasts of burden played major roles in these countries developing to the point where such animals could be replaced by self-propelled mechanisms. Societies today can differ greatly in their socioeconomic development, as a result of the extent to which the pace of their development was facilitated or impeded by geographic factors in centuries past.

Geographic differences alone have been enough to preclude the equal opportunity that many seem to assume would exist in the absence of discriminatory bias or genetic differences. Mountain peoples are not a race, since they exist on different continents around the world, and were isolated from each other for millennia. Yet they share many social characteristics that have made their options and achievements very different from the options and achievements of people in the surrounding lowlands, and still more different from those of people living in coastal areas.

Mountain peoples are about 10 to 12 percent of the world's population,[73] which may seem small, but in absolute numbers that is a population more than twice the size of the population of the United States, and more than ten times the size of Italy's population.[74] But, while Italy has produced such landmark figures in human history as Galileo, da Vinci, Michelangelo, Marconi and Fermi, the world's mountain communities have produced no such individuals, despite having a far larger population than Italy.

This is not a criticism of mountain peoples, but an attempt to demonstrate the consequences of the inherent constrictions of their geographic circumstances. Mountain people *within Italy* have produced no such landmark achievements as those in the rest of that country's population. A classic study of a mountain village in Italy in the mid-twentieth century found the people living there to be not only desperately poor but also largely cut off from the outside world.[75] Most mountain peoples have had nothing resembling equal opportunity, compared to their contemporaries in more favorable geographic settings, even though the cause of their plight was not other human beings but the inherent geographic constraints of their circumstances.

The influence of geography is not limited to the specific geographic characteristics of a given location, such as water transport costs versus land transport costs, or differences in the fertility of the soil. Geographic *location as such* can have a major influence. When agriculture developed in the Middle East during prehistoric times, and with it a more advanced urban civilization with a written language among other things, knowledge of such advances reached Greece long before it reached the British Isles or Scandinavia, simply because Greece was located closer to where such advances originated. Ancient Greek civilization became far more advanced, by almost any standard, than the societies in the British Isles or Scandinavia at that time.

Over the centuries, as other landmark advances took place at various locations around the world, particular peoples located nearer to the source of such advances had opportunities to advance themselves that peoples located farther away did not. Many other historic developments— ranging from wars, political upheavals, devastating epidemics, and mass migrations to landmark voyages of discovery, and both scientific and technological breakthroughs— all combined to present radically different opportunities to different peoples at different places, and even within a given society.

Multi-ethnic societies, with groups from various other societies around the world, can inherit to some extent the cultural consequences of the very different advantages and disadvantages of the geographic locations of those other societies, as well as current influences of the society in which they all live today. Scholars who have devoted themselves to the study of such things have often reached radically different conclusions from those who implicitly assume that an absence of equal outcomes is both unusual and suspicious.

The conclusion of French historian Fernand Braudel— that "In no society have all regions and all parts of the population developed equally"[76]— is a conclusion reached by many others who have done empirical studies of peoples, institutions and societies around the world. A landmark international study of ethnic groups by Professor Donald L. Horowitz of Duke University concluded that the idea of "proportional representation" of such groups was something that "few, if any, societies have ever approximated."[77] The research of Professor Myron Weiner of MIT led him to point out: "All multi-ethnic societies exhibit a tendency for ethnic groups to engage in different occupations, have different levels (and, often, types) of education, receive different incomes, and occupy a different place in the social hierarchy."[78] An international study of the ethnic makeup of military forces found that "militaries fall far short of mirroring, even roughly, the multi-ethnic societies" from which their people are drawn.[79]

Specific locational differences in various socioeconomic outcomes and intellectual achievements have also been found. Professor Angelo Codevilla, for example, divided Europe into various cultural zones and concluded that "a European child will have a very different life" if born "east or west of a line that starts at the Baltics and stretches southward along Poland's eastern border, down Slovakia's western border and along the eastern border of Hungary, then continues down through the middle of Bosnia to the Adriatic Sea."[80]

A monumental empirical treatise, *Human Accomplishment* by Charles Murray, traced differences in historic advancements in the arts and sciences within different parts of Europe and concluded that "80 percent of all the European significant figures can be enclosed in an area that does *not* include Russia, Sweden, Norway, Finland, Spain, Portugal, the Balkans, Poland, Hungary, East and West Prussia, Ireland, Wales, most of Scotland, the lower quarter of Italy, and about a third of France."[81] Within the United States, that same study found similarly skewed locational differences among the origins of notable achievements in the arts and sciences, with the northeast grossly over-represented and most of the South grossly under-represented, except for Virginia.[82]

Demography

Among the most overlooked factors in socioeconomic outcome differences, both within nations and between nations, are such demographic factors as differences in median age. These differences are not small, and neither are their consequences.

In the United States, for example, income differences between middle aged people and young adults are larger than income differences between blacks and whites.[83] Moreover, these income differences among age groups have increased over time, as the physical vitality of youth has become less valuable economically with the replacement of human muscle power by mechanical and electrical power, while the development of human capital— knowledge, skills and experience— has become more valuable, with the development of more advanced technologies and more complex organizations.

Ethnic and other social groups differ in median ages by as much as two decades or more. In the United States, for example, the median age of Japanese Americans is 51 and the median age of Mexican Americans is 27.[84]

How likely is it that these two groups— or others— would have the same proportions of their populations equally represented in occupations, institutions or activities requiring long years of education and/or long years of job experience? Is it surprising if Hispanic Americans are not as well represented as Japanese Americans in the professions, or in managerial careers, for which long years of education and experience are usually required? How many 27-year-olds of any ethnic background meet the requirements for being CEOs in civilian life or generals and admirals in the military?

Even if Japanese Americans and Mexican Americans were absolutely identical in everything else besides age, they would nevertheless differ significantly in incomes and other age-related outcomes. Racial, ethnic and other groups are of course seldom, if ever, identical in everything else. That makes the prospects of equal outcomes even more improbable, and disparities in outcomes even more questionable as *automatic* indicators of discrimination. In terms of capabilities, a man is not even equal to himself at different stages of life, much less equal to the wide range of other people at varying stages of their own respective lives.

In these circumstances, equal rights and equal treatment of all does not mean equal performances— and virtually guarantees *unequal* performances and outcomes. This does not mean that either genes or discrimination can simply be dismissed as a possible factor in any given circumstance, but only that hard evidence would be required to substantiate either of these possibilities, which remain testable hypotheses, without being foregone conclusions.

The Lure of Determinism

The belief that disparities in incomes are indicators of disparities in the treatment of those with lower incomes is part of a more general set of assumptions that some one particular factor is the key or dominant factor behind differences in outcomes. In the early twentieth century, the key factor behind economic, intellectual and other disparities among different groups was assumed to be genetics.[85] That view was as dominant then as the opposite view today that disparities in outcomes imply discrimination. American colleges and universities had hundreds of courses on eugenics then,[86] just as many academic institutions today have courses— and whole departments— teaching that outcome disparities imply discrimination.

Nor was genetic determinism peculiar to the United States or confined to any particular part of the political or ideological spectrum, though American Progressives took the lead in promoting genetic determinism in the United States then, as they later took the lead in promoting the opposite presumption that disparities imply discrimination in the second half of the twentieth century. On both sides of the Atlantic, and in both eras, leading intellectual and political figures were in the forefront of those promoting the prevailing presumption of their times.

In England, for example, John Maynard Keynes was one of the founders of the eugenics society at Cambridge University, and such other internationally renowned British writers on the political left as H.G. Wells, George Bernard Shaw, Julian Huxley, Harold J. Laski and Sidney and Beatrice Webb were also advocates of eugenics. Among British conservatives, Winston Churchill and Neville Chamberlain, who would later differ on other issues, were both supporters of eugenics.[87]

In the United States, leading figures in the eugenics movement included founders and leading officials of the American Sociological Association and the American Economic Association.[88] Among the pioneers in the development of mental tests, Professor L.M. Terman of Stanford University concluded from his study of minorities in the southwestern United States that "They cannot master abstractions"[89] and Carl Brigham, creator of the Scholastic Aptitude Test (SAT), declared that U.S. Army mental test results during the First World War tended to "disprove the popular belief that the Jew is highly intelligent."[90]

In short, stampedes toward one-factor explanations do not exempt even the leading intellectuals of an era. Nor are one-factor explanations confined to disparities among human beings. It extends to issues about differences in nature. No one can dispute that sunlight is hotter in the tropics, but that scientific fact does not prevent the highest temperature ever recorded in Asia, Africa, North America and South America from all having been recorded *outside* the tropics on all these continents.[91] No part of Europe is in the tropics, but there are European cities whose highest recorded temperatures are higher than any temperature ever recorded in Singapore, located virtually on the Equator.[92]

In general, even a major factor— unchallenged as a scientific fact— can be outweighed by some combination of other factors. It is no denial of the influence of differences in north-south locations on temperatures to point out that the average high temperature in December is the same in London as in Washington, even though London is located more than 850 miles farther north than Washington.[93] The warm waters of the Gulf Stream, flowing through the Atlantic Ocean, transfer warmth northeastward past Western Europe, including London, creating milder winters in that part of the world than at the same latitudes in Asia, North America or Eastern Europe.

Other factors enable many other places in the temperate zones to reach higher temperatures than many places in the tropics.[94] None of this contradicts the scientific fact that sunlight is hotter in the tropics. But that unchallenged fact does not mean that this single factor automatically determines all outcomes. Similarly, among human beings, the unchallenged fact of discriminatory bias against various groups in countries around the world does not preclude outcomes from being determined by a wider range of other factors in particular places and times.

While we find skewed distributions of outcomes in many dimensions of human activities around the world, we find assumptions of equal or comparable outcomes as a default setting in many social theories that regard the absence of equality of outcomes as automatic signs of some sinister influences which have prevented this natural equality from taking place. But neither equality of achievements nor equality of crimes is common.

The murder rate in Eastern Europe has been some multiple of the murder rate in Western Europe for centuries.[95] Today, according to the British publication *The Economist*, Latin America has "8% of the world's people but 38% of its recorded murders." Moreover, "80% of violent killings in Latin American cities occur on just 2% of streets."[96]

Neither genetics nor discrimination is either necessary or sufficient to account for all skewed outcomes among human beings. But, given how widely, how long and how strongly each of these two explanations— that is, genes or discrimination— has dominated thinking, laws and policies in various parts of the world, it is no small matter to escape from having painted ourselves into a corner with either of these sweeping preconceptions.

Two of the monumental catastrophes of the twentieth century— Nazism and Communism— led to the slaughter of millions of human beings by their own governments, in the name of either ridding the world of the burden of "inferior" races or ridding the world of "exploiters" responsible for the poverty of the exploited. While each of these beliefs might have been testable hypotheses, their greatest political triumphs came as dogmas placed beyond the reach of evidence or logic.

Neither Hitler's *Mein Kampf* nor Marx's *Capital* was an exercise in hypothesis testing. While Karl Marx's vast three-volume economic treatise was a far greater intellectual achievement, "exploitation" was at no point in its 2,500 pages treated as a testable hypothesis. Exploitation was instead the foundation assumption on which an elaborate intellectual superstructure was built— and that proved to be a foundation of quicksand. Getting rid of capitalist "exploiters" in Communist countries did not raise the living standards of workers even to levels common in many capitalist countries, where workers were presumably still being exploited, as Marxists conceived the term.

Discrimination as an explanation of economic and social disparities may have a similar emotional appeal for many. But we can at least try to treat these and other theories as testable hypotheses. The historic consequences of treating particular beliefs as sacred dogmas, beyond the reach of evidence or logic, should be enough to dissuade us from going down that road again— despite how exciting or emotionally satisfying political dogmas and the crusades resulting from those dogmas can be, or how convenient in sparing us the drudgery and discomfort of having to think through our own beliefs or test them against facts.

Chapter 2

Discrimination: Meanings and Costs

Some people are said to have discriminating tastes when they are especially discerning in detecting differences in qualities and choosing accordingly, whether choosing wines, paintings or other goods and services. But the word is also used in an almost opposite sense to refer to arbitrary differences in behavior toward people, based on their group identities, regardless of their actual qualities as individuals.

Both kinds of discrimination can result in large differences in outcomes, whether judging people or things. Wine connoisseurs can end up choosing one kind of wine far more often than another, and paying far more for a bottle of one kind of wine than for a bottle of the other.

Something similar can often be observed when it comes to people. It is common, in countries around the world, for some groups to have very different outcomes when they are judged by others in employment, educational and other contexts. Thus different groups may end up with very different incomes, occupations and unemployment rates, or very different rates of admissions to colleges and universities, among many other group disparities in outcomes.

The fundamental question is: Which kind of discrimination has led to such disparate outcomes? Have differences in qualities between individuals or groups been correctly discerned by others or have those others made their decisions based on personal aversions or arbitrary assumptions about members of particular groups? This is ultimately an empirical question, even if attempts to answer that question evoke passionate feelings and passionate certainty by observers reaching opposite conclusions.

Another way of saying the same thing is: Are group disparities in outcomes a result of *internal* differences in behavior and capabilities, accurately assessed by outsiders, or are those disparities due to *external* impositions based on the biased misjudgments or antagonisms of outsiders?

The answers to such questions are not necessarily the same for all group disparities, nor necessarily the same for a given group at different times and places. Seeking the answers to such questions is more than an academic exercise, when the ultimate purpose is to enable more fellow human beings to have better prospects of advancing themselves. But, before seeking answers, we need to be very clear about the words in which the question is asked.

MEANINGS OF DISCRIMINATION

At a minimum, we need to know what we ourselves mean when we use a word like "discrimination," especially since it has conflicting meanings. The broader meaning— an ability to discern differences in the qualities of people and things, and choosing accordingly— can be called Discrimination I. The narrower, but more commonly used, meaning— treating people negatively, based on arbitrary aversions or animosities to individuals of a particular race or sex, for example— can be called Discrimination II, the kind of discrimination that has led to anti-discrimination laws and policies.

Ideally, Discrimination I, applied to people, would mean judging each person as an individual, regardless of what group that person is part of. But here, as in other contexts, the ideal is seldom found among human beings in the real world, even among people who espouse that ideal. If you are walking at night down a lonely street, and see up ahead a shadowy figure in an alley, do you judge that person as an individual or do you cross the street and pass on the other side? The shadowy figure in the alley could turn out to be a kindly neighbor, out walking his dog. But, when making such decisions, a mistake on your part could be costly, up to and including costing you your life.

In other contexts, you may in fact judge each person as an individual. But that this depends on context means that people have already been implicitly pre-sorted by the context, and only after that pre-sorting are they then judged as individuals. For example, a professor entering a classroom on the first day of the academic year may judge and treat each student as an individual. But that same professor, walking down a lonely street at night, may not judge and react to each stranger on the road ahead as an individual.

The students in a college classroom are not likely to be a random sample of the full range of variations found in the general population, and are more likely to represent a narrower range of people assembled there for a narrower range of purposes, and with a narrower range of individual characteristics, as well as being in a setting less dangerous than a dark street at night.

In short, one of the differences between the applicability of Discrimination I and Discrimination II is cost— and this is not always a small cost, nor a cost measured solely in money. Everyone might agree that Discrimination I is preferable, other things being equal. Nevertheless, one may still be aware that other things are not always equal, and sometimes other things are very far from being equal.

Where there is a difference in costs when choosing between Discrimination I and Discrimination II, much may depend on how high those costs are, and especially on who pays those costs. People who would never walk through a particular neighborhood at night, or perhaps not even in broad daylight, may nevertheless be indignant at banks that engage in "redlining"— that is, putting a whole neighborhood off-limits as a place to invest their depositors' money. The observers' own "redlining" in their choices of where to walk may never be seen by them as a different example of the same principle.

In short, Discrimination I can have prohibitive costs in some situations, especially when it is applied at the individual level. However, Discrimination II— the arbitrary or antipathy-based bias against a group, is not the only other option. Another way of making decisions is by weighing empirical evidence about groups as a whole or about the interactions of different groups with one another.

To take an extreme example, for the sake of illustration, if 30 percent of the people in Group X are alcoholics and 2 percent of the people in Group Y are alcoholics, an employer may well prefer to hire people from Group Y for work where an alcoholic would be not only ineffective but dangerous. This would mean that a majority of the people in Group *X*— 70 percent— would be more likely to be denied employment, even though they are not alcoholics. What matters, crucially, to the employer is the *cost* of determining which individual is or is not an alcoholic, when job applicants all show up sober on the day when they are seeking employment.

This also matters to the customers who buy the employer's products and to society as a whole. If alcoholics produce a higher proportion of products that turn out to be defective, that is a cost to customers, whether the customer gets the defective product or whether the number of products that have to be discarded at the factory because they are defective means higher prices for the products that are sold, because the costs of defective products that are screened out at the factory must be covered by the prices charged for the good quality products that emerge from that process and are sold.

To the extent that alcoholics are not only less competent but dangerous, the costs of those dangers are paid by either fellow employees or by the customers who buy dangerously defective products, or both. In short, there are serious costs inherent in the situation, so that either 70 percent of the people in Group *X* or employers or customers— or all three— are going to end up paying the cost of the alcoholism of 30 percent of the people in Group *X*.

This is certainly not judging each job applicant as an individual, so it is not Discrimination I in the purest sense. On the other hand, it is also not Discrimination II in the sense of decisions based on a personal bias or antipathy toward that whole group. The employer might well have personal friends from Group *X*, based on far more knowledge of those particular individuals than it is possible to get about job applicants, without prohibitive costs.

The point here is neither to justify nor condemn the employer but to *classify* different decision-making processes, so that their implications and consequences can be analyzed.

A real-life example of the effect of the cost of knowledge in this context is a study which showed that, despite the reluctance of many employers to hire young black males, because a significant proportion of them have had criminal records, those particular employers who automatically did criminal background checks on *all* their employees tended to hire more young black males than did other employers.[1] In other words, where the nature of the work made criminal background checks worth the cost for all employees, it was no longer necessary to use group data to assess whether individual young black job applicants had a criminal background.

Discrimination I— basing decisions on empirical evidence— thus has two variations. The ideal, and more costly, variation is seeking and paying the cost for information that would permit judging each individual as an individual, regardless of the group from which that individual comes. This we can call Discrimination I*A*.

In other cases, where such information is too costly to be worth it, individuals may be judged by empirical evidence on the group they are part of. This can be called Discrimination I*B*. Both variations are different from Discrimination II, where the reason for treating individuals from different groups differently has no empirical basis but is due to personal bias or aversion to members of particular groups.

Even employers who have no animosity or aversions against particular groups may nevertheless engage in Discrimination I*B*— empirically based generalizations— when the employer knows that various groups react differently in the presence of other groups.

Back in nineteenth-century America, for example, when there were many immigrants from Europe in the workforce, some groups brought their mutual animosities in Europe with them to America. To have a workforce including both Irish Protestants and Irish Catholics working together was to risk animosities and even violence, with negative effects on productivity. In other words, a workforce consisting exclusively of either group was more efficient than a workforce consisting of both.

The same principle applies where different groups have especially positive reactions to one another. For example, the employer may be indifferent as to whether the work to be done is done by men or by women, and yet be well aware that men and women are not indifferent to each other, or else the human race would have become extinct long ago.

Therefore, in the interests of workforce efficiency, when a particular occupation is overwhelmingly chosen by women, such as nursing, the employer may be reluctant to hire a male nurse. Conversely, where lumberjacks are overwhelmingly male, the employer may be reluctant to hire a female lumberjack, even if she is demonstrably as fully qualified as the men.

Observers who point out that particular individuals are equally qualified, regardless of sex, miss the point. An equally qualified individual may do the work just as well as others, but if some of the others are distracted from their work, the net effect can be a less efficient workforce. That is the empirical basis that can lead employers to practice Discrimination I*B*, even if the employers have no bias or aversion to those less likely to be hired.

Misdiagnosing the basis for discrimination produces more than a difference in words. It can produce policies less likely to achieve their goals, or even policies that make matters worse. For example, forbidding employers from checking criminal records of job applicants can mean reducing the job opportunities of those young black males who have no criminal record.

Employment decisions are not the only decisions affected by discrimination of one sort or another. Where there are real differences between groups, with potentially dire consequences, such as murder rates several times higher in one group than in the other, Discrimination I*B* may be carried to the point of "redlining" a neighborhood or group, even when a majority of the group avoided are not guilty of the behavior feared.

Even in a high-crime neighborhood, for example, most people are not necessarily criminals.* But the costs of sorting the local population individually can be prohibitively high. Therefore decisions are likely to be made through a cruder decision-making process, relying on empirically based generalizations— Discrimination I*B*— rather than

---

* As a personal note, some years ago an elderly relative was crossing a busy thoroughfare in the Bronx, when she lost consciousness and fell to the ground in a high-crime neighborhood. People on the sidewalk rushed out into the street, to direct traffic around her. One of the women in the group took charge of her purse and returned it after my unconscious relative revived. Not a cent was missing from the purse.

the more discerning, but costly, Discrimination I*A* or an antipathy-based or bias-based Discrimination II.

One of the consequences of such situations is that a law-abiding majority in a high-crime neighborhood can end up paying a high price for the presence of a criminal minority among compatriots living in their midst. Some businesses will not deliver their products— whether pizzas or furniture— to high-crime neighborhoods, rather than risk bodily harm, including death, to their drivers.

Taxi drivers may avoid taking passengers to such neighborhoods for the same reason, even when these are black taxi drivers refusing to go into black high-crime neighborhoods, especially at night. Supermarkets and other businesses are often reluctant to locate stores in such neighborhoods, for similar reasons.

All this hurts law-abiding people in high-crime neighborhoods, who are, in effect, paying a price for what other people are doing. In addition to being the principal victims of crimes committed by criminals in their midst, they also literally pay a price in hard cash for the behavior of others, in the higher prices usually charged for goods sold in neighborhoods where there are higher costs of doing business, due to higher levels of shoplifting, vandalism, burglary, pilferage and robbery— and higher business insurance premiums because of these and other neighborhood disorders.[2]

A study titled *The Poor Pay More* saw the poor in general as "exploited consumers,"[3] taken advantage of by stores located in low-income neighborhoods. This view was echoed in the media, in government and in academic publications.[4] Yet, because many low-income neighborhoods are also high-crime neighborhoods, *The Poor Pay More* committed an all too common error in assuming that the *cause* of some undesirable outcome can be determined by where the statistical data were collected.

In this case, researchers collected price data in the neighborhood stores. But the *causes* of those high prices were not the people who posted those prices in the stores. Moreover, while prices were higher in inner-city, low-income neighborhood stores, rates of profit on investments in such stores were not higher than average but *lower* than average.[5]

For people unaware of these facts, the higher prices may be seen as simply "price gouging" by "greedy" store owners— Discrimination II against minority neighborhoods. For those who see the situation this way, higher prices may appear to be a problem that the government could solve by imposing price controls, as a Harlem newspaper suggested during the 1960s furor over revelations that "the poor pay more."[6] But if businesses in these neighborhoods do not recover their higher costs of doing business there in the prices they charge, they face the prospect of having to go out of business.

There is often a dearth of businesses in low-income, high-crime neighborhoods, which would hardly be the case if there were higher rates of profit being made from the higher prices charged in such neighborhoods.

It may be no consolation to those law-abiding citizens in a high-crime neighborhood that the higher prices they have to pay are reimbursing higher costs of doing business where they live. Meanwhile, politicians and local activists have every incentive to claim that the higher prices are due to discrimination, in the sense of Discrimination II, even when in fact the community is simply paying additional costs generated by some residents in that community.

Those local residents who created none of those costs can be victims of those who did, rather than being victims of those who charged the resulting higher prices. This is not just an abstract philosophical point or a matter of semantics. The difference between understanding the source of the higher prices and mistakenly blaming those who charged those prices is the difference between doing things to lessen the problem and doing things likely to make the problem worse by driving more much-needed businesses out of the neighborhood. The difference between Discrimination IB and Discrimination II is not just an academic distinction.

Although higher prices in low-income neighborhoods are often discussed in the context of racial or ethnic minorities, the same economic consequences have been found where the people in the low-income neighborhoods were white. As the *Cincinnati Enquirer* reported: "Residents of eastern Kentucky refer to the higher prices and interest rates common in their area as the 'hillbilly tax.'"[7]

Among the things that might be done to reduce the burden of unfairness to law-abiding residents of high-crime neighborhoods could be stronger law enforcement by the police and the courts. But, to the extent that the public— both inside and outside the affected communities— sees the high prices as Discrimination II against the affected community as a whole, due to bias or antipathy by the larger society, the imposition of stronger law enforcement may be seen as just another imposition of injustice on the affected communities.

In short, whether people believe that higher prices in low-income, high-crime neighborhoods are due to Discrimination II or to empirically-based decisions matters in terms of which policies to reduce the unfair burdens on law-abiding residents are politically feasible. Community or ethnic solidarity can be a major obstacle to seeing, believing or responding to the facts.

SIDEBAR: FACTORS BEHIND PRICE DIFFERENCES

Crime is not the only reason why prices are higher in many low-income neighborhoods. To someone unfamiliar with economics, it may seem strange that a store in a low-income neighborhood can be struggling to survive, while selling a product for a dollar that Walmart is getting rich selling for 75 cents. But the costs of running a business are among the many things that are neither equal nor random. Walmart's costs are lower in many ways, of which safer locations are just one.

Even if a local store charging a dollar is making 15 cents gross profit per item, while Walmart is making only 10 cents, if Walmart's inventory turnover rate is three times as high, then in a given time period Walmart is making 30 cents selling that item, while the local store is making 15 cents. Walmart's inventory turnover rate is in fact higher than that of even some other big box chain stores, and much higher than that of a local neighborhood store, where the same item may sit on the shelf much longer before being sold.

> Delivery costs are also likely to be lower per item delivered to a Walmart store. For example, the cost of delivering 100 boxes of cereal to one giant Walmart store may be far lower than the cost of delivering ten boxes of cereal to each of ten different neighborhood stores scattered around the city. It is a hundred boxes of cereal in either case, but the cost of delivering them can be very different.

None of this tells us how much Discrimination I or Discrimination II exists in a given society— or how many disparities in outcomes are due to some other circumstances or some other decision-making process.

In some situations, there may clearly be costs deliberately imposed on a group by outsiders— Discrimination II— such as denying black American citizens the right to vote in many Southern states in times past. The racial segregation laws in those states, forcing black passengers to sit in the back of buses and trolleys, and denying them admissions to state universities, were obvious examples of a wider range of clearly racial discrimination, in the sense of Discrimination II.

The original European ghettos in centuries past, which forced Jews to live in a confined area and banned them from most European universities, were other examples of the same Discrimination II. Innumerable other groups in countries around the world— the "untouchables" in India being a classic example— faced even more and worse restrictions and oppressions.

These are all costs imposed by Discrimination II, and paid by its victims. What also warrants analysis, in order to understand cause and effect, are the costs paid *by the discriminators*, because these costs are factors in how much Discrimination II can persist in particular circumstances and institutions. Such costs have no such moral, political or ideological attraction as the costs paid by victims. But the costs that discriminators have to pay— and the various circumstances in which they do or do not have to pay those costs— can affect how much Discrimination II is in fact likely to be inflicted.

Understanding the costs paid by discriminators also presents opportunities for policies that can ensure that these costs cannot be evaded, as well as warnings that other policies may inadvertently free discriminators from paying such costs, if the circumstances are not understood.

COSTS OF DISCRIMINATION

Neither the amount nor the severity of Discrimination II is fixed permanently. It varies greatly from country to country and from one era to another in the same country. There was an era in which many American employers' advertisements for some jobs said "No Irish Need Apply" or "Whites Only." There was a time when some shops in Harlem, back when that was an upscale white community, had signs that read, "No Jews, and No Dogs."[8]

Nor were Americans unique. In many other places and times around the world, group discrimination— that is, Discrimination II— was so pervasive and so widely understood that no such signs were necessary. For a woman, a Jew or members of some other groups to apply for certain jobs would have been considered a presumptuous waste of the employer's time.

Discrimination II in hiring and promotion raises questions about both causation and morality. Both kinds of questions deserve to be examined— separately.

Causation

In trying to understand the causes and the consequences of discrimination in hiring and promotion, it is necessary to again consider whether this is Discrimination I or Discrimination II. This is not always an easy question to answer, and in fact easy answers such as automatically equating statistical disparities in outcomes with Discrimination II can be a major obstacle to getting at the truth.

An employer who judges each job applicant individually, without regard to the applicant's group membership, can nevertheless end up with employees whose demographic makeup is very different from the demographic makeup of the local population.

One major demographic fact that is often overlooked by those who automatically equate statistical disparities in outcomes with Discrimination II is that different ethnic groups have very different median ages. As already noted, Japanese Americans have a median age more than *two decades* older than the median age of Mexican Americans.[9] Even if every individual of the same age had the same income, regardless of which group that individual was part of, nevertheless there would still be serious disparities in income between Japanese Americans and Mexican Americans— as well as between many other groups.

A group with a median age in their twenties will obviously not have nearly as large a proportion of their population with 20 years of work experience as a group whose median age is in their forties. One group may therefore have a disproportionate number of people in high level occupations requiring long years of experience, while the other group may be similarly over-represented in professional sports or in violent crimes, both of which are activities disproportionately engaged in by the young.

Such disparities in outcomes are not automatically evidence of either outsiders' biases or internal deficiencies in the groups. Either or both may be present or absent, but that requires empirical evidence going beyond gross statistical differences in outcomes.

In short, conditions *prior* to job applicants reaching an employer can have a "disparate impact" on the chances of someone from a particular group being hired or promoted, even if the employer judges each applicant on that applicant's own individual qualifications, without regard to the group from which the applicant came. Put differently, even Discrimination I*A* can produce "disparate impact" statistics, just as Discrimination II can.

Age is just one of those pre-existing conditions. As already noted, children raised in families where the parents have professional occupations hear nearly twice as many words per hour as children raised in working-class families, and more than three times as many words per hour as children raised in families on welfare.[10]

Can we believe that such differences— and others— compounded over many years while growing up, make no difference in individual capabilities and social outcomes, when those children become adults seeking employment? All these individuals may have been very similar at birth, but many things happen between birth and applying for a job or for college admissions. And those things seldom happen the same for everybody. As we have seen, they happen differently for children born and raised in the same family.

More generally, you cannot tell where the disparity in outcomes originated from where the statistics were collected. The data may be collected at the employer's place of business, but that does not preclude disparities in individual capabilities from having originated in the home in or in the local cultures where people were raised.

Not only differences in child-rearing, but also decisions made by individuals themselves, affect their outcomes. When more than three-quarters of all college degrees in education go to women and more than three-quarters of all college degrees in engineering go to men,[11] the statistical predominance of women in teaching and men in engineering cannot automatically be attributed to employers' biases. More fundamentally, the cause of a given outcome is an empirical question, whose answer requires untangling many complex factors, rather than simply pointing dramatically to statistical disparities in outcomes.

Costs and Their Effects

It is easy to understand how being denied an opportunity to be hired or promoted for some jobs can lead to some groups having lower incomes than others, and why that can arouse moral objections, not only from those denied jobs but also from others who find such practices morally repugnant.

From a causal perspective, other questions arise as to the reasons for such practices. Here the cost of discrimination *to the discriminator* plays a causal role in the outcome. There is also a cost for society at large. A society in which women are arbitrarily banned from many kinds of work can pay a huge cost by forfeiting the productive potential of half its population.

"Society," however, is seldom a decision-making unit, except perhaps at election time or during a mass uprising. To understand decisions in general, or employment decisions in particular, requires understanding the incentives and constraints confronting the particular decision-makers in particular kinds of institutions, who cannot simply choose to do whatever they wish, without regard to the costs of their decisions to themselves.

In a competitive market for labor, or for the sale of the employers' products, the validity of the beliefs behind a business owner's decisions can determine whether that business operates at a profit or a loss, or whether it survives or is forced to go out of business. In short, we cannot simply go directly from attitudes to outcomes— even if these attitudes involve racism or sexism— as if there were no intermediate factor of *costs* for decisions made in a competitive market. A systemic analysis of markets cannot proceed as if there were no other factors involved besides what individual decision-makers happen to prefer.

Economists who have recognized this have ranged from followers of Adam Smith to followers of Karl Marx. The point was perhaps best expressed by Friedrich Engels, co-author with Marx of *The Communist Manifesto*. Engels said: "what each individual wills is obstructed by everyone else, and what emerges is something that no one willed."[12] An analysis of systemic causation is concerned with what emerges.

Adam Smith, patron saint of free-market capitalism, likewise had a systemic analysis of causation. He did not attribute the benefits of a capitalist economy to good intentions by capitalists.[13] On the contrary, a case could be made that Adam Smith's view of capitalists as individuals was even more negative than that of Karl Marx.[14] Smith and Marx reached opposite conclusions as to the benefits or harm done by free-market capitalism, but neither based his conclusions on the intentions of capitalists. Each based his conclusions on the systemic incentives and constraints of economic competition.

Too many other observers, including some academic scholars, reason as if intentions automatically translate directly into outcomes. Thus, in his book *The Declining Significance of Race*, sociologist

William Julius Wilson pointed out the various organized ways in which white Southern landowners and employers in the post-Civil-War South sought to keep down the earnings of black workers and black sharecroppers.[15] But there was no reference in that book to empirical evidence on how those intentions actually turned out— in other words, on "what emerges," as Engels put it.

By contrast, economist Robert Higgs, who researched the actual consequences of those efforts of white employers and landowners in the postbellum South, found that such organized efforts often collapsed, as a result of competition among white employers and landowners for black workers and sharecroppers.[16] It might seem as if newly freed blacks— desperately poor, usually illiterate and unfamiliar with working as free people in labor markets— would be easy prey for whites united to enforce whatever wage and sharecropper conditions they wanted. But that ignores the inherent, systemic competitive pressures in a market economy.

In agriculture, especially— and the South was largely agricultural at the time— there is an inherent urgency about getting the land plowed and the seeds planted in the spring, or else there will be no crop in the fall. Those white landowners who were the first to violate the terms to which other white landowners sought to limit black workers and sharecroppers stood to be the first to assure themselves of a workforce sufficient in both quantity and quality to maximize the size of the crop that could be grown on a given piece of land.

Other white landowners, who stuck by the restrictions and/or who cheated the black workers and sharecroppers in various ways, tended to find themselves having to make do with whatever quantity and quality of black workers and sharecroppers remained, after other white landowners had skimmed the cream by paying higher wages and higher crop shares, in order to improve their own prospects of a profitable crop. Black workers and sharecroppers did not have to know economics in order to know where friends and relatives were getting a better deal, and go there.[17]

It is hardly surprising that these efforts at suppressing black workers' pay and black sharecroppers' shares often broke down under such economic pressures. "What emerges" in this case was that black incomes per capita in 1900 were, at a minimum, "almost half again" higher than they had been in 1867–68. This represented a rate of growth higher than that in the American economy as a whole during that period.[18] Because they started from a far lower economic level, blacks remained poorer than whites. But Professor Higgs' data indicated that "black incomes grew more rapidly than white incomes over the last third of the nineteenth century."[19]

Businesses in general, making decisions in a labor market or a product market, are not like professors voting at a faculty meeting, because those votes seldom have any costs for the professors themselves, despite whatever good or bad results such votes may have for students or for the academic institution. The difference is the difference between decisions made subject to consequential feedback in a competitive market and decisions made with insulation from such feedback in academia and in other insulated venues.

South Africa Under Apartheid

To avoid endless and inconclusive debates about the presence or magnitude of racism, we can test our hypotheses about the costs of discrimination in a historical context where there was no ambiguity on the subject— namely, South Africa during the era of apartheid, ruled by a white minority government, elected with the black majority denied a vote, and openly promoting white supremacy.

Apartheid laws limited how many blacks could be employed in particular industries and occupations, and forbad their being hired for work above certain levels in those industries and occupations. Yet white South African employers in competitive industries often hired more blacks than they were allowed to under the apartheid laws, and in higher occupations than those laws permitted.

A government crackdown during the 1970s led to hundreds of firms in South Africa's construction industry being fined for violating those laws. Nor was the construction industry the only one in which competitive businesses were fined for hiring more blacks, and in higher occupations, than allowed under the law. In some other industries blacks even outnumbered whites in particular job categories where it was illegal for blacks to be hired at all.[20]

There is no compelling evidence that the white employers violating those laws had different racial views than the white legislators who passed such laws. What was different was that employers who failed to hire black workers whom it was profitable to hire paid a price for Discrimination II, in the form of lost opportunities to make money, while the legislators who passed laws imposing Discrimination II paid no price at all. Indeed, legislators who failed to pass such laws could pay a price politically, in a situation where only whites could vote, and white workers wanted protection from the competition of black workers.

Both the employers and the legislators were rationally pursuing their own self-interests. It was just that the institutional incentives and constraints were different in a competitive market from the incentives and constraints in a political institution. Nor were labor markets the only markets affected by the costs confronting discriminators in South Africa.

Apartheid laws also made it illegal for non-whites to live in certain areas set aside by law for whites only. Yet many non-whites in fact lived in these whites-only areas. These included black American economist Walter E. Williams during a three month stay in South Africa, doing research.[21] There was at least one whites-only area in South Africa where non-whites were a majority of the residents.[22] Here again, costs were the key. The costs to owners of rental property in whites-only areas who forfeited economic benefits available by renting to non-whites competed with the costs of disobeying apartheid laws, and the latter did not always prevail.

While racists, by definition, prefer their own race to other races, individual racists— like other people— tend to prefer themselves most of all. That is what led to widespread violations of apartheid laws by white employers and landlords in competitive industries in South Africa. It cost nothing for white South Africans to vote for candidates promoting white supremacy. But the costs of refusing to hire black workers who would make their business profitable could be considerable.

Moreover, the cost of refusing to hire them when their competitors in the product market were hiring them, and therefore could have lower costs of doing business— enabling competitors to undercut the product prices of employers who failed to hire black workers— exposed those who obeyed apartheid laws to the risk of losing profits and potentially losing their whole business.

This is not to say that discriminatory laws and policies have no effect. There are costs to disobeying laws, as well as countervailing costs to following such laws, so outcomes depend on particular circumstances in particular times and places.

However, the costs of Discrimination II to the discriminator— in the context of a competitive market— are far lower, or even non-existent, in situations where free market competition does not exist, such as in (1) public utility monopolies whose prices and profit rates are directly controlled by government, (2) non-profit organizations, and (3) government employment. In all these particular situations, Discrimination II has tended to be far more common than in competitive markets, not only in South Africa under apartheid, but also in other countries around the world.[23]

Unless one believes that decision-makers in these particular institutions have different racial or other views than decision-makers in competitive markets, and that such differences persist over time, as new generations of decision-makers come and go, the reasons for such *institutional* differences must be sought in particular incentives and constraints growing out of differences in the circumstances of those institutions.

Institutional Incentives and Constraints

One of the landmark struggles in the civil rights movement in mid-twentieth-century America was a campaign against laws in most Southern states mandating that black passengers sit or stand only in the back of buses, with the seats up front being reserved for whites. Although many people on both sides of this struggle regarded these laws as though they had existed from time immemorial, they had not. The history of such laws illustrates again the different roles of economic incentives and constraints versus political incentives and constraints.

Three decades after the end of slavery, laws mandating racially segregated seating in municipal transit vehicles *began* to be passed in many Southern communities, toward the end of the nineteenth century. The political situation had changed from that in the period immediately after the Civil War, when U.S. troops were stationed in Southern states, and Southern governments were subject to federal policies granting blacks the right to vote during what was called the Reconstruction era.

With the end of Reconstruction, and the return of local self-government in the South, blacks often lost the right to vote, by methods ranging from laws to organized terrorism. Racially segregated seating on municipal transit vehicles was just one of the political consequences. Before these laws were passed, it was common for blacks and whites to sit wherever they felt like sitting on public transportation vehicles.

Many, if not most, of the streetcar companies during that era were privately owned, and their profits depended on how many people— whether black or white— chose to ride in their vehicles, and how often.

The decision-makers in these privately owned companies understood that they could lose profits if offending black customers by making them sit in the back, or to stand when all the back seats were taken, even if there were vacant seats in the front section that was reserved for whites. Indeed, racially segregated seating could even offend some whites, when all the white section seats were filled but there were vacant seats in the section set aside for blacks.

In short, racially segregated seating in municipal transit vehicles was seen, by those who owned or managed such companies, as something that reduced profits. Not surprisingly, municipal transit companies in the South fought against the passage of laws requiring racially segregated seating in streetcars. After losing politically in the legislatures, some municipal transit companies then took the issue into the courts, where they lost again. Then, after the laws went into effect legally, many Southern municipal transit companies simply did nothing to enforce racially segregated seating. In some places, passengers continued for years to sit wherever they felt like sitting.[24]

Eventually, however, Southern government authorities cracked down. They began charging municipal transit company employees with violations of the law for not enforcing racially segregated seating, and in some cases the owners of those companies were threatened with prosecution if those transit lines did not enforce the racial segregation laws. Only then did the laws that had been passed, in some cases years earlier, finally get enforced.[25]

Railroads were also affected economically by racial segregation laws. When black and white passengers had to be carried in separate coaches, this imposed the considerable cost of buying additional coaches for their passenger trains, as well as the further additional costs of more fuel to move the now heavier trains.

This was especially costly where there were insufficient passengers to fill one coach. If there were only enough black and white passengers for the total to fill two-thirds of the seats in a coach, racial segregation laws could create a situation where there were now two coaches required, each with only one-third of the seats occupied.

Like municipal transit companies, railroad managements in the South opposed the racial segregation laws, in their own self-interest, even if their racial views might have been no different from those of politicians who passed such laws. But the incentives to which the politicians responded were votes— that is, white votes— while the incentives to which railroad owners and managers responded were financial, and money was the same, regardless of the racial source.

The famous Supreme Court case of *Plessy v. Ferguson* in 1896 arose from the cooperation of the railroads with Homer Plessy, who was challenging these racial segregation laws, in order to create a test case.

Although Plessy was part of the black community, he was genetically far more Caucasian than African, and was physically indistinguishable from white men. Had he simply gotten on a train and ridden to his destination, there was little likelihood that he would have been questioned about being seated in a railroad car set aside for whites only. But the attorneys for the railroad and the attorneys for Plessy cooperated in arranging a legal confrontation, so that there would be a case to take into the federal courts.[26] Unfortunately for both, and for the cause of equal rights in general, the Supreme Court majority ruled against them.

There is no predestined outcome of the conflict between economic and political forces. What is important is to recognize the implications of that conflict when crafting or changing laws and policies.

It is not only in political institutions, but also in some economic institutions, that decision-makers are insulated from having to pay the costs of Discrimination II that they impose on others. Public utility monopolies, whose prices and profit rates are directly controlled by government regulatory agencies, are among the institutions insulated from paying the economic costs which a competitive market imposes on discriminatory behavior, whether directed against ethnic minorities, women or others.

Although engaging in Discrimination II when hiring employees could mean lower profits for a firm operating in competitive markets, a government-regulated public utility that has a monopoly in its field would not be allowed to earn a higher profit rate than the government agency deemed proper in any case. So a public utility was not forfeiting any additional profit that it would be allowed to keep, if it hired without regard to the group from which job applicants came.

Discrimination II might require the regulated public utility company to pay additional labor costs from having to offer higher salaries, in order to attract a larger pool of qualified applicants, from which only applicants from groups that the decision-makers preferred would be hired. But, as a government-regulated monopoly, such costs could be passed on to customers who had little choice but to pay those costs.

The history of the telephone industry, back when telephones meant land lines, and all the major phone companies in the United States were subsidiaries of the American Telephone and Telegraph Company (A.T.&T.), illustrates this pattern.

As of 1930, there were only 331 black women in the entire country working as telephone operators, out of more than 230,000 women in that occupation. As late as 1950, black women were still only one percent of all women working for phone companies.[27] However, after creation of "fair employment practices" laws in some Northern states in the 1950s, and then federal civil rights laws and policies in the 1960s, many telephone companies reversed their policies, and blacks began to be hired disproportionately.

Prior to the 1960s, however, the state "fair employment practices" laws existed solely outside the South. Although a *national* sample of employment in the telephone industry showed that the employment of black telephone operators increased more than three-fold between 1950 and 1960,[28] it was 1964 before the first black telephone operator was hired by phone companies in such Southern places as New Orleans, Florida or South Carolina.[29]

These regional differences reflected the fact that individual telephone companies were regulated by *state* governments, and reflected state political forces. In the South during the 1950s, in all 11 states that had once formed the Confederate States of America, the share of blacks among male employees of telecommunications companies actually *declined* during the same decade when telephone companies in Northeastern and Midwestern states were hiring more blacks.[30]

Later data from a *national* sample of telephone companies showed that blacks accounted for one-third of the total growth in telephone companies' employees from 1966 to 1968—a trend that had begun in the 1950s and was concentrated mainly in Northeastern and Midwestern companies.[31] Since all major telephone companies in the country were owned and controlled by A.T.&T., such sharp regional disparities in individual phone company policies were far more consistent with regional political differences between Southern and non-Southern state governments that regulated these companies, rather than with policies handed down from A.T.&T.'s national management.

What was consistent in all these various regions was that additional costs entailed by either preferential or discriminatory treatment of black job applicants were costs that phone companies could pass on to customers, who had little choice but to pay them, since there were only land lines at the time, and each phone company was a monopoly in its own area.

It was much the same story in the government-regulated oil and gas public utilities at that time, where that regulation was also by state agencies, and increased hiring of blacks was confined to states outside the South during that era.[32] They too paid no cost for discriminating against blacks before, nor any cost for preferential hiring of blacks afterwards. The same was true of decision-makers who ran non-profit organizations or officials in charge of government hiring policies.

Similar incentives produced similar outcomes in non-profit organizations such as academic institutions, hospitals and foundations— and different outcomes in profit-based businesses operating in competitive markets. Like decision-makers in regulated public utilities, those in non-profit organizations were able to go along with whatever the prevailing opinions and pressures of the time might be, without having to worry about the costs created by Discrimination II against minorities, which their institutions would have to pay.

Against this background, it is hardly surprising that employment discrimination against blacks and Jews was especially widespread among colleges, universities, hospitals and foundations until after World War II, when a revulsion against Nazi racism set in. Before that happened, however, there were 300 black research chemists employed in private businesses in this earlier era, but only three black Ph.D.s in any field employed by white universities.[33]

As for Jews, they were seldom found on American college and university faculties before World War II. Although Milton Friedman had a temporary academic appointment before the war, it lasted only one year, despite high praise for his work by students and colleagues alike, and he spent the war years working as a statistician before eventually becoming a regular, tenured professor of economics at the University of Chicago after the war.[34]

At about the same time, the University of Chicago had its first black tenured professor.[35] The University of Chicago was exceptional only in doing such things *before* most of the rest of the academic world.*

Decades later, after the political climate had changed considerably, colleges and universities engaged in preferential hiring of black faculty, as well as preferential admissions of black students— again, without the academic decision-makers paying any price for their decisions, just

---

* As a personal note, the first time I encountered a white professor at a white university with a black secretary, it was Milton Friedman at the University of Chicago in 1960— four years before the Civil Rights Act of 1964.

as they paid no price for opposite policies earlier. "Affirmative action" in academia was sooner and more sweepingly adopted than in private industries operating in competitive markets.

All this happened too fast for such sweeping policy reversals in non-profit organizations to have been due to changing personnel in the role of decision-makers. In many, if not most, cases the same decision-makers who had discriminated against blacks were now instituting preferential policies favoring blacks. In neither case was the policy necessarily due to the personal beliefs, biases or values of the individual decision-makers, nor was the change necessarily due to "road to Damascus" conversions of personal views occurring among innumerable decision-makers at the same time.

UNINTENDED CONSEQUENCES

In addition to laws and policies directly concerned with Discrimination II, other laws and policies with very different purposes can also change the amount and impact of adverse consequences on groups defined by race, sex or other characteristics. In short, unintended consequences can affect outcomes as readily as intended consequences, and sometimes even more so. Minimum wage laws and building restrictions are two examples among others.

Minimum Wage Laws

Although minimum wage laws in the United States apply without regard to race, that does not mean that their impact is the same on blacks and whites alike. Where rates of pay are determined, not by supply and demand in a free market, but are imposed by minimum wage laws, that can affect the cost of Discrimination II to the discriminator.

A wage rate set above where it would be set by supply and demand in a freely competitive market tends to have at least two consequences: (1) an increase in the number of job applicants, due to the higher wage rate, and (2) a decrease in the number of workers actually hired, due to labor having been made more expensive. In this situation, the resulting chronic surplus of job applicants beyond the number of jobs available reduces the cost of refusing to hire qualified job applicants from particular groups, so long as the number of qualified job applicants refused employment is not greater than the number of surplus qualified applicants.

When, for example, the number of qualified black job applicants refused employment can be easily replaced by otherwise surplus qualified white or other job applicants, that reduces the cost of Discrimination II to the discriminating employer to virtually zero. On the most basic economic principles, such a situation makes racial or other discrimination far more affordable by employers, and therefore more sustainable, than in a situation where wage rates are determined by supply and demand in a free, competitive market.

In the latter case, where supply and demand leave no chronic surplus or chronic shortage of labor, qualified black job applicants turned away have to be replaced by attracting *additional* other qualified job applicants from other groups by offering higher pay than what that pay would be by supply and demand in a freely competitive and non-discriminatory labor market. In other words, Discrimination II has costs to discriminators in a free market, greater than its costs when a minimum wage law creates a chronic surplus of job applicants.

Empirical evidence is consistent with this hypothesis. The prevailing national minimum wage law in the United States is the Fair Labor Standards Act of 1938. However, high rates of inflation that began in the 1940s put virtually all money wages above the level specified in that Act. As a practical matter, there was no minimum wage in effect a decade after the law was passed. As economist George J. Stigler pointed out in 1946, "The minimum wage provisions of the Fair Labor Standards act of 1938 have been repealed by inflation."[36]

As of 1948, during this period of no effective minimum wage law, the unemployment rates of both black and white teenagers were just a fraction of what they would become in later years, as minimum wage rates began rising in the 1950s, in order to try to catch up, and then keep up, with inflation in later years.

What is particularly striking, however, is that there was no significant difference between the unemployment rates of black and white teenagers in 1948. The unemployment rate for black 16-year-old and 17-year-old males was 9.4 percent. For their white counterparts, the unemployment rate was 10.2 percent. For 18-year-old males and 19-year-old males, the unemployment rate was 9.4 percent for whites and 10.5 percent for blacks. In short, there was no significant racial difference in unemployment rates for teenage males in 1948,[37] when there was no effective minimum wage.

After the effectiveness of the minimum wage law was restored by recurring minimum wage increases in later years, not only did teenage unemployment rates as a whole rise to multiples of what they had been in 1948, black teenage male unemployment rates became much higher than the unemployment rates for white teenage males— usually at least twice as high for most years from 1967 on into the twenty-first century.[38]

Labor force participation rates tell much the same story. As of 1955, labor force participation rates were virtually the same for black and white males, aged 16 and 17. For 18-year-old and 19-year-old males, blacks had a slightly higher labor force participation rate than whites, as was also true of males aged 20 to 24. But this pattern changed drastically, as minimum wage rates rose over the years.

In the mid-1950s, black labor force participation rates for 16-year-old and 17-year-old males began falling below that of their white counterparts, and the gap grew wider in succeeding decades. For males aged 18 and 19, the same racial reversal in labor force participation rates occurred a decade later, in the mid-1960s. For males aged 20 to 24, that same racial reversal occurred at the beginning of the next decade, in 1970. The *magnitude* of the racial difference in labor force participation rates among males, after the racial reversal, followed the same pattern, being greatest for the 16-year-olds and 17-year-olds, less for males aged 18 and 19, and least for males aged 20 to 24.[39]

These labor force participation patterns shed additional light on the basis for racial differences in employment. If the primary reason for that racial difference in labor force participation rates was racism (Discrimination II), there was no reason for such reversals, and especially reversals in different years and with different magnitudes for different age groups. People who are black at age 16 remain black as they get older, so there is no basis for racists to change their treatment of blacks in such patterns as black workers age.

If, however, the real reason for these patterns was that the work experience and job skills of younger black workers made them less in demand than older black workers with more work experience and/or more job skills, then a rising minimum wage rate prices the younger blacks out of jobs first and to the greatest extent.

Unfortunately, when minimum wage laws reduce the employment prospects of inexperienced and unskilled black teenagers, that reduces their labor force participation, and therefore reduces their rate of acquisition of work experience and job skills. Whatever the degree of racism, it cannot explain age differences in employment among young black males, who do not change race as they grow older.

This pattern of virtually no difference in unemployment rates between black and white teenagers when wages were determined by supply and demand in a free market, but with large and enduring racial differences in unemployment rates when minimum wage laws became effective again, also fits the economic principle that a chronic surplus of job applicants reduces the cost of discrimination to the employer.

This pattern establishes correlation between increased minimum wage rates and changing racial differences in unemployment rates, and labor force participation rates, among teenagers. If this does not conclusively prove causation, it does establish a remarkable coincidence, persisting for decades.

Alternative explanations for these changing patterns of racial differences— such as racism, poverty or inferior education among blacks— cannot establish even correlation with changing employment outcomes over the years, because all those things were *worse* in the first half of the twentieth century, when the unemployment rate among black teenagers in 1948 was far lower and not significantly different from the unemployment rate among white teenagers.

Building Restrictions

Severe restrictions on building homes or other structures swept through various parts of the United States during the 1970s, in the name of preserving "open space," "saving farmland," "protecting the environment," "historical preservation," and other politically attractive slogans. But, however they were characterized, what such laws and policies did in practice was forbid, or drastically reduce, the building of either housing or other structures. Coastal California, including the entire peninsula from San Francisco to San Jose, was one of the largest regions where severe building-restriction laws and policies prevailed.

The predictable effect of restricting the building of housing, as the population was growing, was a rise in housing prices, when the supply of housing was not allowed to rise as the demand rose. California home prices were very similar to those in the rest of the country before this wave of building restrictions swept across the coastal regions of the state in the 1970s. But, afterwards, home prices in coastal California rose to become some multiple of home prices in the country as a whole.[40]

San Francisco Bay Area home prices rose to more than three times the national average.[41] In Palo Alto, adjacent to Stanford University, home prices nearly quadrupled during the 1970s, not because more expensive homes were being built— because there were *no* new homes built in Palo Alto during that decade. Existing homes simply skyrocketed in price.[42]

The racial impact of these housing restrictions was more pronounced than many racially explicit restrictions. By 2005, the black population of San Francisco was reduced to less than half of what it had been in 1970, even though the population of the city as a whole was growing.[43] In an even shorter span of time, between the 1990 and 2000 censuses, three other California counties— Los Angeles County, San Mateo County, and Alameda County— had their black populations decline by more than ten thousand people each, despite increases in the general population in each of these counties.[44]

By contrast, Harlem was a predominantly white community as late as 1910, and there were openly proclaimed and organized efforts by white landlords and realtors to prevent blacks from moving into Harlem.[45] But, like the organized white efforts to suppress black earnings in the post-bellum South, the mere presence of such organized efforts was no evidence or proof that they achieved their goal. To call such explicitly racist efforts in Harlem unsuccessful would be an understatement.

Those white landlords and realtors in Harlem who held out while others began to rent to blacks, found themselves losing white tenants who moved out of the neighborhood as blacks moved in, leaving the holdouts' buildings with many vacancies, representing lost rent.[46]

No such economic consequences inhibited those residents and their elected officials in later years who restricted the building of housing in San Francisco and other coastal California communities through the political process, driving up housing prices to levels that many blacks could not afford. On the contrary, such restrictions on new building *increased* the market value of the existing homes of residents in those communities.

Attitudes and beliefs, however strongly held or loudly proclaimed, do not automatically translate into end results— into "what emerges"— especially when there are costs to be borne by discriminators themselves.

It may well be that the racial attitudes and beliefs held by white landlords and realtors in early twentieth-century Harlem were more hostile to blacks than the attitudes and beliefs of white residents and officials in late twentieth-century San Francisco. But, in terms of end results, the actions of the former failed to keep blacks out of Harlem, while the actions of the latter drove out of San Francisco more than half the blacks already living in that city. Costs matter.

Chapter 3

Sorting and Unsorting People

Much empirical evidence suggests that human beings do not interact randomly— nor as frequently or as intensely— with all other human beings as with selected sub-sets of people like themselves. In short, people sort themselves out, both in where they choose to live and with whom they choose to interact most often and most closely.

It is worth examining some of that empirical evidence as to self-sorting, before going on to consider the consequences of third-party sorting or unsorting of other people. The crucial point here is that, when people spontaneously sort themselves, the results are seldom even or random, and are often quite skewed.

RESIDENTIAL SORTING AND UNSORTING

Where people live has, at various times and places, been decided either by the people themselves or by others who imposed various restrictions through a variety of institutional devices, ranging from government laws and policies to many private formal and informal means, ranging from restrictive covenants to homeowners' associations to outright violence against individuals or groups who have sought to live in neighborhoods where they were not welcome.

Residential and Social Self-Sorting

Immigrants have seldom emigrated evenly or randomly from their country of origin. Nor have they settled evenly or randomly in the country they reached. For example, two provinces in mid-nineteenth-century Spain, containing 6 percent of the Spanish population, supplied 67 percent of the Spanish immigrants to Argentina. Moreover, these immigrants tended to live clustered together in particular neighborhoods in Buenos Aires.[1]

Similarly skewed patterns of settlement have been common around the world, among other immigrants moving from their country of origin to their country of settlement.[2] During the era of mass emigration from Italy, for example, Italian immigrants in Australia, Brazil, Canada, Argentina and the United States not only tended to cluster together in predominantly Italian neighborhoods but, more specifically, within those neighborhoods people from Genoa, Naples or Sicily clustered together with other people from those same respective places in Italy.[3]

During that same era, the massive immigration of Eastern European Jews to America was concentrated in New York's Lower East Side. But within those Jewish neighborhoods, Hungarian Jews were largely clustered in their own enclaves, as were Jews from Romania, Russia and other places in Eastern Europe.[4]

German Jews, who had lived in their own enclave on the Lower East Side, decades before the mass arrival of Eastern European Jews, were already leaving that neighborhood as they rose socioeconomically, and were increasingly locating in other parts of New York as the Eastern European Jews arrived. Such spatial and social separation between German Jews and Eastern European Jews was common in New York,[5] Chicago,[6] San Francisco[7] and Boston.[8] In Australia, as well, there have been both institutional and social separation between the earlier arriving Jewish immigrants from Western Europe and the later Jewish immigrants from Eastern Europe, with the latter establishing their own synagogues and pursuing different religious and secular views and agendas.[9]

Lebanese immigrants to Sierra Leone in Africa or Colombia in South America likewise settled in enclaves of other Lebanese from the same parts of Lebanon and of the same religion, with Catholic Lebanese from particular places in Lebanon settling together and separate from enclaves of Orthodox Christians from Lebanon or Lebanese Shiite Muslims.[10]

German immigrants who settled in nineteenth-century New York not only settled in an area of Manhattan called *Kleindeutschland* (little

Germany), Hessians clustered in one part of *Kleindeutschland,* while Prussians clustered in another.[11]

People tend to sort themselves out, not only in their residential patterns but also in their social interactions. Twentieth-century Japanese immigrants to Brazil not only settled in Japanese enclaves, most Okinawan immigrants in Brazil married other Okinawans, rather than marrying fellow Japanese from other parts of Japan, much less marrying members of the Brazilian population at large.[12]

It was much the same story among German immigrants in nineteenth-century New York, where most Bavarians married other Bavarians, and most Prussians married other Prussians. Among the Irish immigrants as well, most nineteenth-century marriages that took place in New York's Irish enclaves were marriages between people from the same county in Ireland.[13]

In the Australian city of Griffith, in the years from 1920 to 1933, 90 percent of Italian men who had emigrated from Venice and gotten married in Australia married Italian women who had also emigrated from Venice. Another five percent married Italian women from other parts of Italy, the same percentage as married "British-Australian" women.[14]

However striking these patterns may be statistically, they are not patterns that most people are made aware of by seeing them with the naked eye, as is the case with differences between black neighborhoods and white neighborhoods in the United States. As a result, black-white residential separations have been seen and treated as if they were unique, as well as being inconsistent with prevailing background assumptions of equal or random outcomes in the absence of discriminatory impositions.

History shows that there have in fact been discriminatory impositions of residential patterns, at various times and places, not only as regards blacks in the United States, but also many other groups in countries around the world. These include the original ghettos imposed on Jews in much of Europe in centuries past. But that does not, by itself, mean that *all* residential sorting and social sorting are externally imposed, or need to be externally eradicated.

Sorting has been as common *within* black neighborhoods as within other neighborhoods around the world. Back in the 1930s, the research of noted black scholar E. Franklin Frazier showed clear patterns of residential clustering of people with different ways of life within the black community in Chicago. After dividing that community into seven zones, Professor Frazier showed empirically that the ratio of adults to children varied greatly from one zone to another, as did the ratio of males to females, and the percentage of mulattoes in the population was several times higher in one zone than in another.[15]

Moreover, these were not simply isolated differences. They were differences reflecting different socioeconomic levels and differences in family stability and individual behavioral standards. Delinquency rates within Chicago's black community ranged from more than 40 percent in some neighborhoods to under 2 percent in others.[16]

In nineteenth-century Detroit, black homeowners lived clustered together and separate from black renters.[17] Similar residential differentiation took place in Cleveland's black community.[18] A history of Harlem pointed out occupational differences among people who returned home from work and got off at different subway stops in Harlem.[19] Mid-twentieth-century data showed income distribution among blacks in the country as a whole to be slightly more unequal than among whites.[20] Later data in 2016 showed that, while the top ten percent of white income earners had incomes nearly *eight* times that of the bottom ten percent of white income earners, the top ten percent of black income earners had incomes nearly *ten* times the income of the bottom ten percent of black income earners.[21]

A 1966 study indicated that among the more than 4 million black American families at that time, just 5.2 *thousand* families produced all the black physicians, dentists, lawyers and academic doctorates in the country.[22] Despite how exceptional such occupations and achievements were among blacks at that time, these particular families averaged 2.25 individuals each in those categories.[23] That is, every four such families averaged nine individuals at these levels.

Awareness of such social and economic differences was both widespread and often acute within the black population.[24] There is a whole literature on exclusive black elites, including such books as

Aristocrats of Color by Willard B. Gatewood, *Our Kind of People* by Lawrence Otis Graham and *Certain People* by Stephen Birmingham.

Particular upscale neighborhoods within mid-twentieth-century Harlem were known as "Strivers' Row" and "Sugar Hill." A luxury apartment building at 409 Edgecombe Avenue was so widely known as a residence of the black elite that it was said to be sufficient to get into a taxi in Harlem and say simply "409" for the driver to know where to take you.[25]

Those blacks born and bred in nineteenth-century Chicago, and living as small enclaves of blacks in an overwhelmingly white population, assimilated culturally to the norms of the surrounding society, as other groups have in similar circumstances. The later massive migrations of Southern blacks to Chicago in the twentieth century created acute polarization within the black community there.[26]

The *Chicago Defender*, a black newspaper, was highly critical of the newcomers for behavior that gave blacks in general a bad name. So were other blacks from the pre-existing black community there and in other Northern cities, where both the existing black residents and the local black press denounced the new arrivals from the South as vulgar, rowdy, unwashed and criminal.[27]

Like other black newspapers in other Northern communities, the *Chicago Defender* published many admonitions to Southern blacks arriving in Chicago, including "Don't use vile language in public places," "Don't allow yourself to be drawn into street brawls," "Don't take the part of law breakers, be they men, women, or children," and "Don't abuse or violate the confidence of those who give you employment."[28]

As with other racial or ethnic groups, in other times and places, blacks in these Northern communities feared that the arrival of less assimilated members of their own group would provoke negative reactions in the larger society that would not only jeopardize the progress of their race, but would even threaten retrogressions, as the larger society turned against blacks in general.[29]

These fears as to how the new black arrivals from the South would behave, and how the local white population would react against blacks in general, both turned out to be all too well founded. A study in early twentieth-century Pennsylvania, for example, showed that the rate of violent crimes among black migrants from the South was nearly five times the rate of such crimes by blacks born in Pennsylvania.[30] The South had long been the country's most violent region, among blacks and whites alike.[31]

Negative reactions from Northern whites set in, as feared, and affected blacks in many ways. Some Northern communities where black children had for years been going to the same schools as white children, now began to impose racial segregation in the schools.[32]

In Washington, blacks were no longer allowed in many white theaters, restaurants or hotels, and their opportunities to work in white-collar occupations shrank.[33] There were similar restrictive trends in Cleveland, Chicago, and St. Louis,[34] among other places. Oberlin College and Harvard, where black students had lived in dormitories with white students before, now excluded black students from their dormitories.[35]

As these retrogressions set in, in Northern cities, black civic organizations, such as the Urban League, sought to assimilate the newcomers to existing norms of behavior, just as civic and religious organizations among the Irish and the Jews did earlier, in order to get Irish and Jewish immigrants assimilated to American cultural standards.[36]

SIDEBAR: FEAR OF RETROGRESSION

Fears of social retrogression from the arrival of less acculturated members of one's own group were not peculiar to blacks or to the United States.

When Jewish refugees from Europe sought to gain entrance to Australia before the Second World War, the Australian Jewish Welfare Society opposed allowing "hordes" of refugees to enter the country, and those Jewish refugees who did in fact enter were handed cards from this organization which read:

> Above all, do not speak German in the streets and in the
> trams. Modulate your voices. Do not make yourself conspicuous
> anywhere by walking with a group of persons, all of whom are
> loudly speaking a foreign language. Remember that the welfare
> of the old-established Jewish communities in Australia, as well
> as of every migrant, depends on your personal behaviour. Jews
> collectively are judged by individuals. You, personally have a
> very grave responsibility.[37]

The conclusion that the widespread retrogressions in racial
opportunities open to blacks in Northern cities in the early twentieth
century were a result of the massive migration of less acculturated
Southern blacks to those communities is reinforced by the history of
the mass migration of Southern blacks to the Pacific coast, decades
later.

In the 1940s, during World War II, industries producing military
equipment and supplies on the Pacific coast attracted vast numbers
of blacks and whites from the South. Henry Kaiser's huge shipyard
in Richmond, California, alone employed more than 90,000 people,[38]
and there were similar war industries in other west coast communities.

As among Northern cities in the nineteenth century, blacks were
a very small percentage of the population on the Pacific coast before
these mass migrations from the South, and were correspondingly
more acculturated to the behavioral norms of the surrounding society
than were Southern blacks arriving there. Prior to the 1940s, racial
discrimination was not on the same scale on the Pacific coast as in
the South, or as in Northeastern cities after the great migrations there
from the South. In San Francisco, black children went to schools that
were not racially segregated and the small black population lived in
neighborhoods with whites, Chinese and other races.[39]

The great migrations of blacks out of the South that reached the
Northeastern and Midwestern cities around the time of the First
World War reached the Pacific coast, decades later, during the Second
World War. In the 1940s, more than four-fifths of the blacks who
arrived in the San Francisco Bay Area shipyards came from the South,
usually the less educated Deep South.[40]

The new black arrivals were overwhelmingly more numerous than the existing black population. In Richmond, California, for example, there were only 270 black residents in 1940 but the Kaiser industries brought in more than 10,000.[41] The black population of Berkeley in the 1950 census was nearly four times what it had been in the 1940 census, before the United States was at war. Over that same span of time, the black population of Oakland rose to more than five times what it had been before, and that of San Francisco rose to approximately nine times its 1940 level.[42]

As in the Northern cities earlier in the twentieth century, the new black arrivals on the west coast were seen by the existing black population there as vulgar and ill-behaved.[43] And, as in Northern cities decades earlier, the arrival of the newcomers was followed by retrogressions in black-white relations.[44]

A timeless explanation of discrimination against blacks, such as racism, cannot account for either the progress or the retrogressions that took place on a large scale at differing times. This is not to deny that there has been racism, but the evidence suggests that the discrimination that took place was not simply Discrimination II, for that would leave unexplained the large swings in the magnitude of discrimination against blacks.

These striking changes in the progress and retrogressions in black-white relations over time have been too large and too numerous in different settings to be simply Discrimination II— based on a false perception by whites— and more closely fit the consequences of Discrimination I*B*, a correct perception of behavioral changes in local black communities outside the South, as those communities began to consist increasingly of people steeped in a culture that originated in the South, and was unwelcome in the North by both black and white Northern communities.

As late as 1944, when a landmark study of American race relations— *An American Dilemma* by Gunnar Myrdal— was published, that study pointed out that most blacks living in the North had been born in the South.[45] Moreover, the sheer size of the greatly enlarged black communities living in places outside the South meant that neither the pace nor the thoroughness of cultural assimilation of these black communities to the behavioral norms of the larger society was likely to be what it had been in the tiny black communities in the North, surrounded by overwhelmingly white communities, during the nineteenth century.

In short, Discrimination I*B* had staying power, despite how much some might prefer depicting it as Discrimination II. To the extent that the cause was misdiagnosed, proposed cures for Discrimination II, such as re-educating the white population to their misperceptions, offered only limited prospects of success.

Many individual blacks were in fact misperceived, given the very high costs of gaining the knowledge required for Discrimination I*A*, judging each individual as an individual.

But to argue that the black population as a whole was misperceived, and that this explains the retrogressions, is to argue that the pre-existing black population and the pre-existing white population were both mistaken when they reached very similar conclusions about the behavior of the incoming migrant population. At the very least, such a conclusion should require at least some empirical evidence.

The Prevalence of Sorting

In countries around the world, innumerable groups have sorted themselves in many ways, socially as well as residentially. This sorting extends right down to the individual level. The correlation between the IQs of husbands and wives is at least as high as the correlation between the IQs of brothers and sisters[46]— even though there is no *biological* reason for the IQs of husbands and wives to be similar, as there is with brothers and sisters. Clearly, people sort themselves out when choosing whom to marry, even though they are highly unlikely to actually know the IQ of the person they marry before the wedding, nor necessarily even afterwards. Yet the net result of their spontaneous and informal sorting produces this statistical correlation nevertheless.

People who shop at stores in the Whole Foods chain have college degrees more than twice as often as people who shop at stores in the Family Dollar chain. The stores in the Whole Foods chain are located in communities with average population sizes more than five times the average population size in communities where stores in the Dollar General chain are located.[47]

There are many other kinds of sorting, including sorting by lifestyle in Bohemian neighborhoods like Greenwich Village, which represents an *unsorting* by such other criteria as race or social class origins. Yet what is far harder to find is the even or random distribution of different kinds of people— in places or endeavors— that is widely treated as a norm, deviations from which are regarded as evidence of discrimination, in the sense of Discrimination II.

From the standpoint of particular individuals, there is no question that, because of pervasive social sorting and Discrimination I*B*, there can be large, and sometimes devastating, costs imposed on individuals because of the actions of other members of the group to which they belong, even when the particular individual has played no part in those actions to which members of other groups object.

Such individuals are clearly victims, but of whom? The hooligans and criminals who have caused other groups to seek to protect their own safety and the security of their homes and families? From a moral perspective, there is no obvious "solution," unless the interests of one set of people automatically trump the interests of another, which hardly seems moral, even if it may be politically expedient or in keeping with whatever the social vogues of the time might be.

An episode involving sociologist William Julius Wilson presents a much milder version of the dilemmas faced earlier during the great migrations. According to Professor Wilson:

> I am an internationally known Harvard professor, yet a number of unforgettable experiences remind me that, as a black male in America looking considerably younger than my age, I am also feared. For example, several times over the years I have stepped into the elevator of my condominium dressed in casual clothes and could immediately tell from the body language of the other residents in the elevator that I made them feel uncomfortable. Were they thinking, "What is this black man doing in this expensive condominium? Are we in any danger?" I once sarcastically said to a nervous elderly couple who hesitated to exit the elevator because we were all getting off on the same floor, "Not to worry, I am a Harvard professor and I have lived

in this building for nine years." When I am dressed casually, I am always a little relieved to step into an empty elevator, but I am not apprehensive if I am wearing a tie.

I get angry each time I have an experience like the encounter in the elevator.[48]

Professor Wilson's sarcasm and anger were directed at people whose reactions reflected a greater concern for their own personal safety than for his sensitivities. His account suggests that they were not racists, for merely by wearing a tie he avoided tensions on both sides, even though wearing a tie did not change his race.

Unlike blacks from an earlier era, who clearly blamed those blacks whose behavior had brought on a retrogression that hurt all blacks, Professor Wilson's account gives no indication of any sense that he was paying the social price for dangers created by black hooligans and criminals.

A very different view of such situations was taken by another black scholar, Professor Walter E. Williams, an economist at George Mason University:

> Information is not costless... People therefore seek to economize on information cost. In doing so, they tend to substitute less expensive forms of information for more expensive forms. Physical attributes are "cheap" to observe. If a particular physical attribute is perceived as correlated with a more costly-to-observe one, the observer might use that attribute as an estimator or proxy for the costly-to-observe attribute.[49]

In a sense, Professor Wilson's reactions were similar to those of people who blame store owners for the high prices charged in low-income, high-crime neighborhoods, rather than blame those whose behavior raised the costs that the stores' prices have to cover. There was a time when ordinary blacks, with far less education than Professor Wilson, saw clearly that the misbehavior of a black underclass would cause other blacks to be burdened with a backlash. They understood what is called here Discrimination I*B*.[50]

Imposed Residential and Social Sorting

In addition to spontaneous self-sorting, there is no question that there has also been residential Discrimination II in the plain sense that governmental regulations have explicitly prescribed where people of a particular race, religion, or other social identity can and cannot live.

These would include the original ghettos to which Jews were consigned in particular European cities in centuries past, or whole geographic regions of the Russian Empire where Jews were permitted or not permitted to settle. The areas where Jews were permitted to live were called "the Pale of Settlement"— a phrase surviving in the English language today in statements about certain things being "beyond the Pale."

Similar residential restrictions were placed on the overseas Chinese minorities in various Southeast Asian communities, as well as other groups in other societies around the world. In the United States, similar governmental restrictions on where black Americans could live were long common in various forms, supplemented by private racial restrictions.[51]

The question is not whether such residential restrictions can exist, or have existed, but whether the presence of such restrictions can be automatically inferred from statistics showing non-random clusterings of particular people living in particular places or concentrated in particular kinds or levels of particular occupations. Such issues involve not only causal questions but also moral questions— the latter being harder to answer.

Causation

Even seeking a causal explanation is by no means simple. We may characterize the behavior of whites who did not want blacks living in their neighborhoods as "racist." But, if we wish to go beyond characterizations to cause and effect, we have entered the world of facts, with its testing of beliefs against evidence. Once again, we confront the difference between Discrimination I and Discrimination II.

Going back to the earliest days of slavery in colonial America, there is no question that slaves simply lived wherever others told them to live. But even in those early times, there were also "free persons of color." In fact, these "free persons of color" existed in the American colonies before slavery existed, even though slavery existed virtually everywhere else in the world at that time. And it developed as a legal institution in seventeenth-century America.

Before that, the relatively few Africans in the colonies were treated like the far larger numbers of indentured servants from Europe, who were held in bondage for a given number of years, usually to pay off the cost of their passage across the ocean, and then released as free people. In early colonial America, more than half the white population in colonies south of New England arrived as indentured servants.[52]

The relative handful of blacks at that time were treated the same legally, in that regard[53]— but not socially. As the numbers of Africans brought to the colonies increased greatly, their fate became that of perpetual slavery for themselves and their descendants.

Thus began a cycle of retrogressions followed by progress, followed by new retrogressions followed by new progress, in the treatment of the black population. The reasons for these oscillations tell us something about Discrimination I and Discrimination II.

Even if racist ideas, assumptions and aversions might fully explain discrimination against blacks, that would still leave unexplained these oscillations— which represented major changes, back and forth, lasting for generations, in both the nineteenth century and the twentieth century.

Major restrictions, both legal and social, against "free persons of color" existed in both the North and the South, during the era of slavery. But, while those restrictions tightened over time in the South during the nineteenth century, they eroded in the North during that same century.

In the South, where plantation slavery was the norm, "free persons of color" were seen as dangers to that whole system, both because their very presence demonstrated to slaves that slavery was not an inevitable fate for black people, and because the fraternization of "free persons of color" with slaves not only spread the idea of freedom, but also provided a source of help for slaves who escaped.

In the North, whose climate was not conducive to plantation slavery, and where blacks were a marginal part of the total population, both legal and social restrictions against blacks were not as severe and— more important— began to erode significantly in the second half of the nineteenth century, after successive generations of Northern-born, free blacks began to acculturate to the behavioral norms of the much larger white population around them. In Illinois, for example, legal restrictions on access to public accommodations for blacks were removed from the law.[54] There were not enough black voters at that time to have brought this about by themselves, so this represented changes in white public opinion.

In nineteenth-century Detroit, blacks were not allowed to vote in 1850, but they were voting in the 1880s, and in the 1890s blacks were being elected to statewide offices in Michigan by a predominantly white electorate. The 1880 census showed that, in Detroit, it was not uncommon for blacks and whites to live next door to each other.[55] The black upper class had regular social interactions with upper-class whites, and their children attended high schools and colleges with the children of their white counterparts.[56]

Writing in 1899, W.E.B. Du Bois noted "a growing liberal spirit toward the Negro in Philadelphia," in which the larger community had begun to "brush away petty hindrances and to soften the harshness of race prejudice"— leading, among other things, to blacks being able to live in white neighborhoods.[57] Both contemporary and later writers commented on similar developments in other Northern communities.[58]

While black children in most Northern communities had long been educated in racially segregated schools during the first half of the nineteenth century, if they were allowed to attend public schools at all, this changed during the second half of that century:

> By 1870, those northern states that had excluded blacks from public schools had reversed course. Moreover, during the quarter century following the end of the Civil War, most northern states enacted legislation that prohibited racial segregation in public education. Most northern courts, when called upon to enforce this newly

enacted antisegregation legislation, did so, ordering the admission of
black children into white schools.[59]

These were not just coincidental mood swings among whites across
the North. *The behavior of blacks themselves had changed.*

As Jacob Riis put it in 1890, "There is no more clean and orderly
community in New York than the new settlement of colored people
that is growing up on the East Side from Yorkville to Harlem."[60] By
the late nineteenth century, most blacks in New York state had been
born in New York state, and grew up with values and behavior patterns
similar to those of the vastly larger white population around them.

However, in this as in other things, a major retrogression set in later,
in Northern cities, with the arrival of large masses of black migrants
from the South in the early twentieth century, concentrated within a
relatively few years and arriving in numbers sufficient to prevent their
becoming as acculturated to the norms of the larger society, either as
quickly or as much as the small nineteenth-century black populations
had in the North. The same retrogressions in race relations seen in
other aspects of life likewise occurred in Northern schools:

> . . .with the migration of hundreds of thousands of southern blacks
> into northern communities during the first half of the twentieth
> century, northern school segregation dramatically increased. Indeed,
> by 1940, northern school segregation was more extensive than it had
> been at any time since Reconstruction.[61]

In most cases, this was *de facto* racial segregation in the North,
as distinguished from the explicit racial segregation by law in
Southern schools. But similar end results were achieved in the North
by gerrymandering school districts and by other means. Among the
reasons cited for this resurgence of racial segregation in the Northern
schools were both educational and behavioral problems of black
children.[62] However, as regards educational problems, surveys in both
Chicago and Detroit indicated that these were primarily problems
with black children whose families had migrated from the South,[63]
where educational standards were lower.

Neither eras of progress in race relations nor eras of retrogression were simply inexplicable mood swings among whites. Both represented responses to demonstrable changes in local black populations. These responses were complicated by the inherent problems of white third parties trying to sort out differences among black children, even though sorting out black children in general from white children in general required nothing more than eyesight. It was very low-cost Discrimination I*B*.

Moreover, in the early twentieth century, the rise to dominance of genetic determinism as a supposedly "scientific" doctrine strengthened the hand of those white officials who were prepared to write off the potential of black and other minority children, as the Progressives of that era did.[64]

UNSORTING PEOPLE

The residential and other outcomes produced by the sorting of people became, in the second half of the twentieth century, widely condemned as wrong in itself, and as creating other social wrongs against the less fortunate groups. This might be considered a special case of the more general assumption that outcomes would tend to be even, or random, in the absence of malign interventions.

But, whatever it was based on, the view became axiomatic among many Americans in the second half of the twentieth century that unsorting people was a high priority, especially in schools, but also in residential neighborhoods.

Educational Unsorting

Perhaps the most famous, and most consequential, Supreme Court decision of the twentieth century was that in the 1954 case of ***Brown v. Board of Education***, declaring that racially segregated schools were unconstitutional. This ended more than half a century of hypocrisy, following the 1896 decision in ***Plessy v. Ferguson*** that government-imposed racial segregation did not violate the Fourteenth Amendment requirement of "equal protection of the laws" for all, so long as the racially segregated facilities provided for blacks were "separate but equal."

For generations, it was widely known that the separate facilities provided for blacks in the racially segregated South were grossly unequal. As courts belatedly began to demand that either equal state institutions be provided for blacks or else blacks must be admitted to the institutions provided for whites, various efforts were made by Southern states to reduce the inequality and, in some cases, blacks were reluctantly granted access to some white institutions, such as a law school in Texas, though with restrictions that did not apply to white students.[65] But even this represented a slow, uphill advance against determined resistance by Southern officials.

Now, in the *Brown v. Board of Education* case, a unanimous Supreme Court decreed that racially segregated schools were, according to Chief Justice Earl Warren, *inherently* unequal,[66] so that the slow and circuitous route to equalizing government facilities was to be replaced by simply outlawing the official sorting of school children by race.

It was now no longer a question of unequal physical facilities or unequal financial support, for the very act of racial segregation was said to reduce the educational prospects of black children: "To separate them from others of similar age and qualifications solely because of their race generates a feeling of inferiority as to their status in the community that may affect their hearts and minds in a way unlikely ever to be undone."[67]

In the heady atmosphere of the times, when the *Brown v. Board of Education* decision was widely hailed by blacks and most whites, except among white Southerners, as a long overdue end to government-imposed racial segregation and discrimination, the ringing assertions made by Chief Justice Warren were widely accepted. Nevertheless, only about a mile from where those pronouncements were made in the Supreme Court, there was an all-black public high school whose history, going all the way back into the nineteenth century, belied the Chief Justice's key assertions about empirical facts.

As of 1954, when Chief Justice Warren declared that separate schools were inherently unequal, all-black Dunbar High School sent a higher percentage of its graduates on to college than any white public high school in Washington.[68] As far back as 1899, when the same test was given in Washington's four academic high schools at that time, this same all-black public high school scored higher than two of the three white public high schools.[69]

Although most of its graduates went to local colleges, some were already beginning to go to some of the leading colleges in the country at the end of the nineteenth century— and graduating Phi Beta Kappa. Over the period from 1892 to 1954, 34 of these graduates were admitted to Amherst College. Of these, 74 percent graduated from Amherst, and 28 percent of these black graduates were Phi Beta Kappas.[70] Among other elite colleges from which students from this high school graduated Phi Beta Kappa during that era were Harvard, Yale, Williams, Cornell, and Dartmouth.[71]

Among the graduates of this high school— known by various names over the years since its founding in 1870, including Dunbar High School since 1916— were "the first black who" had a range of career achievements. These included the first black woman to earn a Ph.D. at an American university, the first black federal judge, the first black general, the first black Cabinet member, the first black tenured professor at a major national university, and Dr. Charles Drew, who won international recognition as a pioneer in developing the use of blood plasma.[72]

Clearly, racially segregated schools were *not* inherently inferior. There is no question that most black schools in the South at that time, and many in the North, had inferior educational outcomes. And no doubt inferior resources supplied to black schools had a role in these outcomes, though not necessarily the sole role or the most important role.

In any event, the crusade to racially integrate public schools, during the decades following the *Brown v. Board of Education* decision, generated much social turmoil, racial polarization and bitter backlashes, *but no general educational improvement* from seating black school children next to white school children.

One of the painful ironies of the racial integration crusade was that Dunbar High School's 85 years of academic achievement came to an abrupt end, in the wake of the *Brown v. Board of Education* decision. To comply with that decision, Washington schools were all made neighborhood schools, so that Dunbar could no longer admit black students from all parts of the city, as it had before, but only students from the particular ghetto neighborhood where it was located. Dunbar quickly became a typical failing ghetto school, with serious academic and behavioral problems.

By 1993, a smaller percentage of Dunbar students went on to college than had done so 60 years earlier[73]— even though 1933 was in the depths of the Great Depression of the 1930s and 1993 was in the midst of the prosperous decade of the 1990s.

Neither racial integration nor general prosperity, nor even a newer, more modern and more expensive school building was a substitute for what was lost. Yet, toward the end of the twentieth century, some new and highly successful schools brought educational excellence to many ghetto communities, not only in Washington but also in New York and other communities across the country. Many of these educational successes were in particular chains of charter schools, such as the Success Academy and KIPP (Knowledge Is Power Program) chains.

Not all charter schools were successful, but those that were successful often produced a level of educational achievement far above those of either most ghetto schools or many of the white schools to which black children were bused in the name of racial integration.

In 2017, for example, the 14,000 students in the Success Academy charter schools in New York passed the statewide examinations in English and mathematics at a higher rate than the students in any regular public school district in the entire state.

What made this especially striking is that an overwhelming majority of the students in the Success Academy schools were either black or Hispanic, and from low-income families, while an overwhelming majority of the students in the regular public school district with the highest proportion of its students passing the same examinations were either white or Asian, and their average family income was four times that of families with children in the Success Academy schools.[74]

What is truly extraordinary about such educational achievements is that the children admitted to the Success Academy charter schools were selected by lottery— by sheer chance— rather than by either tests or by their previous records in school. They differ from a random sample of low-income black and Hispanic youngsters only in that they are the children of parents who cared enough about their education to enter them in the lottery. They were *self-sorted*, contrary to beliefs by many others that low-income minority parents are not qualified to make educational decisions supposedly best made by educational or other "experts."

Here, as with Dunbar High School during its past era of academic achievement, *self-sorting* was crucial. Black students were not simply assigned to go to Dunbar High School during its era of academic achievements. Students had to apply, and those with neither the interest nor the inclination to subject themselves to rigorous educational norms had no reason to apply.

The educational track record of such self-sorting has been far more successful than *third-party* sorting, whether the third parties sorted by race or by residential location, or by a belief that racial diversity would lead to higher educational achievements.

The usual explanations or excuses for grossly inferior educational results in minority neighborhood public schools do not stand up under scrutiny. Whatever the effects of "a legacy of slavery" or of generations of racial discrimination, these black children who succeeded in Success Academy charter schools were no more exempt from these and other negative social influences than other black children from the same communities who have failed abysmally in the regular public schools.

Internal differences have been at least as common among blacks as among other racial or ethnic groups, making self-sorting a way of reducing counterproductive frictions that impede education. Successful charter schools give a glimpse of what can be accomplished by black children in low-income ghettos when self-sorting frees them from the disruptions and violence of unruly classmates, just a small number of whom can prevent a whole class from getting a decent education.

Residential Unsorting

Along with the unsorting of American school children by decades of mandatory busing to racially "integrate" public schools in racially different neighborhoods, there have been parallel efforts to racially "integrate" the neighborhoods themselves.

Among the various government programs to unsort people who have sorted themselves have been programs to build the kind of housing in middle-class neighborhoods that would be affordable to people with lower incomes. Other strategies have included providing subsidies to enable low-income and minority families to be able to rent existing housing in higher income neighborhoods.

The assumption behind such programs has been that social isolation was behind many social pathologies in the ghettos, so that ending that isolation would lead to improvements in the behavior and performances of minority adults and children.

This was essentially the same assumption behind the Supreme Court's *Brown v. Board of Education* decision, that separate facilities were inherently unequal. Although that decision did not explicitly state that racial mixing was essential for black children to get an equal education, that was the logical corollary of what the decision did say.

The idea of racial "integration" or demographic "diversity" spread from education issues to questions of residential unsorting of different racial, ethnic or income groups. Government promotion or imposition of such policies was said to benefit both the newcomers inserted into middle-class neighborhoods and the existing residents who had sorted themselves away from them.

Whatever the plausibility of those assumptions and theories, the crucial question of the empirical validity of such assumptions depends on hard evidence. Contrary to those who attribute social pathologies in the ghettos to external causes in general, and white racism in particular, some of the strongest opposition to government programs that insert people from ghettos into middle-class neighborhoods came from *black* residents in those middle-class neighborhoods.[75] As the *Chicago Tribune* put it:

The harshest criticism of dispersing public housing's tenants comes not from whites but from blacks. In Harvey, a struggling, working-class African-American suburb south of the city, nearly one of every 10 housing units is already occupied by renters with subsidies.[76]

Among the behaviors of the newcomers commonly complained of by the original residents of working-class and middle-class neighborhoods around the country are that the newcomers' teen-aged children "are allowed to hang out on corners, play basketball late into the night, and sit in parked cars blasting profane music,"[77] as in Chicago. Pre-existing residents complain that they "hear frequent gunfire."[78]

In a San Francisco Bay Area community, the charge is that the children of the newcomers are "burglarizing nearby residences, hosting wild parties during the week and weekends, threatening neighbors, and engaging in various forms of criminal activity... robbing and assaulting our kids to and from school."[79] In Louisville, homicides have remained concentrated over the years in areas where housing project people have been concentrated.[80]

Black residents in working-class or middle-class communities have been particularly uninhibited in their denunciations of people from public housing projects and people on welfare that the government inserts into their communities, perhaps because black middle-class residents are not afraid of being called "racists."

According to the *Chicago Tribune*, the resistance of working-class and middle-class blacks "in some cases has been fierce." Black homeowners have "protested, loudly" at public meetings that they "didn't want 'those people' moving back into their rejuvenated neighborhood." Often homeowners at public gatherings "would shout at officials that they'd worked hard to get where they were and that they didn't want to live next door to people who would just tear up their homes. They called them 'project people,' 'lowlifers' and 'freeloaders.'"[81]

"Some blacks feel that 'those people' make it tough on those of us trying to make something of ourselves," says Shirley Newsome, a homeowner in Kenwood-Oakland and a longtime voice of moderation. "That's why white America doesn't want me living next to them, because they look at me and figure I'm from a place like public housing."[82]

Like so many social patterns that are usually discussed in terms of race, this pattern of inserting underclass newcomers into neighborhoods where they are resented by the pre-existing residents also exists when the underclass newcomers are white, and are resented by white pre-existing residents. In the best-selling memoir *Hillbilly Elegy*, the author— a white man from a hillbilly background— reported that his grandmother saw the government's placing underclass people in their midst "as a betrayal, ensuring that 'bad' people would move into the neighborhood," even though they "looked a lot like us," but they were the kind of hillbillies who "gave our people a bad name."[83]

Among other things, she resented "the drugs and the late-night fighting" among the new neighbors that the government had placed in their neighborhood, and said of the woman who lived next door: "She's a lazy whore, but she wouldn't be if she was forced to get a job." More pointedly: "I can't understand why people who've worked all their lives scrape by while these deadbeats buy liquor and cell phone coverage with our tax money."[84]

Advocates of unsorting neighborhoods, whether by race or by class, argue that living in a better neighborhood will produce benefits for both the adults and the children who are moved in, and benefits of "diversity" for society at large. But these expected benefits to the newcomers from housing projects and high-crime neighborhoods have repeatedly failed to show up in extensive empirical studies by a wide variety of researchers on the federal government's "Moving to Opportunity" program.

A study of that program published in the *Journal of Human Resources* concluded: "We did not find evidence of improvements in reading scores, math scores, behavior or school problems, or school engagement, overall or for any age group."[85] Another study of the same program published in the *American Journal of Sociology* concluded that "there is no evidence that extra time spent in low-poverty integrated neighborhoods improves economic outcomes."[86]

Yet another study of the "Moving to Opportunity" program, published in the economic journal *Econometrica* likewise concluded, "we found no significant evidence of treatment effects on earnings, welfare participation, or amount of government assistance after an average of 5 years since random assignment."[87] The *American Economic Review*, the official journal of the American Economic Association, reached similar conclusions about the same federal program— "no consistent detectable impacts on adult economic self-sufficiency or children's educational achievement outcomes" from the movement of thousands of people into higher income neighborhoods than the ones they came from.[88]

The *Quarterly Journal of Economics*, the oldest American journal in economics, likewise concluded that "the changes in neighborhoods induced by MTO ("Moving to Opportunity" program) have not affected the employment rates, earnings, or welfare usage by a statistically detectable amount for household heads."[89]

In addition to these scholarly journals, a study published by the U.S. Department of Housing and Urban Development (HUD) was based on research on that same program which "followed more than 4,600 very low-income families in five U.S. cities over a 10- to 15-year period to examine the short- and long-term effects of moving to low-poverty neighborhoods." Its conclusion was: "No discernible benefit to economic self-sufficiency, employment outcomes, and risky and criminal behavior for adults and children was observed as a result of moving. Similarly, moving had few positive effects on educational achievement for youth."[90]

Nevertheless, Secretary of Housing and Urban Development Shaun Donovan in 2013 "vowed to help urban blacks relocate to suburban neighborhoods, where they can have access to 'good schools, safe streets, jobs, grocery stores,' among other things." Secretary Donovan claimed that realtors and landlords still discriminate against blacks. "African-Americans," Donovan said, "are being denied their freedom of choice."[91] According to *Investor's Business Daily*:

Earlier this year, HUD broadened the authority of two anti-discrimination laws— the Fair Housing Act and the Equal Credit

Opportunity Act— making illegal any housing or credit policy
that results in disproportionately fewer blacks or Latinos receiving
housing or home loans than whites, even if those policies are race-
neutral and evenly applied across all groups.[92]

Here, yet again, we see the implicit assumption that there would
be no disparate outcomes unless there were disparate treatment.
Moreover, that assumption seems almost impervious to evidence.

One major difference between people sorting or unsorting
themselves, on the one hand, and government officials sorting or
unsorting them, on the other hand, is that people who sort or unsort
themselves receive both the benefits and the costs of doing so. But
government officials receive neither the benefits nor the costs of
unsorting other people— and so may persist in the process, in utter
disregard of benefits or costs that fall on others. Indeed, the *political*
costs of admitting to having inflicted socially counterproductive
policies are a powerful incentive to keep on inflicting those policies
and ignoring or denying their consequences.[93]

It would be wrong to say that there have been literally no benefits
at all to anyone from government-subsidized or government-enforced
unsorting of people. While some studies have found some benefits
to some segments of the low-income groups placed into middle-class
neighborhoods by the government,[94] these have seldom, if ever, been
of the scope or magnitude envisioned when these programs were
instituted.

More fundamentally, negative consequences to the pre-existing
residents of the communities into which they have been placed are
seldom, if ever, mentioned— much less measured— in these studies. It
is as if any benefit, however small, to the new residents automatically
outweighs any costs, however large, to the pre-existing residents.

"Disparate Impact" in Employment

If a given prerequisite for employment or promotion— a high
school diploma, for example— has a "disparate impact" on some group,
such as ethnic minorities, then the burden of proof falls on the accused

employer to provide a justification of the requirement or else be judged guilty of discrimination.

This process represents a major departure from American legal principles in both criminal and civil cases, where the burden of proof is usually put on those making an accusation, rather than expecting the accused to prove their innocence. There are serious practical consequences of this very different legal standard in civil rights cases. There are costs to both employers and workers seeking employment, when the assortment and proportions of employees differ from the assortment and proportions of groups in the surrounding area.

For the employer, the fact that a charge of discrimination can be made, based solely on statistics about his employees, without even a single flesh-and-blood human being actually claiming to be discriminated against, means that employers can be put through a costly and time-consuming legal process that can drag on for years, consuming millions of dollars in legal costs alone, quite aside from costs imposed if this uncertain process leads to an unfavorable verdict.

For example, a case charging the Sears department store chain with sex discrimination cost the company $20 million in legal fees[95] and took 15 years to resolve through the federal courts— without the government having to produce even one woman, from any of Sears' hundreds of department stores around the country, claiming to have been discriminated against. Statistical disparities alone were sufficient to keep this costly process going for more than a decade.

In the end, Sears prevailed in the appellate courts. But few employers are in any position to sustain such financial costs for so many years, all the while operating under the public stigma of discrimination accusations that can affect public opinion and the sale of the company's products.

Most employers, including large corporations, find it expedient to settle such cases out of court, even when they have not violated anti-discrimination laws— and the number of such settlements is then used by critics to claim that employment discrimination is widespread. In 2012, for example, PepsiCo paid more than $3 million to settle a charge by the Equal Employment Opportunity Commission that the big soda and snacks company's use of criminal background checks was discrimination against blacks.[96]

This was a bargain compared to the cost to Sears of fighting a charge of discrimination against women, even though Sears eventually won the case. Moreover, having a charge of racial discrimination hanging over PepsiCo for years, while the case dragged on through the federal courts, could have cost more millions, as individuals and institutions decided to buy their sodas and snacks from some other company.

In short, the outcome of "disparate impact" cases does not necessarily depend on either the quantity or the quality of the evidence. By the time of the PepsiCo settlement, an empirical study had already shown that companies using criminal background checks tended to hire *more* blacks than companies which did not use such checks.[97] The crucial factor in such cases is not the trial, but the costliness of going to trial, both in legal fees and in the loss of business due to bad publicity. The only way for the accused to win, in any economically meaningful sense, is for the case to be thrown out of court instead of going to trial.

Rarely does a judge refuse even to let a case go to trial, though that did happen in 2013 when the evidence presented by the Equal Employment Opportunity Commission was called by District Court judge Roger Titus "laughable" because of its "mind-boggling-number of errors" and because of the inconsistency of EEOC's lawsuit against a company for using criminal background checks on job applicants, when the EEOC itself used such checks.[98]

The implications of the use of a "disparate impact" basis for costly lawsuits in civil rights cases does not end with employers. Workers can also be adversely affected, and not just with reduced employment opportunities for black workers who have no criminal record.

When a federal agency can so easily make charges of discrimination on behalf of workers from racial or ethnic minorities— charges that can be costly and time-consuming to defend against in the courts, or charges that can force costly settlements out of court— that reduces the value of hiring black or other minority workers, even when their job qualifications are equal to the job qualifications of other workers who present no such legal risk.

Employers therefore have incentives to locate their businesses away from concentrations of minority populations, so that they will not be as legally vulnerable to costly charges of discrimination if their work force does not end up with the same demographic makeup as that of the surrounding population.

Some Japanese firms seeking to find locations for their first businesses in the United States have specified that they do not want to locate near concentrations of blacks in the local population.[99] American firms that do the same thing, being more familiar with both the legal and the social atmosphere in the United States, may be less likely to leave a paper trail. Nevertheless, this raises the question whether anti-discrimination laws, as applied in the courts, provide incentives to discriminate against racial minorities as well as incentives not to discriminate, with their net effect being uncertain.

Many observers who see racism as both widespread and widely effective in the job market fail to account for the fact that employers in competitive markets have actively sought out black workers, even in places and times where racism was rampant and undisguised, such as in South Africa during the era of apartheid, under a white minority government openly proclaiming white supremacy.

Similarly, black American workers were sufficiently in demand more than a century ago, in the Jim Crow South, that the organized attempts of white employers and landowners to suppress black earnings often collapsed under the pressure of that demand for black workers and sharecroppers.

Northern white employers sent recruiters into the South during the Jim Crow era to recruit black workers, on such a scale as to cause many laws to be passed in the South, restricting the activities of these recruiters by charging them licensing fees and imposing other restrictions, and with serious penalties for violating those restrictions.[100] This clearly indicated a strong demand for black workers in both regions of the country.

Within Northern communities, the demand for black workers was sufficient in the 1920s to cause Henry Ford and his executives to establish connections with clergy in Detroit's black community, in order to get their help in sorting black job applicants. Similar arrangements existed in Chicago and Pittsburgh.[101] The Ford Motor Company was, in effect, seeking low-cost access to knowledge of individuals' qualities, in order to judge each individual individually, instead of having to rely on information about group characteristics. Contacting black clergy was one way of getting the benefits of Discrimination I*A* without paying the usual very high costs.

In short, racism has not been sufficient to prevent a demand for black workers in a competitive market. It would be painfully ironic if anti-discrimination laws have been among the factors which reduced that demand in later times. Intentions, whether good or bad, do not predestine outcomes.

Chapter 4

The World of Numbers

There are three kinds of lies:
lies, damned lies, and statistics.

Mark Twain

When trying to understand economic and social disparities, statistics are often used, both to convey the magnitude of those disparities and to try to establish their causes. To some, numbers may convey a sense of objective, hard facts. But, even when the numbers are correct, the words that describe what the numbers are measuring may be incorrect or misleading. These include such basic numbers as income, unemployment rates and rates of arrest.

Numbers may also be misleading, not because of any intrinsic defects in either the numbers themselves or in the words describing them, but because of implicit assumptions about the norms to which those numbers are being compared. Here the seemingly invincible fallacy of assuming an even or random distribution of outcomes as something to expect, in the absence of such complicating causes as genes or discrimination, can make many statistics that show very disparate outcomes be seen as indicating something fundamentally wrong in the real world, rather than something fundamentally wrong with the assumptions behind the norms to which those outcomes are being compared.

Neither logic nor empirical evidence provides a compelling reason for expecting either equal or random outcomes among individuals, groups, institutions or nations— or of natural phenomena such as tornadoes or earthquakes, for that matter.

When used with an awareness of their pitfalls, statistics can be enormously valuable in testing competing hypotheses about disparate outcomes. But statistics may nevertheless be grossly misleading when they are distorted by errors of omission or errors of commission.

ERRORS OF OMISSION

The mere omission of one crucial fact can turn accurate statistics into traps that lead to conclusions that would be demonstrably false if the full facts were known. This often happens in comparisons of different ethnic groups and different income classes, among other comparisons.

Group Disparities

In the course of a long and heated campaign in politics and in the media during the early twenty-first century, claiming that there was rampant discrimination against black home mortgage loan applicants, data from various sources were cited repeatedly, showing that black applicants for the most desirable kind of mortgage were turned down substantially more often than white applicants for those same mortgages.

In the year 2000, for example, data from the U.S. Commission on Civil Rights showed that 44.6 percent of black applicants were turned down for those mortgages, while only 22.3 percent of white applicants were turned down.[1] These and similar statistics from other sources set off widespread denunciations of mortgage lenders, and demands that the government "do something" to stop rampant racial discrimination in mortgage lending institutions.

The very same report by the U.S. Commission on Civil Rights, which showed that blacks were turned down for conventional mortgages at twice the rate for whites, contained other statistics showing that whites were turned down for those same mortgages at a rate nearly twice that for "Asian Americans and Native Hawaiians."

While the rejection rate for white applicants was 22.3 percent, the rejection rate for Asian Americans and Native Hawaiians was 12.4 percent.[2] But such data seldom, if ever, saw the light of day in most newspapers or on most television news programs, for which the black-white difference was enough to convince journalists that racial bias was the reason.

That conclusion fit existing preconceptions, apparently eliminating a need to check whether it also fit the facts. This one crucial omission enabled the prevailing preconception to dominate discussions in politics, in the media and in much of academia.

One of the very few media outlets to even consider alternative explanations for the black-white statistical differences was the *Atlanta Journal-Constitution*, which showed that 52 percent of blacks had credit scores so low that they would qualify only for the less desirable subprime mortgages, as did 16 percent of whites. Accordingly, 49 percent of blacks in the data cited by the *Atlanta Journal-Constitution* ended up with subprime mortgages, as did 13 percent of whites and 10 percent of Asians.[3] In short, the three groups' respective rankings in terms of the kinds of mortgage loans they could get was similar to their respective rankings in average credit ratings.

But such statistics, so damaging to the prevailing preconception that intergroup differences in outcomes showed racial bias, were almost never mentioned in most of the mass media. With credit ratings being what they were, the statistics were consistent with Discrimination I*A* (judging each applicant as an individual), but were reported in the media, in politics and in academia as proof of Discrimination II, arbitrary bias against whole groups.

While the omitted statistics would have undermined the prevailing preconception that white lenders were biased against black applicants, that preconception at least seemed plausible, even if it failed to stand up under closer scrutiny. But the idea that white lenders would also be discriminating against white applicants, and in favor of Asian applicants, lacked even plausibility. What was equally implausible was that black-owned banks were discriminating against black applicants. But in fact black-owned banks turned down black applicants for home mortgage loans at a *higher* rate than did white-owned banks.[4]

Household Income Statistics

It is, unfortunately, not uncommon to omit statistics that are discordant with prevailing preconceptions. This has become a common practice in politics, in the media and even in much of academia. Such errors of omission are not confined to mortgage loan issues, but are also common in many discussions of income statistics.

Household income data, for example, are often used to indicate the magnitude of economic disparities in a society. But to say that the top 20 percent of households have X times as much income as the bottom 20 percent of households exaggerates the disparity between flesh-and-blood human beings, which can be quite different from disparities between income brackets. That is because, despite equal numbers of *households* in each 20 percent, there are far more *people* in the top 20 percent of households.

Census data from 2002 showed that there were 40 million people in the bottom 20 percent of households and 69 million people in the top 20 percent of households.[5] Such facts are usually omitted in statistics about disparities in incomes.

No doubt people in the top quintile average higher incomes than people in the bottom quintile. But the fact that there were also 29 million more people in this top quintile exaggerates the disparity in incomes among *people*. Later data for 2015 from the U.S. Bureau of Labor Statistics indicated that there were now over 36 million more people in the top quintile than in the bottom quintile.[6]

Moreover, the number of people earning income was four times as large in the top quintile as in the bottom quintile.[7] Most households in the bottom quintile have no one working.[8] How surprising is it when four people working earn more income than one person working? That is yet another of the errors of omission, when the truth would undermine a prevailing preconception.

There are not only different numbers of people per household at different income levels, there are also different numbers of people per household from one ethnic group to another, and different numbers of people per household from one time period to another. Omitting those differences when drawing sweeping conclusions can distort the meaning or implications of those statistics.

As the Bureau of the Census pointed out, more than half a century ago, the number of American households has been increasing faster than the number of people.[9] In short, American households tend to contain fewer persons per household over time— a trend continuing into the twenty-first century.[10] There are not only smaller families in later times, more individuals are financially able to live in their own individual households, rather than live with relatives or roommates, or live as individual roomers or in boarding houses, as average incomes rise from generation to generation.

When income per person is rising over the same span of years when the average number of persons per household is declining, that can lead to statistics indicating that the average household income is *falling*, even if every individual in the country has a higher income.

For example, if per capita income rises by 25 percent over some span of years, during which the average number of persons per household declines from 6 persons to 4 persons, then four people in the later period have as much income as five people had in the earlier period. But that is still not as much as *six* people had in the earlier period, so average household income *falls*, statistically, even if everyone's income has risen by 25 percent.

Household income statistics can be misleading in other ways. If two low-income people are sharing an apartment, in order to make the cost of rent less burdensome to each, and if either or both has an increase in income, that can lead to one tenant moving out to live alone in another apartment— and that, in turn, can lead to a *fall* in average household income.

If, for example, each of the two tenants had an income of $20,000 a year initially, and later both reach an income of $30,000 a year, leading to each living in a separate apartment afterwards, that will mean a *fall* in household income for these individuals from $40,000 a year to $30,000 a year. There will now be two low-income households instead of one, and each household will be poorer than the one they replaced. Again, a rise in individual income can be reflected statistically as a fall in household income.

Since most income is paid to individuals, rather than to households, and "individual" always means one person while "household" can mean any changeable number of persons, why would household income statistics be used so often instead of individual income statistics?

Clearly, omitting individual income statistics, and using household income statistics instead, is less useful to someone seeking the truth about economic differences among human beings. But household income statistics can be very useful for someone promoting political or ideological crusades, based on statistics that exaggerate income disparities among people.

For purposes of seeking the truth about the economic well-being of the American people, among the simplest and most straightforward statistics are data on per capita real income— that is, total money income divided by the number of people in the population, and adjusted for inflation. This is, however, a statistic seldom cited in income controversies, and seldom featured in official U.S. Bureau of the Census publications.

Time and Turnover

Among the factors often omitted, or distorted, in discussions of income disparities is the *time* dimension. People in the bottom 20 percent are often spoken of as "the poor" and, if the income in that quintile has not changed much over some span of years, it may be said that the income of "the poor" has stagnated. But the great majority of people initially in the bottom quintile do not stay there. There is nothing mysterious about the fact that most people tend to begin their working years in a lower occupation, with lower incomes than they will have in later years, after they have acquired more experience, skills and maturity, as well as a longer track record by which they can be judged.

A University of Michigan study that followed a given set of working Americans from 1975 to 1991 found that 95 percent of the people initially in the bottom 20 percent were no longer there at the end of that period. Moreover, 29 percent of those initially in the bottom quintile rose all the way to the top quintile, while only 5 percent still remained in the bottom 20 percent.[11]

Since 5 percent of 20 percent is one percent, only one percent of the total population sampled constituted "the poor" throughout the years studied. Statements about how the income of "the poor" fared during those years would apply only to that one percent of the people.

Similar distortions of reality occur when the time dimension is ignored in discussing people in the upper income brackets, who are often also spoken of as if they were a permanent class of people, rather than transients in those brackets, just like "the poor" in lower brackets. Thus a *New York Times* essay in 2017 referred to "This favored fifth at the top of the income distribution" as having collected "since 1979" a far greater amount of income than others.[12]

Considering how much turnover there was among people in different quintiles from 1975 to 1991, the implicit assumption that the same people were in the top quintile over the even longer period from 1979 to 2017 is a staggering assumption. But of course the very idea of turnover was omitted.

Another of the relatively few statistical studies that followed a given set of Americans over a span of years found a reality very different from what is usually portrayed in the media, in politics, or in academia: "At some point between the ages of 25 and 60, over three-quarters of the population will find themselves in the top 20 percent of the income distribution."[13]

For most Americans in other quintiles to envy or resent those in the top quintile would mean envying or resenting *themselves*, as they will be in later years. What the *New York Times* chose to call a "favored fifth" is in fact a substantial majority of all Americans. Moreover, it seems doubtful that three-quarters of all Americans receive their income as a favor, rather than by working for it.

Calling people in particular income brackets "the poor" or "the rich" implicitly assumes that they are enduring residents in those brackets, when in fact most Americans do not stay in the same income quintile from one decade to the next.[14] Similar patterns of transience in low-income brackets have been found by studies in Australia, Canada, Greece, Britain and New Zealand.[15]

The turnover rate among people in the highest income brackets is even greater than that of the population in general. Fewer than half of those Americans who were in the much-discussed "top one percent" in income in 1996 were still there in 2005.[16] Although people in that bracket have been referred to as "the best-off one in one hundred,"[17] that is true only as of a given instant. Over the course of a lifetime, the proportion of people in that bracket is one in nine, since 11 percent of Americans are in that bracket at some point in their lives.[18] People initially in the top *one hundredth of one percent* had an even faster turnover, and those with the 400 highest incomes in the country turned over fastest of all.[19]

Crime Statistics and Arrest Statistics

Some of the most gross distortions of reality through errors of omission have involved quite simple omissions. No one needs to be an expert on the complexities of statistical analysis in order to see through many statistical fallacies, including those based on simple omissions. But it does require stopping to think about the numbers, instead of being swept along by a combination of rhetoric and statistics.

Statistics cited in support of claims that the police target blacks for arrests usually go no further than showing that the proportion of black people arrested greatly exceeds the roughly 13 percent of the American population who are black.

If anyone were to use similar reasoning to claim that National Basketball Association (NBA) referees were racially biased, because the proportion of fouls that referees call against black players in the NBA greatly exceeds 13 percent, anyone familiar with the NBA would immediately see the fallacy— because the proportion of black players in the NBA greatly exceeds the proportion of blacks in the American population.

Moreover, since blacks are especially over-represented among the star players in the NBA, the actual playing time of black players on the basketball court would be even more disproportionately higher, since it is the players on the court who get cited for fouls more so than secondary players sitting on the bench.

What would be relevant to testing the hypothesis that blacks are disproportionately targeted for arrest by the police, or disproportionately convicted and sentenced by courts, would be objective data on the proportions of particular violations of the law committed by blacks, compared to the proportions of blacks arrested, convicted and sentenced for those particular violations.

Such objective data are not always easy to come by, since data reflecting actions by the police would hardly be considered valid as a test of whether the actions of the police were warranted. However, there are some particular statistics that are both relevant and independent of the actions of the police.

The most reliable and objective crime statistics are statistics on homicides, since a dead body can hardly be ignored, regardless of the race of the victim. For as long as homicide statistics have been kept in the United States, the proportion of homicide victims who are black has been some multiple of the proportion of blacks in the population. Moreover, the vast majority of those homicide victims whose killers have been identified were killed by other blacks, just as most white homicide victims were killed by other whites.

Since the homicide rate among blacks is some multiple of the homicide rate among whites, it is hardly surprising that the arrest rate of blacks for homicide is also some multiple of the rate of homicide arrests among whites. What is relevant in such statistical comparisons is not the proportion of blacks in the general population, but the proportion of blacks among people who commit a particular crime.

Another violation of the law that can be tested and quantified, independently of the police, is driving in excess of highway speed limits. A study by independent researchers of nearly 40,000 drivers on the New Jersey Turnpike, using high-speed cameras and a radar gun, showed a higher proportion of black drivers than of white drivers who were speeding, especially at the higher speeds.[20]

This study, comparing the proportion of blacks stopped by state troopers for speeding with the proportion of blacks actually speeding, was not nearly as widely accepted, or even mentioned, by either the media or by politicians, as other studies comparing the number of blacks stopped by state troopers for speeding and other violations with the proportion of blacks in the *population*.[21]

Yet again, specific facts have been defeated by the implicit presumption that groups tend to be similar in what they do, so that large differences in outcomes are treated as surprising, if not sinister. But demographic differences alone are enough to lead to group differences in speeding violations, even aside from other social or cultural differences.

Younger people are more prone to speeding, and groups with a younger median age tend to have a higher proportion of their population in age brackets where speeding is more common. When different groups can differ in median age by a decade, or in some cases by two decades or more,[22] there was never any reason to expect different groups to have the same proportion of their respective populations speeding, or to have the same outcomes in any number of other activities that are more common in some age brackets than in others.

The omission of data on the proportion of blacks— or any other racial group— engaged in a given violation of law, as distinguished from the proportion of blacks or others in the population at large, is sufficient to let racial profiling charges prevail politically, despite their inconsistency with either logic or evidence.

Some professional statisticians have refused to get involved in "racial profiling" issues because these issues are so politically charged. As a professor of criminology explained: "Good statisticians were throwing up their hands and saying, 'This is one battle you'll never win. I don't want to be called a racist.'"[23]

Among the other consequences is that many law enforcement officials also see this as a politically unwinnable battle, and simply back off from vigorous law enforcement, the results of which could ruin their careers and their lives. The net result of the police backing off is often a rise in crime,[24] of which law-abiding residents in black communities are the principal victims.

Some people may think that they are being kind to blacks by going along with unsubstantiated claims of racial bias and discrimination by the police and by the criminal justice system. But, as distinguished black scholar Sterling A. Brown said, long ago: "Kindness can kill as well as cruelty, and it can never take the place of genuine respect."[25]

ERRORS OF COMMISSION

Statistical errors of commission include lumping together data on things that are fundamentally different, such as salaries and capital gains, producing numbers that are simply called "income." But calling things by the same word does not make them the same things.

Other errors of commission include discussing statistical brackets as if they represented a given set of flesh-and-blood human beings called "the rich," "the poor" or "the top one percent," for example. Errors of commission also include using survey research to resolve factual issues that the inherent limitations of survey research make it unable to resolve.

Capital Gains

While annual income statistics for individuals avoid some of the problems of household income statistics, both of these sets of statistics count as income (1) annual wages, salaries and other incomes earned and paid during the same year and (2) income from capital gains accrued over some previous span of years, and then turned into cash income during a given year. Treating the incomes earned by some individuals over various numbers of years as being the same as incomes earned by other individuals in just one year is like failing to distinguish apples from oranges.

Capital gains take many forms from many very different kinds of transactions. These transactions range from sales of stocks and bonds that may have been bought over a span of prior years to sales of a home or business that has increased in value over the years.

If a farm was purchased for $100,000 and then, 20 years later— after the farmer has built barns and fences, and made other improvements to the land and the structures on it— the farm is sold for $300,000, that sale will result in a net increase of the owner's income by $200,000 in the particular year when the farm is sold. Statistically, that $200,000 that was earned over a period of 20 years will be recorded the same as a $200,000 salary earned by someone else in just one year.

Looking back, that farmer has in reality earned an average of $10,000 a year for 20 years, as increases in the value of the farm, through the investment of time, work and money on the farm. Looking forward, the farmer cannot expect to earn another $200,000 the following year, as someone with a $200,000 annual salary can.

Capital gains in general are recorded in income statistics as being the same as an annual salary, when clearly they are not. Nor is there some easy formula available to render salaries and capital gains comparable, because capital gains by different individuals accrue for differing numbers of years before being turned into cash income in a given year.

If capital gains were equally present at all income levels— say, 10 percent of all incomes being capital gains— then the disparities in income statistics might not be affected as much. But, in reality, low annual incomes are far more likely to be salaries or wages, and very high annual incomes are far more likely to be capital gains. For example, someone making twenty *thousand* dollars a year is probably getting that from a pay check, while someone making twenty *million* dollars a year is more likely to be making that much money from capital gains of one sort or another.

The exceptionally high rates of turnover of people at very high income levels reinforce this conclusion. Internal Revenue Service data show that half the people who earned over a million dollars a year, at some time during the years from 1999 through 2007, did so just *once* in those nine years.[26]

This does not imply that all the others in that bracket made a million dollars every year. Another study, also based on tax data, showed that, among Americans with the 400 highest incomes in the country, fewer than 13 percent were in that very high bracket more than twice during the years from 1992 to 2000.[27] The highest incomes are usually very transient incomes, reinforcing the conclusion that these are transient capital gains rather than enduring salaries.

All of this distorts the implications of income statistics that treat annual earnings and multi-year capital gains as if they were the same. Talk of how much of a country's income is received by the top ten percent, or by the top 400, proceeds as if this is a given set of people.

But, because of the high turnover rate in high income brackets, there can be thousands of people in the "top 400" during just one decade.

During the period from 1992 to 2014, for example, there were 4,584 people who were in the top 400 income earners, according to Internal Revenue Service data. Of these, 3,262 were in that bracket just one time during those 23 years.[28] When incomes received by thousands of people are reported statistically as if these were incomes received by hundreds of people, that is a severalfold exaggeration of income disparities— in this case, more than a tenfold exaggeration.

Such data are also relevant to the oft-repeated claim that "the system is rigged" by the wealthy. That claim certainly fits the prevailing social vision. But if the question is whether it also fits the facts, then it can be tested like any other hypothesis. In light of these data, if the top 400 income recipients in the United States rigged the system, and 71 percent of the people in the "top 400" are in that category just one time during a period of more than two decades, why would anyone rig the system in such a way that they themselves would be unlikely to remain in the topmost income bracket? It would have to be some of the most incompetent rigging imaginable.

It is a similar story as regards the 400 richest people in the world, who had net losses of $19 billion in 2015.[29] As of 2016, the number of billionaires in the world was slightly fewer than in 2015, while the total wealth held by all the world's billionaires declined by $570 billion on net balance.[30] If the world's richest people had in fact "rigged the system," surely they could have done better for themselves than that.

SIDEBAR: CAPITAL GAINS AND INEQUALITY

A hypothetical example may illustrate how income statistics can exaggerate inequality when they make no distinction between (1) people who receive annual earnings in a given year and (2) people who receive capital gains in that same year, representing income earned over a previous span of years.

If, for example, there are 10 people who are in a high income bracket, each earning $500,000 a year, while there are also 10 people in a lower income bracket, each earning $50,000 a year, it might seem as if there is a ten-to-one difference in income between people in these two brackets. But, if only one of the ten people in the higher bracket is earning $500,000 *every* year in a decade, while the others are there for just one year each in that decade— the year in which their accrued capital gains are turned into cash income— then, given the very high rate of turnover in very high income brackets, the situation is very different from what it would be if there were the same ten people in the higher bracket every year of the decade.

If most of the people in the higher income bracket have a one-year spike in income from capital gains, after which they return to some lower level of income, which may still be above the national average— say, an individual income of $100,000 a year— then, over the course of a decade, the income disparity between *people* is substantially less than the income disparity between *income brackets*.

In this hypothetical example, where there are nine people initially in the higher income bracket, earning $500,000 each in the first year covered, and $100,000 in each of the subsequent nine years of the decade, that adds up to a total of $1.4 million each during that decade, which in turn adds up to $12.6 million for all nine people collectively. The tenth member of the top bracket, who is in that bracket every year of the decade, receiving $500,000 a year in all ten years, has a total income of $5 million. For all these particular ten people put together, that adds up to $17.6 million received collectively in a decade by the ten people initially in the higher bracket.

Meanwhile, among the ten people in the lower income bracket, receiving $50,000 a year each initially and throughout the decade, that adds up to $500,000 each in a decade, for a total income of

$5 million as a group. With the ten people initially in the higher bracket earning a total of $17.6 million during that same decade, and the ten people initially in the lower bracket earning a total of $5 million during that decade, the disparity in income between *people* is less than four-to-one, while the disparity in income between their respective income *brackets* is ten-to-one.

That is because nine of the ten people in the higher bracket are replaced each year by someone else having a one-year spike in income from capital gains, for an income of $500,000 in this example. Counting all 91 people who are in the higher income bracket at some point during the decade, their average annual incomes in that decade are less than *three* times that of people in the lower bracket.[31]

Although this illustration assumes, for the sake of simplicity, that people in the lower income bracket have constant incomes throughout the decade, data from the real world show the incomes of people initially in lower income brackets to usually be rising over time more sharply than the incomes of people initially in higher brackets.[32] This would make the disparity in incomes between people in these two brackets even less than that in this example.

A hypothetical example obviously cannot pretend to be an exact replica of the real world. The point is merely to illustrate how, under some approximation of these conditions, the disparities between income brackets can be much greater than the disparities between actual flesh-and-blood human beings.

Racial and Ethnic Disparities

In trying to determine the reasons for economic and social disparities between blacks and whites, some observers attribute these differences primarily to policies and practices by people outside the black community, while other observers attribute these same differences to internal differences in behavior between black and white Americans.

In seeking to resolve this issue, sociologist William Julius Wilson relied heavily on statistics from opinion surveys. These surveys, according to Professor Wilson, show that "nearly all ghetto residents, whether employed or not, support the norms of the work ethic."[33] In one survey, "fewer than 3 percent of the black respondents from ghetto poverty census tracts denied the importance of plain hard work for getting ahead in society, and 66 percent expressed the view that it is very important."[34]

After admitting that "surveys are not the best way to get at underlying attitudes and values,"[35] Professor Wilson nevertheless presented— as a refutation of "media perceptions of 'underclass' values and attitudes" in inner-city ghettos— the fact that "residents in inner-city ghetto neighborhoods actually verbally endorse, rather than undermine, the basic American values concerning individual initiative."[36]

Despite Professor Wilson's reliance on opinion surveys to refute claims that ghetto residents have different cultural values from those of the American population as a whole, there is no necessary correlation between what people say and what they do. A survey of low-income people by Columbia University researchers showed that 59 percent regarded buying goods on credit as a bad idea. Nevertheless "most of the families do use credit when buying major durables."[37]

Economists tend to rely on "revealed preference" rather than verbal statements. That is, what people *do* reveals what their values are, better than what they *say*. Even when people give honest answers, expressing what they sincerely believe, some people's conception of hard work, for example, need not coincide with other people's conception, even when both use the same words.

When black students in affluent Shaker Heights spent less time on their school work than their white high school classmates did, and spent more time watching television,[38] that was their revealed preference. Data from other sources show even greater differences between the time devoted to school work by black Americans and by Asian Americans in high school.[39] Nor are such differences peculiar to blacks or to the United States. In Australia, for example, Chinese students spent more than twice as much time on their homework as white students did.[40]

How surprised should we be that Asian students in general tend to do better academically than white students in general, *in predominantly white societies* such as Australia, Britain or the United States? The same pattern can be seen among whole nations, as such Asian countries as Japan, South Korea and Singapore likewise show patterns of hard work by their students and academic results on international tests that place these countries above most Western nations.[41]

Statistics compiled from what people express verbally may be worse than useless, if they lead to a belief that such numbers convey a reality that can be relied on for serious decision-making about social policies.

Incidentally, the high correlation between the amount of work that different groups put into their education and the quality of their educational outcomes does not bode well for theories of genetic determinism. When we find some race whose students spend less time and effort on their school work than students in some other race, and yet get educational results superior to the results of hard-working students in that other race, this would be evidence supporting the genetic hypothesis. But such evidence does not seem to be available.

When trying to determine, from statistics, how much discrimination— in the sense of Discrimination II— is involved in income differences between groups, one of the common errors of commission that can make such comparisons unreliable is to compare individuals with supposedly the "same" education or other qualifications, when the qualifications are in fact *not* the same in any meaningful sense. Comparing blacks and whites with the "same" number of years of schooling was obviously not a comparison of blacks and whites with the same education during much of the early twentieth century.

Most blacks were concentrated in the South during that era, and their racially segregated schools usually had shorter school years, among other disparities.[42] According to a study of that era, "A black pupil attending school three months of the year for six years would have finished at most half the grades completed by a white attending six months for six years."[43] Statistically, however, they both had the "same" number of years of education.

Clearly there was Discrimination II in such situations, but *where* the discrimination took place cannot be determined by where the statistics were collected. That is, when black and white workers with the "same" amount of schooling received different pay, that was not necessarily all due to employers' biased discrimination, as distinguished from biased discrimination that took place for years in the school system, before black workers reached an employer.

Similarly in a later era, after schools were no longer racially segregated by law, but black high school graduates had scores on education tests that were lower than the scores of white students who were years younger.[44] Here the failure of employers to pay black workers what white workers with the "same" education were being paid need not be due to Discrimination II in the workplace, even if the statistics were collected at the workplace. But, when comparing individuals with the same results on mental tests, blacks and whites received comparable pay.[45]

Statistics often do not have nearly as much detail as would be necessary to compare people who were truly comparable. A very similar problem can affect comparisons of male and female workers with the "same" qualifications in gross terms. But when a higher proportion of women are part-time workers, and they are workers with fewer years of continuous employment experience (due to taking time out to care for small children), or with college degrees in subjects that do not prepare them for careers in high-paying professions, comparisons of women and men with the "same" qualifications in gross terms are comparisons of apples and oranges.

In situations where data are available on a wider range of work qualifications, so that truly comparable individuals from different groups can be compared, income disparities tend to shrink, often to the vanishing point, and sometimes the inequality reverses.[46] As far back as academic year 1972–73, for example, white faculty members had higher incomes than black faculty members. But, when comparing those faculty members with Ph.D.s in the same fields, from similarly high-ranked departments in their respective disciplines, and with similar numbers of published articles, black faculty members had higher incomes than their white counterparts.[47] Similarly, male faculty members in general had higher incomes than female faculty members in general. But, among similarly qualified faculty, women who never married earned higher incomes than men who never married.[48]

Minimum Wages and Unemployment

One of the important areas in which survey research has done major damage has been in trying to resolve differences of opinion as to the effect of minimum wage laws on unemployment. Advocates of minimum wage laws argue that such laws raise the incomes of the poor, while critics argue that these laws cause more of the poor to be unemployed, because low-income workers tend to be workers with few skills and/or little work experience, so that employers find them worth employing only at low wage rates. Despite an abundance of detailed statistics on unemployment, this controversy has raged for generations.

Part of the problem is that, as we have seen in other contexts, most of what are called "the poor" are not permanent residents in low-income brackets, any more than other people are permanent residents in other income brackets. About half of all Americans earning at or near the minimum wage rate are from 16 to 24 years of age,[49] and of course they do not remain young permanently. So, when people say, as Senator Ted Kennedy once said, "Minimum wage workers have waited almost 10 long years for an increase,"[50] they are not talking about a given set of human beings, but about a statistical category containing an ever-changing mix of people.

Because young people are usually, almost by definition, less experienced as workers, their value to a prospective employer tends to be less than the value of more experienced workers in the same line of work. Some young people may acquire valuable work skills through education, but education also takes time, and people grow older with the passage of that time.

Often what younger, inexperienced workers acquire from an entry-level job is primarily the habit of showing up every day and on time, and the habit of following instructions and getting along with others. After having acquired work experience in some simple, entry-level job, most young beginners go on to other jobs, with different employers, where work experience of some sort may be a prerequisite for getting hired. Simple as such things may seem, the absence of a work experience prerequisite can negate whatever other good qualities a young worker may have, but which have not yet had a chance to manifest themselves in a work situation.

High rates of employee turnover, sometimes exceeding 100 percent per year, are common in many entry-level jobs in retail businesses or fast-food restaurants.[51] These jobs are stepping stones to other jobs with other employers, though some observers falsely call entry-level jobs "dead-end jobs."[52] If workers in fact stayed on permanently in such jobs, which usually have no automatic promotions ladder, those workers would in fact be in dead-end jobs. But, when the average tenure of supermarket employees has been found to be 97 days, that is clearly not the case.[53]

Like most things in a market economy, inexperienced and unskilled workers are more in demand at a lower price than at a higher price. Minimum wage laws, based on what third parties would like to see workers paid, rather than being based on those workers' productivity, can price unskilled workers out of a job. This traditional economic analysis has been challenged by advocates of minimum wage laws, and survey research data have been a major part of that challenge.

Back in 1945, Professor Richard A. Lester of Princeton University sent out questionnaires to employers, asking how they would respond to higher labor costs. Their responses, which were not along the lines of traditional economic analysis, convinced Professor Lester that the traditional economic analysis was either incorrect or not applicable to minimum wage laws.[54] However, what traditional economic analysis seeks to do is predict economic outcomes, not predict how people who are surveyed will answer questionnaires. Moreover, outcomes are not just the fruition of beliefs or intentions, as we have seen in discussions of the costs of discrimination.

Decades after Professor Lester's challenge to traditional economic analysis, other economists, also at Princeton, again challenged traditional economic analysis on the basis of survey research, though now by surveying the same employers before and after a minimum wage increase, and asking each time how many employees they had. The answers convinced the Princeton economists that the minimum wage increase had not reduced employment. They and their supporters therefore declared the traditional analysis to be a "myth" that had now been "refuted."[55]

Devastating criticisms of the Princeton economists' conclusions were made by some other economists, who challenged both the accuracy of their statistics and the logic of their conclusions.[56] But, even if the Princeton economists' statistics were completely accurate, that would still not address the key weakness of survey research in general— which is that *you can only survey survivors*. And what may be true of survivors need not be true of others in the same circumstances who did not survive in those particular circumstances.

An extreme hypothetical example may illustrate the point that is applicable in less extreme situations. If you wished to determine empirically whether playing Russian roulette was dangerous, and did so through survey research, you might send out questionnaires to all individuals known to have played Russian roulette, asking them for information as to their outcomes.

After the questionnaires were returned and the answers tabulated, the conclusion from these statistics might well be that no one was harmed at all, judging by the answers on the questionnaires that were returned. Not all questionnaires would have been returned, but that is not uncommon in survey research. Basing your conclusions on the statistical data from this research, you might well conclude that you had "refuted" the "myth" that playing Russian roulette was dangerous. This is the kind of result you can get when you can only survey survivors.[57]

In the case of minimum wage studies, if all the firms in an industry were identical, then any reduced employment resulting from the imposition of a minimum wage, or the raising of an existing minimum wage rate, would appear as a reduction of employment in all the firms. But, in the more usual case, where some firms in a given industry are quite profitable, others are less profitable and still others are struggling to survive, unemployment resulting from a minimum wage can push some struggling firms out of the industry— and reduce the number of their replacements, now that labor costs are higher and profits are more problematical.

The only firms that can be surveyed for their employment data, both before and after the minimum wage was imposed or raised, are the firms that were there in both time periods— that is, the survivors. If there has been a net decrease in the number of firms, the employment in these surviving firms need not have gone down at all, regardless of a decline in employment in the industry as a whole. The firms surveyed are like the people who survived playing Russian roulette, which may well be a majority in both cases, though not an indicative majority in terms of the issue at hand.

Empirically, a study of the effect of raising local minimum wage rates on employment in restaurants in the San Francisco Bay Area found that the principal effect was through some restaurants going out of business— and reducing the number of new firms entering to replace them. Those restaurants going out of business were primarily restaurants rated lower in quality. Employment in five-star restaurants was unaffected.[58] In Seattle as well, the response to a local minimum wage rate increase was that a number of restaurants simply closed down.[59] These now non-existent restaurants obviously cannot be surveyed.

The amount of labor demanded can be measured either by the number of workers employed or by the number of hours that they work, or both. A study published by the National Bureau of Economic Research measured employment by hours of work, as well as by the number of workers employed, and concluded that "the minimum wage ordinance lowered low-wage employees' earnings by an average of $125 per month in 2016."[60] Thus a theoretical increase in income from a higher minimum wage rate became, in the real world, a significant *decrease* in income. That is, even workers who kept their jobs worked fewer hours and therefore earned less money.

Another problem with trying to determine the effect of a minimum wage law on unemployment is that the proportion of the work force directly affected by a minimum wage is often small. Therefore unemployment among that fraction of the work force can be swamped by the normal fluctuations in the unemployment rate among the larger number of other employees around them.

This is less of a problem in situations where most of the employees are earning a wage low enough to be directly affected by a minimum wage law. But five-star restaurants were unlikely to be having inexperienced teenagers delivering food to their upscale customers' tables, even if restaurants like McDonald's or Burger King often have teenagers delivering food over the counter to their customers.

Other ways of assessing the effect of a minimum wage on unemployment would include gathering data restricted to just the kinds of inexperienced and unskilled workers directly affected, such as teenagers. We have already seen, in Chapter 2, how minimum wage laws affect both the teenage unemployment rate in general and racial disparities in teenage unemployment rates as well.

Yet another way of assessing the effect of minimum wage laws on unemployment would be to gather unemployment data on places and times where there have been no minimum wage laws at all, so that these unemployment rates could be compared to unemployment rates in places and times where there have been minimum wages laws— especially where these have been comparable societies or, ideally, the very same society in the same era, with and without a minimum wage law.

By focusing on teenagers in general, or black teenagers in particular, it is possible to see the effects of minimum wage laws more clearly and precisely, since these are workers on whom such laws have their greatest impact, because these are a population most lacking in education, job skills and experience, and therefore earning especially low wage rates. Moreover, there are extensive statistics on what happened to these populations in the labor markets from the late 1940s to the present.

As we have seen, what is most striking about statistics on American teenage unemployment rates in the late 1940s is that (1) these unemployment rates were only a fraction of the levels of unemployment to which we have become accustomed to seeing in later decades, and (2) there was little or no difference between the unemployment rates of black and white teenagers then.

Internationally, unemployment rates have been markedly lower in times and places where neither governments nor labor unions set most wage rates. Most modern nations have had minimum wage laws, but the few that have not have tended to have strikingly lower unemployment rates. These would include Switzerland and Singapore today, and Hong Kong under British rule, prior to the 1997 return of Hong Kong to China. There was also no national minimum wage law in the United States before the Davis-Bacon Act of 1931, which impacted wage rates in the construction industry.

As for hard data on unemployment rates in these places and times, *The Economist* magazine reported in 2003: "Switzerland's unemployment neared a five-year high of 3.9% in February."[61] But this "high" (for Switzerland) unemployment rate returned to a more normal (for Switzerland) 3.1 percent in later years.[62]

In 2013, Singapore's unemployment rate was 2.1 percent.[63] In 1991, when Hong Kong was still a British colony, it too had no minimum wage law, and its unemployment rate was under 2 percent.[64] In the United States, the last administration with no national minimum wage law at any time was the Coolidge administration in the 1920s. During President Coolidge's last four years in office, the annual unemployment rate ranged from a high of 4.2 percent to a low of 1.8 percent.[65]

Yet discussions of minimum wage laws, even by some academic scholars, are often based on the intentions and presumed effects of these laws, rather than being based on empirical evidence as to their actual consequences.

IMPLICATIONS

The emphasis on complex statistical analysis in economics and other fields— however valuable, or even vital, such statistical analysis may be in many cases— can lead to overlooking simple but fundamental questions as to whether the numbers on which these complex analyses are based are in fact measuring what they seem to be measuring, or claim to be measuring. "Income" statistics which lump together annual salaries and multi-year capital gains are just one of many sets of statistics which could stand much closer scrutiny at this fundamental level— especially if laws and policies affecting millions of human beings are to be based on statistical conclusions.

What can be disconcerting, if not painful, are the simple and obvious fallacies that can pass muster in intellectual circles when these fallacies seem to advance the prevailing vision of what is called "social justice." Among prominent current examples is French economist Thomas Piketty's large international statistical study of income inequality, which was instantly acclaimed in many countries, despite such obvious and fundamental misstatements as one pointed out by Professor Steven Pinker of Harvard:

> Thomas Piketty, whose 2014 bestseller *Capital in the Twenty-First Century* became a talisman in the uproar over inequality, wrote, "The poorer half of the population are as poor today as they were in the past, with barely 5 percent of total wealth in 2010, just as in 1910." But total wealth today is vastly greater than it was in 1910, so if the poorer half own the same proportion, they are far richer, not "as poor."[66]

In addition to speaking of percentages as if they represented a given amount of income or wealth over the course of a century, Professor Piketty also made such assertions as that, in income, "the upper decile is truly a world unto itself,"[67] when in fact just over half of all Americans are in that upper decile at some point in their lives.[68] When Piketty said that the top one percent sit atop the "hierarchy" and "structure of inequality,"[69] he again verbally transformed a changing mix of people in particular income brackets into a fixed *structure* rather than a fluid *process*, in which most Americans do not remain in the same quintile from one decade to the next.

Such misstatements are different expressions of the same fundamental misconception. As an empirical study of the 400 richest Americans pointed out, Piketty "naively assumes that it's the same people getting richer."[70] But the majority of the 400 richest Americans have earned their fortunes in their own lifetimes, rather than being heirs of the 400 largest fortunes of the past.[71]

Such misconceptions are not peculiar to Professor Piketty. Nor are these the only problems with his statistics. But that such simple and obvious misstatements can pass muster in intellectual circles is a problem and a danger that goes far beyond Thomas Piketty.

Whether income differences are measured before taxes or after taxes can change the degree of inequality. If inequalities are measured both after taxes and after government transfers, whether in money or in goods and services, that can reduce the inequality considerably, when high-income people pay higher taxes and low-income people receive most of the government transfers.

Statistics on tax rates themselves can be grossly misleading when changes in tax rates are described in such terms as "a $300 billion increase in taxes" or "a $300 billion decrease in taxes." In reality, all that the government can do is change the tax *rate*. How much tax *revenue* that will produce depends on how people react. There have been times when higher tax rates have produced lower tax revenues, and other times when lower tax rates have produced higher tax revenues,[72] as well as times when tax rates and tax revenues moved in the same direction.

During the 1920s, for example, the tax rate on the highest income Americans was reduced from 73 percent to 24 percent— and the income tax *revenue* rose substantially[73]— especially income tax revenues received from people in the highest income brackets. Under the older and much higher tax rate, vast sums of money from wealthy investors were sheltered in tax-exempt securities, such as municipal bonds. The total amount of money invested in tax-free securities was estimated to be three times the size of the annual budget of the federal government, and more than half as large as the national debt.[74]

Such vast and legally untaxable sums of money caught the attention and aroused the ire of Secretary of the Treasury Andrew Mellon, who declared it "repugnant" in a democracy that there should be "a class in the community which cannot be reached for tax purposes."[75] Failing to get Congress to take steps toward ending tax exemptions for incomes from particular securities,[76] Secretary Mellon sought instead to lower the tax *rates* to the point where it would in fact lead to collection of more tax *revenues*.

Tax-exempt securities tend not to pay as high a rate of return on investments as other securities, whose earnings are taxed. It made sense for wealthy investors to accept these lower rates of return from tax-exempt securities when the tax rate was 73 percent, but not after the tax rate was lowered to 24 percent. In terms of *words on paper*, the official tax rate on the highest incomes was cut from 73 percent to 24 percent in the 1920s. But, in terms of *events in the real world*, the tax rate actually paid— on staggering sums of money previously untouchable in tax shelters— *rose* from zero percent to 24 percent. This produced huge increases in tax revenues received from high-income people, both absolutely and as a percentage of all income taxes collected.[77]

This increase in income taxes collected from high-income taxpayers was a result of the plain fact that 24 percent of something is larger than 73 percent of nothing. Tax rate cuts in some later administrations also led to increases in tax revenues.[78] For example, a front-page news story in the *New York Times* of July 9, 2006 said: "An unexpectedly steep rise in tax revenues from corporations and the wealthy is driving down the projected budget deficit this year."[79]

However unexpected this increase in tax revenues may have been to the *New York Times* and others decrying "tax cuts for the rich," this was precisely the kind of outcome predicted and expected by others in various administrations over the years, who had urged that tax *rates* be cut, in order to get money disgorged from tax shelters and invested in the market economy. This included people in the Coolidge, Kennedy, Reagan and George W. Bush administrations, where there were similar outcomes.[80] But the very possibility that tax rates and tax revenues can move in opposite directions is seldom mentioned in the media— a crucial error of omission.

These are not simply arguments about history. Among the consequences in our own time is that proposals to reduce income tax *rates* are automatically met with objections to reducing income tax *revenues*. In the *Wall Street Journal* of January 31, 2018, for example, economist Alan Blinder objected to tax rate cuts on grounds that "the deficit is already too large."[81]

This is in defiance of what the *New York Times* reported about the unexpected *reduction* of the deficit by increased tax revenues during the administration of President George W. Bush. It is also in defiance of a record-breaking budget surplus after tax rates were reduced in the 1920s— a surplus large enough to allow about one-fourth of the national debt to be paid off.[82] Like many others, Professor Blinder proceeded as if it were axiomatic that tax rate reductions mean tax revenue reductions.

There is, of course, no guarantee of what any given tax rate reduction will lead to in a given set of circumstances. But Professor Blinder's assertion was not based on any argument that a tax rate reduction under particular current circumstances would lead to a reduction in tax revenues. There was in fact no argument whatever on that point, nor apparently any sense of need to make such an argument. Similarly, a twenty-first century book on President Calvin Coolidge likewise asserted that, as a result of the tax rate cuts during his administration, "the bounty that the rich enjoyed sapped the U.S. Treasury of funds it might have used for other ends."[83] Thus a record-breaking budget surplus under President Coolidge was verbally transmuted into a deprivation of funds, with the turn of a phrase.

All the voluminous and detailed statistics on tax rates and tax revenues published by the Internal Revenue Service, going back more than a hundred years, might as well not exist, as far as many of those with the prevailing social vision are concerned. This is ultimately not a question about history, but about what such heedlessness implies for the present and still more so for the future.

Chapter 5

The World of Words

For words are wise mens counters,
they do but reckon by them: but
they are the mony of fooles...

Thomas Hobbes, 1651

While numbers can be used in ways that are deceptive as regards particular issues, words can be used in ways that can be more sweepingly deceptive as regards how a whole society is seen.

Numbers may deceive us because of their apparent objectivity, but words can deceive more comprehensively because of their emotional appeals that numbers seldom have. There may be very legitimate reasons to react adversely to words like "war," "racism" or "murder," but it is the illegitimate invoking of emotionally charged words that is especially dangerous— as anything that overrides thought, or substitutes for thought, can be dangerous. Emotional manipulation is, however, only one of the dangers when words are used in ways that obscure both realities and the connections of cause and effect behind those realities.

EMOTIONS VERSUS CAUSATION

Decent people can be appalled by the many oppressions and persecutions that have abounded throughout history. But to weigh the current *causal* effects of such oppressions and persecutions of the past— or even of the present— is very different from simply reciting a litany of wickedness, as if that automatically establishes causation for other events.

In seeking to establish the causes of poverty and other social problems among black Americans, for example, sociologist William Julius Wilson pointed to factors such as "the enduring effects of slavery, Jim Crow segregation, public school segregation, legalized discrimination, residential segregation, the FHA's redlining of black neighborhoods in the 1940s and '50s, the construction of public housing projects in poor black neighborhoods, employer discrimination, and other racial acts and processes."[1]

These various facts might be summarized as examples of racism, so the causal question is whether racism is either *the* cause, or one of the major causes, of poverty and other social problems among black Americans today. Many might consider the obvious answer to be "yes." Yet some incontrovertible facts undermine that conclusion. For example, despite the high poverty rate among black Americans in general, *the poverty rate among black married couples has been less than 10 percent every year since 1994.*[2]

The poverty rate of married blacks is not only lower than that of blacks as a whole, but in some years has also been lower than that of *whites* as a whole.[3] In 2016, for example, the poverty rate for blacks was 22 percent, for whites was 11 percent, and for black married couples was 7.5 percent.[4]

Do racists care whether someone black is married or unmarried? If not, then why do married blacks escape poverty so much more often than other blacks, if racism is the main reason for black poverty? If the continuing effects of past evils such as slavery play a major *causal* role today, were the ancestors of today's black married couples exempt from slavery and other injustices?

As far back as 1969, young black males whose homes included newspapers, magazines, and library cards, and who also had the same education as young white males, had similar incomes as their white counterparts.[5] Do racists care whether blacks have reading material and library cards?

Highly successful chains of charter schools, like the KIPP (Knowledge Is Power Program) schools and the Success Academy schools, are places where minority children from low-income families often score much higher on educational tests than other low-income and minority youngsters in the regular public schools. Sometimes they also score higher than students in school districts where most of the children are white and from families with higher incomes. On statewide tests in 2013, fifth-graders in one of the Success Academy schools in Harlem were reported in the *New York Times* as having "surpassed all other public schools in the state in math, even their counterparts in the whitest and richest suburbs, Scarsdale and Briarcliff Manor." [6]

These charter schools cannot change the facts of history, however. Their highly successful educational results, with ghetto children selected by *lottery* rather than ability, suggest that historic injustices— however deserving of condemnation— are not automatically current destiny. The stark question then is whether we want a better future for such children, and for blacks in general, or do we want the continued repetition of a "legacy of slavery" mantra, in order to preserve a social vision and the political careers, institutional fiefdoms and shakedown opportunities based on that mantra and that vision?

The crucial question is not whether evils exist but whether the evils of the past or present are automatically the *cause* of major economic, educational and other social disparities today. The bedrock assumption underlying many political or ideological crusades is that socioeconomic disparities are automatically somebody's fault, so that our choices are either to blame society or to "blame the victim." Yet whose fault are demographic differences, geographic differences, birth order differences or cultural differences that evolved over the centuries before any of us were born?

If we are serious about seeking causation, we must look beyond emotional words, which are not necessarily intended to inform or convince, but often achieve their goal if they simply overwhelm through repetition or silence through intimidation.

To his credit, Professor Wilson has noted that, when making comparisons of different *time periods*, the degree of various adverse economic factors in black communities has not corresponded with changes in the behavior of the people living in those communities:

> Despite a high rate of poverty in ghetto neighborhoods throughout the first half of the twentieth century, rates of inner-city joblessness, teenage pregnancy, out-of-wedlock births, female-headed families, welfare dependency, and serious crime were significantly lower than in later years and did not reach catastrophic proportions until the mid-1970s.[7]

Fear of violence in black communities was demonstrably less in earlier years, as Professor Wilson also noted:

> Blacks in Harlem and in other ghetto neighborhoods did not hesitate to sleep in parks, on fire escapes, and on rooftops during hot summer nights in the 1940s and 1950s, and whites frequently visited inner-city taverns and nightclubs.[8]

Many examples from other sources reinforce the same conclusion, that black communities were not nearly as dangerous in the past as they became in the second half of the twentieth century.[9] In short, the supposed causes of major social pathologies in black ghettos today were much worse in the first half of the twentieth century than in the second half— and yet it was in the second half of that century that social pathologies became more widespread and ghettos more dangerous. In fact, this pattern extends far beyond black ghettos and far beyond the United States, as we can see when examining similar social degeneration, during the same time period, among low-income whites in England.

Meanwhile, what are we to make of the fact that blacks who are married or who have library cards have had such different economic outcomes than blacks as a group?

It seems unlikely that marriage, as such, or library cards, as such, directly cause the difference. What seems more probable is that these are *indicators* of cultural lifestyle choices in general that make for better economic prospects. Further evidence for this is that, while the labor force participation rate of black males as a whole has in recent times been lower than the labor force participation rate of white males as a whole, the labor force participation rate of *married* black males has been *higher* than the labor force participation rate of white males who never married. Moreover, this has been true for more than 20 consecutive years.[10]

Apparently individual lifestyle choices have major consequences for both blacks and whites. Marriage, library cards, labor force participation and entering one's children in lotteries for charter schools are among the indicators of the cultural values behind those lifestyle choices and socioeconomic outcomes.

Alternative explanations might be advanced as hypotheses to be tested empirically. But what is far more common is the deploying of a whole vocabulary of words and phrases which evade any such empirical confrontation of opposing explanations. Instead, it is often simply asserted that a "web of rules and institutions" is what leads to "unequal outcomes." These outcomes include "racial and gender pay gaps" and that blacks are "overrepresented among unemployed and low-wage workers and underrepresented in the middle class."[11]

No one on either side of these issues has denied that there are different outcomes in different groups of Americans, as there have been different outcomes in different groups in other countries around the world, and over thousands of years of recorded history. What is at issue here, as in other times and places, are the *causes* of those differences. Merely reciting these differences and arbitrarily attributing them to whatever the prevailing social vision of the time declares to be the cause— whether genes or discrimination— is hardly hypothesis-testing. Slippery words are among the many ways of evading an empirical confrontation of opposing explanations.

CHANGING WORDS AND MEANINGS

In many discussions of social visions and social policies, familiar words have often been used in new ways, to mean something very different from what those words meant before. Among the words given new and often misleading meanings are such common and simple words as "change," "opportunity," "violence" and "privilege." Conversely, old meanings have been expressed by new words, as vagrants became "the homeless," exultant young thugs became "troubled youths," and Balkanization became "diversity."

As one of the most often used, and least often examined, words of our time, "diversity" may be as good a place as any to begin an examination of the world of words, and its contrast with the world of reality.

"Diversity"

A fragmented society of people polarized into separate group identities used to be called a "Balkanized" society, and the painful history of strife, bloodshed and atrocities in the Balkans stood as an example of how destructive that can be to all. But that was before the word "Balkanization" was replaced by the much nicer-sounding word "diversity," from which all sorts of wonderful benefits have been assumed and incessantly proclaimed, *without any empirical test of those claims*. This new and nicer-sounding word has also avoided having the painful history of the Balkans— and of similar places elsewhere around the world— being called to mind.

By "diversity" those who incessantly proclaim that word, and its presumed benefits, mean more than simply people with different cultures interacting. The word "diversity" is used to imply positive interactions, with benefits for the various participants and for society at large. But we cannot simply define our way into beneficial outcomes. Whether the promotion of separate identities— by race, sex or other characteristics— is beneficial or harmful in its consequences is an empirical question— and a question almost never confronted by apostles of "diversity." The actual track record of promoting separate group identities, whether called "Balkanization" or "diversity," has been appalling, in countries around the world.

Among the most disturbing social realities are societies in which different groups live with at least forbearance toward each other for years, or even generations, until some spark— whether a particular incident or a talented demagogue— comes along and suddenly sets off a nightmare of horrors.

In India— a country severely cross-cut by differences in castes, religions, languages and cultures— the country's emergence into national independence in 1947 was marked by hundreds of thousands of people killed in mob violence against each other. Since then, there have been innumerable local outbreaks of lethal violence among India's many discrete groups at various times and places. Outbreaks of intergroup violence in Mumbai (Bombay) in 1992–93, for example, were reported in *The Times of India* as including "neighbours leading long-time friends to gory deaths."[12]

Nor was India unique in this regard. A study of twentieth century genocides in the Balkans noted that "outbursts of hatred and great violence occurred between people who had also known times of harmony or at least passive acceptance of each other."[13]

Sri Lanka was another country with a very similar pattern. When colonial Ceylon became the independent nation of Sri Lanka in the middle of the twentieth century, many observers— both inside and outside the country— pointed to the good, and even cordial, relations between the Sinhalese majority and the Tamil minority as a model of what intergroup relations should be. As a result, many people predicted not only a peaceful transition to independent nationhood, but a happier future than in other multi-ethnic Third World countries.[14]

Nevertheless, before the first decade of Sri Lanka's independence was over, a Sinhalese politician promoted resentments against the more prosperous Tamil minority, during his campaign to become prime minster. Ethnic polarization led first to discriminatory laws against the Tamils, and then to a cycle of violence and counter-violence that ultimately escalated into a decades-long civil war, in which there were unspeakable atrocities on both sides.[15]

At a minimum, history shows how dangerous it can be, to a whole society, to automatically and incessantly attribute statistical differences in outcomes to malevolent actions against the less successful. That the charge can often be false and misleading might also carry some weight, and merit closer attention to the specific facts of particular cases. Not only the society in general, but lagging groups in particular, can benefit from knowing what is true, as distinguished from what is currently in vogue. Not only does the truth offer a clearer path to advancement, the breakdown of law and order brought on by constantly stirred bitter resentments almost invariably leads to more suffering among the less fortunate.

Ex Ante Words and *Ex Post* Meanings

In addition to individual transformations of words and meanings, sometimes a particular change of meaning has been imposed on a whole category of words, creating very different implications. For example, some words that refer to initial conditions have been used to describe outcome conditions, making it appear that individuals or groups who did not do as well as others had barriers placed in their paths that others did not have.

Such barriers may in fact be the reason various groups have lagged in educational, economic and other endeavors at various times and places. But the extent to which it is true in any particular case is something to be determined by empirical evidence, not by redefining words that refer to *ex post* results as if they referred to *ex ante* conditions. For example, some people have been said to have been denied "opportunity" or "access" to some benefit— mortgage loans, for example— when in fact they have simply failed to meet qualifying standards met by other people who had the same options available at the outset as themselves.

Just as some people have been said to have been denied "opportunity" or "access" because their outcomes have been less favorable, so some other people who have had more positive outcomes have been called "privileged," even if individuals from such groups had no more numerous, nor more favorable, options available at the outset than others whose outcomes have not been as positive.

In each of these cases, there is a confusion between words that apply to conditions beforehand and words that apply to outcomes afterwards. Because someone ended up failing at some endeavor, that does not automatically mean that he was denied opportunity or access at the outset. Whether or not that was true in reality is a major *empirical* question, and a question too important to be answered by simply shifting the meanings of words.

In some cases, those who succeeded have had even fewer or less favorable options at the outset than others who did not succeed as well. Thus the Chinese minority in Malaysia, who have higher average incomes than the Malay majority, have been referred to as "privileged"[16] and the Malay majority as "deprived"[17]— even though laws and government policies in Malaysia impose preferential treatment of Malays in university admissions and in both government and private employment. Moreover, this particular usage of the terms "privileged" and "deprived" was not taken from political demagoguery but from serious academic studies.

In the ordinary sense of words, it is the Malays who have been privileged, even if they have not used their privileges to produce as beneficial outcomes for themselves as the Chinese have, when using their more limited opportunities. This was in fact a conclusion reached, in his later years, by a Malay leader who had long advocated the creation of preferential policies for Malays.[18]

Verbal usages, turning reality upside down, have not been confined to Malaysia or to people writing about Malaysia. The confusion of the *ex ante* with the *ex post* has become common in America, not only among journalists or politicians, but among academic scholars as well. Even though an achievement is, by common usage, something that has been achieved— that is, an *ex post* result— the word "privilege" has often been substituted, even though a privilege is something that exists *ex ante*.

The notion that those who achieved must have been privileged at the outset may be consistent with the prevailing social vision, but the more fundamental question is whether or to what extent, that vision itself is consistent with empirical facts. However, merely by changing the usage of a word, that empirical test is circumvented.

If the issue were simply one of differences of opinion as to the causes of disparate achievements, differences of opinion have been common among human beings for thousands of years, and are in principle capable of being resolved by empirical evidence. But when beliefs are anchored in a social vision protected by redefined words, empirical tests are finessed aside.

It has become increasingly common to refer to achievement as "privilege" throughout the American educational system, where crusades against "white privilege" abound, along with demands for statistical parity based on demographic representation rather than individual productivity.

This is consistent with the seemingly invincible fallacy that social groups would tend to have equal, or at least similar, outcomes in the absence of biased treatment or genetic differences in ability. Here, yet again, there is an inversion of criteria, so that the prevailing social vision is not judged by whether it is consistent with facts but, instead, facts are redefined to make them verbally consistent with the vision.

The phrase "white privilege" is not the only verbal sleight of hand used to make achievement differences vanish. Even racial or ethnic groups that arrived in the United States destitute during the nineteenth century, and were forced to live in a desperate poverty and squalor almost inconceivable today, have had their later rise from such dire conditions verbally erased by calling their eventual achievement of prosperity a "privilege."[19]

The histories of Irish, Jewish, Chinese and Japanese immigrants in America are classic examples of this process— and of their achievements being verbally air-brushed out of history by simply calling them "privilege." Even middle-class blacks today have likewise been characterized by some as "privileged,"[20] even though their ancestors arrived as slaves.

Achievements are a threat to a social vision and a political agenda based on that vision, and so are often kept off the hypothesis-testing agenda by adherents of that vision. Redefining words is a key part of that process.

Worse yet, children who are currently being raised with the kinds of values, discipline and work habits that are likely to make them valuable contributors to society, and a source of pride to themselves and to those who raised them, are called "privileged," and are taught in schools to feel guilty when other children are being raised with values, behavior and habits that are likely to leave them few options as adults, other than to live at the expense of other people, whether via the welfare state or through a life of crime, or both.

Social mobility is another issue distorted verbally, by simply shifting the meaning of the word "mobility." In the ordinary usage of words, an automobile is considered to be mobile, because it is capable of moving. Even when it is parked, an automobile remains capable of moving, so that no one is surprised to see someone get into a parked car and drive off. The car was always *mobile*, even when it was not always *moving*.

Mobility is an *ex ante* concept, independent of whether movement is actually taking place *ex post*. But, if a car's motor is too damaged to function, then that car is no longer mobile, even if a tow truck is moving it at highway speeds. In short, mobility and movement are two fundamentally different things. One is *ex ante* and the other is *ex post*.

How much *movement* takes place does not tell us how much *mobility* there is. Nevertheless, empirical studies of social movement are cited as a test of social mobility, even by a Nobel Prize-winning economist, Joseph Stiglitz, who says that social mobility in America is a "myth," based on data showing little *ex post* movement upward among poor people. In his own words, "when social scientists refer to equality of opportunity, they mean the likelihood that someone at the bottom will make it to the top."[21]

That likelihood, however, is affected not only by external impediments but also by internal factors such as individual skills and efforts. *Social* mobility is the extent to which a society permits upward and downward movement. How much movement actually takes place depends also on the extent to which individuals and families avail themselves of the opportunities.

Measuring social *mobility* by how much *movement* takes place proceeds as if nothing depends on how individuals and families behave. That certainly avoids complications for those promoting the prevailing social vision. But it also avoids empirically testing that vision. Yet the very possibility that internal factors may be at work disappears, by verbal sleight of hand, when results *ex post* are equated with opportunity *ex ante*. Another Nobel Prize-winning economist, Angus Deaton, used the same *ex post* criterion to measure opportunity *ex ante*,[22] thereby sealing off the prevailing vision from the danger of contamination by discordant facts.

One of the things that sometimes seems to threaten to puncture the verbally sealed bubble of the prevailing vision is the presence of some poor immigrant group with a culture very different from that of domestic low-income groups. Cuban refugees to the United States have been one of a number of such groups, who have initially been at least as poor as domestic groups living at the official poverty level. But when the newcomers have been unencumbered by the welfare state vision and its values, such groups have often risen socioeconomically above the domestic poor, and sometimes above the native population as a whole, as the descendants of the Cuban refugees have.

The children of some very poor immigrant groups have risen educationally in the schools, not only above the level of native-born children from families at the same income level, but even above the educational level of the children from the native population as a whole. In New York City, for example, while students who pass the demanding tests to get into the most elite public high schools tend to be from high-income neighborhoods, an exception are students from low-income neighborhoods with concentrations of immigrants from Fujian province in China.[23]

Such groups represent a threat to the prevailing social vision. Among the ways of meeting that threat are (1) ignoring such social results that are so discordant with the assumptions of that vision, (2) making statements attributing the newcomers' success to "privilege," using the word in the redefined sense that turns this into a circular argument, and (3) stigmatizing the making of comparisons between successful ethnic groups and unsuccessful ones as manifestations of implicit racism against such groups as blacks in the United States.

However politically effective this third tactic may be within the United States, it is not nearly so effective in countries where the underclass is predominantly white, and the poverty-stricken newcomers who succeed in the schools and in the economy include groups that are non-white. In England, for example, among children whose families' incomes were low enough to qualify for free lunch programs, the children of immigrants from Africa and Bangladesh met educational test standards nearly 60 percent of the time, while white, native-born children from families at the same low economic level met the standards only 30 percent of the time.[24]

Viewed in racial terms, these educational results in England might seem to be very different from those in the United States. But viewed in terms of low-income, native-born children, raised in a culture long steeped in the welfare state vision and its values, as compared to those low-income immigrant children who have been spared that culture and those values, the results are remarkably similar on both sides of the Atlantic.*

In Britain, immigrants who have been successes in school have often also had successes in higher education and in their careers:

> The children of immigrants from the Indian sub-continent make up a quarter of all British medical students, twelve times their proportion in the general population. They are likewise overrepresented in the law, science, and economics faculties of our universities.[25]

While empirical studies of American society that measure mobility *ex ante* by movement *ex post* have often been cited by those claiming that social mobility in contemporary America is a "myth,"[26] one of the often-cited empirical studies of social mobility, by the Pew Charitable Trust, pointed out that its sample did *not* include immigrant families. The study itself added that, for immigrant families, "the American Dream is alive and well."[27] This statement is seldom, if ever, quoted by those like Professor Stiglitz who cite the Pew studies to claim that social mobility is a myth.[28]

In England, physician-author Theodore Dalrymple noted: "I cannot recall meeting a sixteen-year-old white from the public housing estates that are near my hospital who could multiply nine by seven (I

---

*   In neither England nor the United States are all immigrant groups the same. Some immigrant groups are far more prone to become dependent on welfare than others, and may even exceed the rate of welfare dependency among the native population. But those particular immigrant groups with a different cultural orientation— one resistant to the welfare state vision and values— have risen in both countries, even when these particular immigrant groups have been non-whites.

do not exaggerate). Even three by seven often defeats them."[29] *The Economist* magazine reported that white 16-year-olds in the borough of Knowsley had worse test results "than do black 16-year-olds in any London borough."[30]

In the course of treating his patients, Dr. Dalrymple has had occasions to ask young, lower-class Britons if they can read and write. When he has asked, "they do not even regard my question as to whether they can read and write as in the least surprising or insulting."[31] Such educational deficiencies have been sufficiently widely known in Britain that there was a popular song there whose first line was "We don't need no education," and another popular song whose title was "Poor, White, and Stupid."[32] Dr. Dalrymple also observed that the average Polish immigrant who has been in Britain six months "speaks better, more cultivated English" than lower-class young Britons do.[33]

Not all British youngsters are lower class, of course. But, comparing foreign youngsters for whom English is not their native language with native white British youngsters as a whole shows a striking pattern. Foreign students whose native language is not English typically do not initially do as well in their early schooling as native white British students as a whole. However, by the end of secondary school "white British pupils are overtaken by ten other ethnic groups." At that time, Chinese pupils "are twice as likely to score 50 points or higher than their white British peers" on a standard educational test.[34]

In the United States, particular minority groups also outperform the majority population. Asian American students outnumber white students in each of New York City's three premier elite public high schools— Stuyvesant, Bronx Science and Brooklyn Tech.[35]

On the other hand, the percentage of black American students at Stuyvesant High School declined over the years from 1979 to 2012 to just under *one-tenth* of their proportion in the latter year of what it was three decades earlier.[36] At New York's highly selective Hunter College, blacks were 12 percent of the students in 1995 and Hispanics were 6 percent. But, in 2009, black students were only 3 percent of the students at Hunter College and Hispanic students only 1 percent.[37] Among the various external factors usually blamed for substandard academic performances by black or Hispanic students, none has been getting worse over time on such a scale as to account for such a sharp decline.

Despite an abundance of literature blaming disparate educational outcomes on the schools, the society or others, in keeping with the prevailing social vision, statistics on the average number of hours per week spent studying by high school students from different ethnic backgrounds show Asian American students spending more hours studying than either white or black American students.[38]

How surprised should we be that academic outcomes show a pattern of disparities similar to the pattern of disparities in the amount of time devoted to school work? And how surprised should we be that such input data seldom see the light of day in the media?

Yet all such data, so discordant with the premises of the prevailing social vision, can be turned aside by simply redefining a word, or by redefining a whole category of words whose *ex ante* and *ex post* meanings are very different in their implications.

"Violence"

It may not be surprising that an incessant drumbeat of declarations that disparities of outcomes among groups demonstrate malicious treatment of the less successful can promote resentments and violence. What is remarkable is how even outbreaks of violence fail to lead promoters of the invidious social vision to reconsider what they are saying. Instead, it often leads to simply redefining violence. After Harlem riots shocked many people in the 1960s, for example, Professor Kenneth B. Clark declared:

> The real danger of Harlem is not in the infrequent explosions of random lawlessness. The frightening horror of Harlem is the chronic day-to-day quiet violence to the human spirit which exists and is accepted as normal.[39]

A similar equating of social problems with violence occurred in *The Nation* magazine, where it was said that the "institutional form of quiet violence operates when people are deprived of choices in a systematic way by the very manner in which transactions normally take place."[40] An advertisement in the *New York Times* by a committee of black clergymen likewise condemned "the silent and covert violence which white middle-class America inflicts upon the victims of the inner city."[41] Books with such titles as *Savage Inequalities* promote the same notion.

Whatever the substantive merits or demerits of such claims of social injustices, they are not violence. Some might consider such things better or worse than violence but, in either case, that does not make them be violence. In the same sense, some people might consider mountains to be more important than rivers or less important than rivers. But, in any case, nothing can make a mountain be the same as a river or a river be the same as a mountain.

This vogue of equating social problems with violence has spawned such spin-offs as justifying campus speech codes and campus riots as responses to "micro-aggression" by visiting speakers saying things considered offensive by those who believe in a particular social vision.

Even when these things are not said to the people who claim to be offended, but are said by visiting speakers on campus to those who invited them, it is still called "micro-aggression." But how can A talking to B be considered to be aggression— much less equivalent to violence— against C? Clever people might say that A could be saying things to B that could lead to violence against C. Even if that were true— and it has not been proved, or even tested, in most cases— in the same sense a match can start a forest fire. But nobody calls a match a forest fire.

Verbal vogues have more than verbal consequences. In so far as they create a false equivalence between violence and socioeconomic conditions, they excuse lawlessness and social disorders, whose principal victims are the less affluent, both immediately and in the longer-run repercussions.

"Change"

For those promoting a particular vision of society, the word "change" often does not refer to changes in general, or even to all changes of a given magnitude or consequence in the lives of people. In practice, even if not in explicit definition, change for many of the intelligentsia often tends to mean only the particular kinds of changes conceived and promoted by their particular social vision.

Other changes, even changes that revolutionize the lives of the great majority of the people, are omitted in many discussions of change by people committed to a particular vision. Eras in which sweeping changes occur may be seen as stagnant or even retrograde eras if, for example, such eras did not include government policies aimed at reducing income disparities. Even widespread improvements in prosperity are no substitute for policies aimed at redistributing income, for those with the prevailing social vision that is focused on invidious comparisons.

When intellectual elites discuss eras of change in the United States, for example, the decade of the 1920s is seldom, if ever, included. Yet there have been few decades with so many, and so large and such consequential changes in the lives of millions of Americans as the 1920s.

The 1920 census was the first census to show more Americans living in urban, rather than rural, communities. While the urban majority of the population was just over 51 percent at the beginning of the 1920s decade, the rate of increase of the urban population was more than eight times the rate of increase of the rural population.[42] The 1920s marked a historic transition to a very different kind of society.

At the beginning of the 1920s, just 35 percent of American homes had electric lights— the same proportion that had gaslight, while another 27 percent of those homes were lit by lamps using either kerosene or coal oil.[43] But, after that decade ended, 68 percent of the homes in America were lit by electricity in 1930. Home radios were virtually non-existent at the beginning of 1920; the first commercial radio station began broadcasting to the general public that autumn.[44] Subsequently, 24 percent of American homes had radios by 1925 and 40 percent in 1930.[45]

Most American families also had an automobile for the first time during that decade. As of 1920, 26 percent of American families had an automobile. But so many more families were able to buy cars during the 1920s that, when that decade was over, 60 percent of American families had an automobile in 1930.[46]

The number of Americans attending colleges and universities doubled between 1920 and 1930.[47] The 1920s were also the first decade of regularly scheduled airline passenger service, which had fewer than 6,000 passengers in 1926, but more than 170,000 passengers by 1929.[48]

Sports and entertainment were also revolutionized in the 1920s. Motion pictures talked for the first time during that decade, greatly boosting attendance at movies— which was twice as large in 1929 as it had been just seven years earlier.[49] This was also the decade when American popular music was revolutionized by jazz, which not only swept the country but spread internationally. In major league baseball, attendance records for every year of the 1920s exceeded the attendance in any year before 1920.[50] The National Football League was founded in the 1920s, and attendance per NFL game in 1928 was three times what it was in 1921.[51]

Chains of department stores and grocery stores spread rapidly across the country during the 1920s,[52] usually selling at lower prices than independent stores,[53] reflecting economies of scale that reduced the costs of getting merchandise from the producer to the consumer. There had been chains of stores before, but the decade of the 1920s was the decade when they expanded severalfold, displacing many small independent stores, whose costs of doing business were not low enough to enable them to match the low prices charged by chain stores.

None of these sweeping changes, however, was "change" to many, if not most, of the elite intelligentsia, because these were not the particular kinds of changes they sought, predicted or recognized. The decade of the 1920s was barely over before a widespread denigration of it as a stagnant or reactionary decade began— a view that has continued since then to the present day.

Noted historians Henry Steele Commager and Richard Brandon Morris, for example, compared the decade of the 1920s to a stagnant region of the north Atlantic known as the Sargasso Sea. They referred to the preceding and succeeding decades as "positive" but to the 1920s as "negative," and "like some Sargasso Sea on the ocean of history."[54] Professor Edward A. Ross, regarded as one of the founders of the profession of sociology in the United States, analogized the years from 1919 to 1931 to the "Great Ice Age."[55]

Despite its high economic growth rate, rising real incomes and low unemployment rates, famed historian Arthur M. Schlesinger, Jr. was among many intellectuals who put the word "prosperity" in quotation marks as regards the 1920s.[56] Professor Schlesinger referred to wages in the 1920s as "unsatisfactory,"[57] without specifying any criterion by which wages might be considered satisfactory otherwise, or some preceding era when wages were higher. Real per capita income in fact increased by nearly one third from 1919 to 1929.[58]

Even those writers who admitted the material progress of the 1920s often struggled to depict this as not "real" progress in some elusive and undefined sense. The people who denigrated the 1920s have not been little-known figures on the fringes of society but, in many cases, have been among the elite scholars in their respective fields. It was in discussions of government policies in the 1920s that the reasons for the dissatisfaction of many intellectuals with that decade became apparent. Calvin Coolidge, who was President of the United States for just over half of the decade of the 1920s, was widely excoriated and/or ridiculed in later histories.

President Coolidge believed in neither of the two government policies that were fundamental to the Progressives— redistribution of income and government intervention in the economy. The reduction of the 73 percent tax rate on the highest incomes to 24 percent that took place as a result of tax rate cuts during the Harding and Coolidge administrations was denounced then, and has continued to be denounced, as "tax cuts for the rich," despite the fact that this change in tax *rates* brought much higher tax *revenues* from high-income people, both absolutely and as a percentage of all income tax revenues collected. Moreover, this outcome was precisely what President Coolidge said beforehand was his objective.[59]

As for the effects of the Coolidge administration's policies on working-class people, in President Coolidge's last four years in the White House, the annual unemployment rate ranged from a high of 4.2 percent to a low of 1.8 percent.[60] This hardly fit a depiction of the Coolidge administration as "unashamedly the instrument of privileged groups,"[61] as claimed in a widely used history textbook by Professors Allan Nevins and Henry Steele Commager.

The other key policy of the Progressives, as exemplified in the Woodrow Wilson administration that preceded that of Harding and Coolidge, was government intervention in the economy, as exemplified by the creation of such institutions as the Federal Reserve System and the Federal Trade Commission, as well as innumerable controls over the economy by the Woodrow Wilson administration during the First World War.

Neither President Warren G. Harding, who succeeded President Wilson, nor Vice President Coolidge who became President after Harding's death, believed in government interventions. But their Secretary of Commerce, Herbert Hoover— who later became President after Coolidge— was more activist-minded in his cabinet role and later made unprecedented interventions in the economy as President, after the 1929 stock market crash.[62] Such interventions were then escalated further by his successor, President Franklin D. Roosevelt.

To the intellectual elites of that time and later, relying more on market processes than on political interventions in the economy was abdicating responsibility for the public welfare, rather than simply a different belief by Presidents Harding and Coolidge that the public welfare would be better served by letting markets function under known and stable laws, rather than with unpredictable *ad hoc* government interventions. The latter policy was perhaps best expressed during the 1930s by President Franklin D. Roosevelt:

> The country needs and, unless I mistake its temper, the country demands bold, persistent experimentation. It is common sense to take a method and try it; if it fails, admit it frankly and try another. But above all, try something.[63]

However more congenial President Roosevelt's approach might be to the prevailing vision of the intellectuals, both then and now, the opposite approach in the 1920s was based on different assumptions— which the intelligentsia refused to see as different assumptions, but only as a calloused failure to promote the public interest and kowtowing to business and the wealthy. As with many other issues in other places and times, a desire to test the actual consequences of fundamentally different beliefs and policies has seldom matched the fervor of pronouncements defending one view or the other.

In any event, to the intellectuals the decade of the 1920s did not deserve the honorific title of an era of "change." It was the decade of the 1930s which brought that kind of political change, and which has since been celebrated as much as the 1920s were denigrated.

SIDEBAR: THE CRASH AND THE INTERVENTIONS

In many, if not most, histories of the United States, the stock market crash in 1929 is presented as the cause of the Great Depression of the 1930s, with its massive unemployment. But, in fact, unemployment never reached double digits in any of the 12 months that followed the stock market crash in October 1929. Unemployment peaked at 9 percent, two months after the crash, and began an irregular decline that brought it down to 6.3 percent in June 1930.[64]

That was when a massive increase in tariffs was passed, despite widely publicized warnings from more than a thousand economists that this would make matters worse. Five months after the Smoot-Hawley tariff bill was passed, unemployment hit double digits— and remained in double digits for every subsequent month during the rest of the decade of the 1930s.[65]

This was not all due to the tariffs, which were just one of many government interventions begun under President Herbert Hoover and escalated by his successor, Franklin D. Roosevelt.

The highest annual rate of unemployment in the 1920s was 12 percent in one year, while unemployment in the 1930s peaked at 25 percent, and was at or above 20 percent for 35 consecutive months.[66] Then, after subsiding somewhat— but still continuously in double digits for years— unemployment rose again to 20 percent or above during six months in 1935, four months in 1938 and one month in the spring of 1939, almost a decade after the stock market crash of 1929 that supposedly caused the high unemployment of the 1930s. In short, unemployment was at or above 20 percent for 46 months— the equivalent of nearly four years— or 38 percent of the much celebrated decade of the 1930s.[67]

In the wake of many business bankruptcies, thousands of bank failures, mass unemployment and lower total output during the early 1930s, the rising standard of living of the much disdained 1920s was replaced by much lower standards of living for millions of people. This was most strikingly illustrated by numerous breadlines and soup kitchens set up by charitable organizations in communities across the country, for people unable to buy food. An especially painful spectacle was that of vast numbers of Americans, in many regions of the country, scavenging in garbage dumps for food during the Great Depression.[68]

An economic study of the Great Depression in a leading scholarly journal in 2004 concluded that the effects of government policies had prolonged the Great Depression by several years.[69] But the contrary view has largely prevailed by sheer repetition and by its consonance with the prevailing social vision.*

These two past decades are not the fundamental issue. The crucial point for us today is understanding the continuing ability of many intellectuals to ignore blatant realities which threaten their cherished vision. It has been an on-going triumph of words over demonstrable realities. We are expected today to automatically follow the kinds of government interventionist policies of the 1930s and to disdain the policies of the 1920s when, in the world of words, there was no "change" because there was no government income redistribution policy.

---

*   It is not only conservative or libertarian economists who see dangers in government interventions. Liberal economist J.K. Galbraith referred to the Federal Reserve's policies during the Great Depression as showing "startling incompetence." John Kenneth Galbraith, *The Great Crash* (Boston: Houghton Mifflin, 1961), p. 32. In the previous century, Karl Marx said that "crackbrained meddling by the authorities" can "aggravate an existing crisis." Karl Marx and Frederick Engels, *Collected Works*, Vol. 38 (New York: International Publishers, 1982), p. 275.

OTHER PEOPLE'S WORDS

Despite the wonders that can be performed in the world of words by those with verbal virtuosity— for example, making ugly and/or dangerous behavior vanish by saying the magic word "stereotypes"— all human beings are nevertheless forced to live their lives in the world of reality, outside the sealed bubble of a vision.

Among the impediments to clearly seeing that world of reality are not only the redefining of words, but also twisting other people's words and meanings— extending in some cases to attributing to people things the direct opposite of what they actually said. Like other verbal distortions, this one is not confined to unscrupulous politicians or irresponsible journalists, but includes academic scholars renowned within their own respective specialties.

As J.A. Schumpeter said, long ago: "We fight for and against not men and things as they are, but for and against the caricatures we make of them."[70] No clearer example of this can be found than those who fight against what they call the "trickle-down theory" that, by government policies to benefit those who are already rich, their prosperity will somehow "trickle-down" to others, including the poor.

"Trickle-Down" Theory

The first and most important thing to understand about the "trickle-down" theory is that *there is no such theory*. Anyone who doubts this can begin by asking themselves whether they have ever— even once in their entire life— seen, heard or read any human being who actually espoused that theory.

If a negative answer to that question does not suffice, one might consult the monumental, 1,260-page *History of Economic Analysis* by J.A. Schumpeter, and look in vain for the "trickle-down" theory there. Finally, one can consult the many writings of those critics who have opposed and denounced the "trickle-down" theory to see whom they quote— and discover that they have not quoted any specific individual espousing that theory.

Such prominent contemporary critics as economists Joseph Stiglitz, Alan Blinder and Paul Krugman, for example, have repeatedly denounced this non-existent theory,[71] without quoting or even citing anyone who had actually proposed such a theory. Nor were they unique in this. The "trickle-down" theory has been denounced repeatedly in numerous books by numerous authors. It has been denounced in *New York Times* editorials, by leading columnists and writers in numerous other publications, by politicians, teachers and television commentators. It has been denounced as far away as India.[72]

Surely the people who have been denouncing this theory for years can tell us who has advocated it, and where the advocates' own words can be found— *if there are any such advocates.*

What has sometimes occasioned these denunciations has been an entirely different theory, which has led to proposals and policies to reduce tax *rates*, in order to collect more tax *revenues*— especially more tax revenues from high-income people— and spur increased investments that can lead to greater output and employment. Like any other theory, this theory can turn out to be correct or incorrect in a given set of circumstances. But it has nothing to do with existing wealth trickling down, and everything to do with attempts to create *additional* wealth in the country as a whole, so that, in a phrase popularized by President John F. Kennedy, "a rising tide lifts all the boats."[73]

Any given individual might argue for or against that conclusion as well, on either analytical or empirical grounds. But all too often critics instead denounce a non-existent "trickle-down" theory and "tax cuts for the rich" supposedly based on that theory.

This was not always a partisan political issue, nor always even an ideological issue. While today it is usually conservative or free market economists who urge reducing tax *rates*, in order to collect more tax *revenues* and spur economic growth, it was none other than John Maynard Keynes— hardly a conservative or free-market economist— who said in 1933 that "taxation may be so high as to defeat its object," that "given sufficient time to gather the fruits, a reduction of taxation will run a better chance, than an increase, of balancing the Budget."[74]

Even earlier, it was two Secretaries of the Treasury during the Democratic administration of Woodrow Wilson who pointed out that tax *rates* above a certain level no longer necessarily bring in more tax *revenue*, as President Wilson himself also noted in an address to Congress.[75]

The first tax rate cuts based on that theory occurred in the Republican administration of President Warren G. Harding in the 1920s, and those cuts were advocated most prominently by Secretary of the Treasury Andrew Mellon. As already noted in Chapter 4, income tax *revenues* did in fact rise after income tax *rates* were cut in the 1920s— and both the amount and the proportion of income taxes paid by people with higher incomes rose dramatically.

In 1920, when the highest tax rate on the highest incomes was 73 percent, people with incomes of $100,000 or more paid 30 percent of all income tax revenues. After the tax rate on the highest incomes was cut to 24 percent, people in that same income bracket paid 65 percent of all income tax revenues in 1929.[76] Nevertheless, in the world of words, these were called "tax cuts for the rich"— and have remained so ever since, in utter disregard of empirical evidence as to the actual amount of tax *revenues* collected from high-income taxpayers at different tax *rates*. There were similar results from later tax rate reductions during the Kennedy, Reagan and George W. Bush administrations.[77]

Whether this will happen again in other circumstances is something that might be debated, instead of fighting a straw man like a non-existent "trickle-down" theory. Back in 1899, long before the income tax rate controversies arose, Oliver Wendell Holmes advanced the general proposition that catchwords can "delay further analysis for fifty years."[78] The catchwords "trickle-down theory" have been going strong for decades, and show no sign of weakening.

Fictitious Villains

Among the essential requirements for the success of fervent social crusades are grievances, villains and victories over those villains. Given the universality of sins among human beings, grievances are the most assuredly supplied of these essentials. But maintaining a sufficiently dependable supply of villains as broader causal explanations of perceived grievances can be a challenge, especially if accuracy is taken seriously as a constraint.

A widely used history textbook, co-authored by a number of well-known historians, two of whom won Pulitzer Prizes, said of Secretary of the Treasury Andrew Mellon: "It was better, he argued, to place the burden of taxes on lower-income groups" and that a "share of the tax-free profits of the rich, Mellon reassured the country, would ultimately trickle down to the middle- and lower-income groups in the form of salaries and wages."[79]

There was neither a quotation nor a citation of any statement in which Secretary Mellon actually made this argument, even though it is a matter of public record what Mellon actually proposed, as regards tax rates on low-income people— and it bears no resemblance to what these historians said.[80]

Mellon's own book, *Taxation: The People's Business* in fact argued just the opposite, that *higher*-income people should pay *more* tax *revenue* to the government,[81] rather than having high tax *rates* on paper that were merely a "gesture" of taxing the rich,[82] while allowing them to escape actually paying those high tax rates by investing in tax-exempt securities.[83] He said, quite plainly, that "wealth is failing to carry its share of the tax burden; and capital is being diverted into channels which yield neither revenue to the Government nor profit to the people."[84]

Mellon argued that what he called the "evil" of tax-exempt securities should be ended.[85] He asserted that it was "repugnant" in a democracy that there should be "a class in the community which cannot be reached for tax purposes,"[86] because of "a refuge in the form of tax-exempt securities, into which wealth that has been accumulated or inherited can retire and defy the tax collector."[87] He also called it "incredible" that a man with an income of a million dollars a year would be permitted "to pay not one cent to the support of his Government"[88] and an "almost grotesque" consequence that people of more modest incomes would therefore have to make up for the tax shortfall.[89]

Nevertheless, another widely used history textbook, a best-seller titled *The American Pageant*, with multiple authors and multiple editions over the decades, declared: "Mellon's spare-the-rich policies thus shifted much of the tax burden from the wealthy to the middle-income groups."[90] Here as well, there was neither a quotation nor a citation of anything that Secretary Mellon actually said, much less a citation of Internal Revenue Service data that told an opposite story from that of the "tax cuts for the rich" scenario.

After the 1920s income tax rate cuts, people with an income of $5,000 and under paid less than half of one percent of the income tax revenues collected in 1929, while people with incomes of a million dollars or more paid 19 percent. Before, under the higher tax rates on high incomes, people with incomes of $5,000 and under paid 15 percent of all income tax revenues collected in 1920, while people with incomes of a million dollars or more paid less than 5 percent.[91]

None of these facts requires extraordinary research in esoteric places. One need only read Mellon's book *Taxation* to see what he advocated, and look at the published records of the Internal Revenue Service to see what happened. Both of these sources are available in libraries or on the Internet. That renowned historians and economists failed to check these readily available sources is just one sign of what can happen in an academic monoculture where the promotion of a social vision takes precedence over the search for facts— and where there are few people with fundamentally different views who would challenge what was said.

Andrew Mellon was by no means the only person whose views differed from that of the prevailing social vision, and whose words, policies or consequences of those policies were not merely criticized but falsified by those with that vision. This practice has continued on into our own times on a whole range of other issues.

Among those demonized in the second half of the twentieth century was a very unlikely candidate for the role of villain, Daniel Patrick Moynihan. He had two careers, one as an academic intellectual writing about social issues, and a political career as a liberal Democrat supporting civil rights for blacks and social programs designed to help the poor. In the 1960s he held an appointed office as Assistant Secretary of Labor in the Lyndon Johnson administration, and was in later years elected as a Democratic Senator from New York, serving in that capacity for 24 years.

One of the disturbing social problems that caught Assistant Secretary of Labor Moynihan's attention in the 1960s was that one-third of black children were growing up in broken homes.[92] He saw great personal and social dangers in that situation, and prepared a paper for internal use, pointing out the dangers he saw and urging government action to help deal with that problem. His paper was later published as a U.S. Department of Labor document titled *The Negro Family* and subtitled *The Case for National Action*. As was common in such government publications, no author was mentioned.

Only after a firestorm of criticism by those angered that black family problems had been aired as contributing to social pathology, was the author revealed to the public, and the document became known thereafter as "the Moynihan Report." Daniel Patrick Moynihan was fiercely denounced in the public media[93] and "bitterly attacked in private" at a White House planning session:

> Moynihan sat in and suffered the assaults in silence— though, said a government friend, "he came out of one conference with tears in his eyes. They called him a racist and a fascist."[94]

Far from singling out blacks for criticism, Moynihan pointed out the problems of "family disorganization" in the earlier history of his own ethnic group, Irish Americans.[95] He also had his own painful personal experience, as a child ten years old, when his father deserted the family during the Great Depression of the 1930s, plunging them from middle-class suburban comfort to dire poverty in one of Manhattan's poorest and roughest neighborhoods. Though only ten years old at the time, he and his even younger brother tried to earn some much-needed money to bring home by shining shoes in Times Square and Central Park.[96]

His younger brother cried one day when he came home without money to buy milk, and young Pat Moynihan was on some other occasions robbed of the money he had earned by neighborhood toughs.[97] As he grew older and bigger, he was able to take on other jobs, including working as a stevedore on New York's waterfront.[98]

The trauma of fatherlessness was something that Moynihan tried to warn others about. Ironically, the one-third of black children who were raised in broken homes, which alarmed Moynihan in the 1960s, became *two-thirds* in later years— and, among blacks in poverty, more than four-fifths.[99]

What happened to Mellon and Moynihan, among others in the past, continues to happen to those who deviate from the prevailing vision in the present. Among the prime targets today is Charles Murray, whose many books on social issues have led to attempts to prevent his speaking on college campuses to students who invited him. Many of these attempts have involved disruptions or violence, and virtually all have involved accusing him of having said vile things— none of which has been quoted from any of the books he has written, and some of which are the direct opposite of what he actually said in those books.[100]

Such practices have become commonplace as regards others, on issues large and small. In 2015, for example, an Associated Press account of an interview with Professor William Julius Wilson of Harvard contained this:

> Wilson's childhood gave him firsthand knowledge of poverty and how to escape it. Referring to Supreme Court Justice Clarence Thomas, who also grew up poor, he says, "He'll say he pulled himself up by his own bootstraps. I say I was in the right place at the right time."[101]

In this case, as in others, there was no quotation or citation of Justice Thomas ever having said any such thing. On the contrary, the Justice's memoir, *My Grandfather's Son*, credited his grandfather, who raised him, with making his advancement possible. When Judge Thomas was sworn in as a Supreme Court Justice, he invited nuns who had taught him in a Southern Catholic school to Washington for his swearing-in ceremony, where they could see that what they did for him was not in vain.[102]

The word "bootstraps," like the word "trickle-down," is almost invariably *attributed* to somebody else, rather than being either quoted or cited. These catchwords tell us more about those who resort to such straw men than about those to whom they attribute these terms or the ideas behind them.

Black American economist Walter E. Williams, who— like Justice Thomas— has opposed the prevailing social vision, has been said by economist Lanny Ebenstein of the University of California at Santa Barbara to be among those "committed to the welfare of the top few."[103] Professor Ebenstein has every right to disagree with Professor Williams' analyses or policies, but that is very different from making sweeping claims without providing substantiation.

As someone who has known Walter Williams as a colleague and friend for half a century, I have seen nothing in any of his writings, or in anything that he has said verbally, whether in public or in private, that has indicated the slightest interest in promoting the welfare of the wealthy.[104] Anyone who wishes to check for themselves can read any of his books, from *Race and Economics* to *South Africa's War Against Capitalism*, the latter resulting from his research in South Africa during the era of apartheid.

People who attribute to others things that are the opposite of what they actually said are not necessarily lying. They may simply not have bothered to check out what was actually said, but based their conclusions instead on widespread beliefs among like-minded people— beliefs sometimes called what "everybody knows." But the net result is no less misleading.

When scholars who are also educators do such things, the most important damage that is done is not to those they attack, but to those whom they are paid to educate. Moreover, that damage is not limited to whatever particular false conclusions may be produced, but to the whole way of thinking— and *not* thinking— that they demonstrate, and which may be emulated by their students.

If students do not acquire systematic methods and standards for testing conflicting beliefs, this can be a major deficiency in their education, for nothing is more certain than that they will encounter conflicting beliefs on many subjects in the years after they have left the politically correct monoculture on many academic campuses.

SIDEBAR: A PROJECT FOR STUDENTS

It could be a valuable project for a student to go to a library, or to the Internet, and check what Andrew Mellon actually said in his little book *Taxation*. After which a check of Internal Revenue Service data would enable the student to find out how much tax revenue was collected from people in different income brackets, before and after the highest tax rate was reduced from 73 percent to 24 percent. The lifelong benefits to the student might include a healthy skepticism toward political slogans and a healthy desire to check out the facts before repeating rhetoric on other issues.

INSINUATION

What words openly *declare* can be tested against empirical evidence, but what words *insinuate* can bypass that safeguard. Even an innocent-sounding phrase like "income distribution," endlessly repeated, can suggest a process in which income exists *somehow* and is then distributed, as one might distribute food at a dinner table or gifts at Christmas.

In reality there is only a figurative "distribution" of income, in the statistical sense in which there is a distribution of heights among people, ranging from the heights of little toddlers to the heights of professional basketball players more than seven feet tall. But no one imagines that heights exist *somehow* as independent entities, and are then literally "distributed"— in the sense of being handed out— to individuals.

In the plain, straightforward sense, most income is not *distributed* at all, either justly or unjustly. Most income in a market economy is *earned* directly by providing something that someone else wants, and values enough to pay for it, whether what they are paying for is labor, housing or diamonds. People who are unable to understand why John D. Rockefeller in the past, or Bill Gates in the present, received so much money might ask what each of them supplied to others that millions of others were willing to pay for, with their individually modest payments that added up to gigantic fortunes. But that question is seldom asked by most people, and especially not by income redistributionists.

Far more common expressions are like those of economist Joseph Stiglitz, who referred to "the share of income grabbed by the top 1 percent" or a *New York Times* editorial which referred to the top one percent as having "cornered an ever-larger share of the nation's wealth."[105] In a similar vein, President Barack Obama said, "The top 10 percent no longer takes in one-third of our income— it now takes half."[106] Such expressions are not peculiar to Americans. An Oxford professor, for example, referred repeatedly to income that people in the top one percent somehow "take" from a presumably pre-existing and collective "national income."[107]

In each case, the key trick is to verbally collectivize wealth produced by individuals and then depict those individuals who produced more of it, and received payment for doing so, as having deprived others of their fair share. With such word games, one might say that Babe Ruth took an unfair share of the home runs hit by the New York Yankees.

Sometimes these word games are played on an international scale. The wealth created in the United States by Americans is rhetorically transformed into part of "the world's wealth," from which Americans *take* an unfairly large share. But Americans, like other peoples, essentially consume what they themselves produce. What they import from other countries is exported by those countries in exchange for part of what Americans have produced. But such mundane facts cannot compete, in the world of words, with melodramatic rhetoric conveying a toxic message that disparities in outcomes imply some people being wronged by others.

Someone once said of nineteenth-century French economist Jean-Baptiste Say that "affected *ways of talking*" constituted a large part of Say's "doctrine."[108] That charge might more readily apply to many of our contemporaries today, who refer to income that people in the top brackets somehow "take" from a presumably pre-existing and collective "national income," or "our income," rather than income they earned directly as payments from those who voluntarily purchased the particular goods or services that those in the top brackets offered for sale.

Although such verbal displays— insinuations as distinguished from arguments— may be in aid of a redistributionist agenda, neither income nor wealth can be *re*distributed when it was not distributed in the first place, but earned directly from those who valued whatever was sold. What is being promoted by such verbal displays is not simply a different set of income or wealth outcomes but a whole fundamentally different *process* for determining how much income or wealth everyone receives. In that alternative world, third-party surrogates, armed with the power of government, can override whatever valuations millions of individuals might place on innumerable goods and services they purchase, and substitute instead the notions in vogue among the surrogates.

Euphemisms are another form of insinuation that enables ideas to bypass factual or analytical tests. When John Rawls, in his *A Theory of Justice* repeatedly referred to outcomes that "society" can "arrange,"[109] these euphemisms finessed aside the plain fact that only government has the power to override millions of people's mutually agreed transactions terms. Interior decorators **arrange**. Governments **compel**. It is not a subtle distinction.

Nor is Rawls the only income redistributionist to evade the reality of compulsion— which is to say, the loss of millions of people's freedom to make their own decisions about their own lives, when an inequality of economic outcomes is replaced by a far more dangerous increased inequality of power. Unequal economic outcomes nevertheless permit even the less fortunate to have rising standards of living. But power is inherently relative, so that more power for some means less freedom for others.

Concealing that crucial trade-off has led many intellectuals to define the proposed benefits of expanded government power as a "new freedom," as Woodrow Wilson called it.[110] Succeeding generations of intellectuals have continued to change the historic definition of freedom to include the supposed benefits of increased government scope and power.

For example, one cannot be free "if one cannot achieve his goals," according to an influential book by two Yale professors.[111] In their definition, consumers "are not free in the market if high costs prohibit a choice that could be made available to them by sharing the commodity through collective choice"[112]— with "collective choice" apparently being another euphemism for government. Professor Angus Deaton used a similar results-oriented definition of freedom:

> In this book, when I speak of freedom, it is the freedom to live a good life and to do the things that make life worth living. The absence of freedom is poverty, deprivation, and poor health— long the lot of much of humanity, and still the fate of an outrageously high proportion of the world today.[113]

Freedom is not some new or esoteric concept. It is a concept widely understood and deeply felt for centuries— especially deeply felt by those who did not have freedom, such as slaves, serfs, prisoners and people living under totalitarian dictatorships. Many such people have made desperate attempts to escape to freedom, even at the risk of their lives. This was not done to get government benefits. Spartacus was not fighting to get farm subsidies or housing vouchers.

Yet many intellectuals, living in the safety and comfort of free societies, have found it expedient to redefine freedom, so that an expansion of government determination of economic outcomes, through an expansion of government compulsion, is not seen as a trade-off of freedom, but as simply an expansion of freedom, as conveniently redefined.

In the world of words, the hardest facts can be made to vanish into thin air by a clever catchword or soaring rhetoric. In a public discourse where slogans and images have too often replaced facts and logic, words have indeed become for some what Hobbes called them, centuries ago— the money of fools,[114] often counterfeit money created by clever people. Our educational system, which might have been expected to develop students' ability to "cross-examine the facts," as the great economist Alfred Marshall once put it, has itself become one of the fountainheads of insinuations and obfuscations.

Chapter 6

Social Visions and Human Consequences

They went to work with unsurpassable efficiency. Full employment, a maximum of resulting output, and general well-being ought to have been the consequence. It is true that instead we find misery, shame and, at the end of it all, a stream of blood. But that was a chance coincidence.

J.A. Schumpeter

Most people do not have simply a random assortment of opinions on various subjects. More commonly, there is a certain coherence among their views on different issues, suggesting that there is some underlying vision of the world, and that particular opinions on particular issues are more or less corollaries of the premises of that vision.

In constructing social visions, the temptation is great to seek some one key factor that supposedly explains it all— whether that factor is genes, exploitation, racism or whatever. But, in the real world, even a single feature of a given individual may have many very different possible causes. For example, young children who are years late in beginning to speak may be late because they are severely mentally retarded or autistic. But many highly intelligent people have also been years late in beginning to speak, including geniuses such as Einstein.[1]

This does not deny that some severely mentally retarded children may in fact be years late in beginning to speak as a result of their affliction. But it does deny that *all* children, or even *most* children, who are late in speaking are late for that particular reason. Highly disparate reasons may also exist for some social phenomenon, such as economic or other disparities, despite how fervently some people may prefer a given reason, on which to build a particular social vision to explain it all.

During the early twentieth century, the key factor behind socioeconomic disparities, as seen by leading Progressive intellectuals of that era, was genetics.[2] Alternative explanations tended to be dismissed, rather than seriously examined. By the late twentieth century, discrimination— in the sense of Discrimination II— had become the prevailing explanation, and alternative views have been similarly dismissed.

There is nothing intrinsically wrong with having visions. While we live in the world of reality, we often advance through the world of visions. In even the hardest of the hard sciences, advances often begin with new conceptions, beliefs, hunches and hopes— in short, visions. What makes science scientific are the rigorous, systematic processes by which those visions can be tested, both logically and empirically. Many, if not most, of those visions may fail such tests, but the benefits from those visions whose premises and corollaries are verified empirically, thereby advancing our understanding, are what make the whole process worthwhile.

Social visions have often been analogized to visions in science, but the elastic words used to describe statistics in what are called the "social sciences" can make even accurate numbers misleading. Words can also be misleading when insinuating a fictitious sameness among things that happen to be called by the same name— such as "income" that includes both salaries and capital gains, or "education" measured by years of schooling rather than by the amount, kind or quality of learning that takes place.

When people with the "same" education receive different incomes, that is often called discrimination— in the sense of Discrimination II— even if some people's years of schooling took place in schools that were a bedlam of rowdy, disruptive and violent behavior, or in college courses offering no skills that are much in demand in the job market.

Justice Oliver Wendell Holmes' repeated admonition, "think things instead of words"[3] applies as much today as when he said it.

FOUNDATIONS OF THE PREVAILING VISION

At the heart of the prevailing social vision of our times is the seemingly invincible fallacy that group outcomes in human endeavors would tend to be equal, or at least comparable or random, if there were no biased interventions, on the one hand, nor genetic deficiencies, on the other. The essence of the invincible fallacy was perhaps best expressed by Jean-Jacques Rousseau in the eighteenth century, when he wrote of "the equality which nature established among men and the inequality which they have instituted among themselves."[4] But nature, in the form of geographic isolation, doomed whole peoples to lagging for centuries, or even millennia, behind the progress of the rest of the world.

Yet Rousseau, like many later believers in this seemingly invincible fallacy, took it as axiomatic that only human biases create inequalities. Geography, demography, cultural differences and differences in the quantity and quality of parenting all vanish from this vision, in favor of one causal factor, for which many have imagined that they had a "solution."

SIDEBAR: GEOGRAPHIC ISOLATION

When the Spaniards took over the isolated Canary Islands in the fifteenth century, they found a native population described as people of a Caucasian race, living as people had lived thousands of years earlier, back in the Stone Age.[5] On the other side of the world, in the isolated island continent of Australia, the British who arrived there in the eighteenth century found a black aboriginal race that was likewise described as living at a Stone Age level[6]—as contrasted with black Africans, who had produced iron centuries earlier[7] and despite Australia's having large deposits of iron ore.

Before the British arrived, Australia was one of the relatively few large areas in the world more isolated than much of sub-Saharan Africa. The extreme degree of human isolation in both Australia and the Canary Islands may be indicated by evidence of extreme isolation in nature, shown by the fact that both places had species that had evolved there, but were not indigenous anywhere else in the world.[8] Conversely, species common in other parts of the world— such as cats, ranging from common house cats to leopards, cheetahs, lions and tigers— were totally non-existent in Australia, as were horses and other hoofed animals. Various species of fish, birds, trees and other vegetation were likewise uniquely indigenous to Australia.

These extreme signs, in nature, of geographic isolation for millennia have implications for the isolation of human beings in that same setting. The correlation between geographic isolation and lagging socioeconomic development has also been found in other natural settings, such as mountains, jungles and deserts.[9] Nature seems to have created at least as much inequality of opportunity as humans have.

Among the many reasons for skewed distributions of outcomes, both among humans and in nature, are multiple prerequisites for particular outcomes, which make a normal bell curve distribution of outcomes unlikely, even if all the individual prerequisites themselves are normally distributed as in a bell curve.

That is because people with various numbers of prerequisites, short of the full ensemble required, all have the same outcome— failure. In nature, having *most* of the prerequisites for tornadoes does not produce any tornadoes, which are accordingly highly concentrated in one country where *all* the prerequisites come together often, so that 90 percent or more of all the tornadoes in the world occur in the United States. Yet many other countries around the world have a general climate not very different from that of the United States, and a similar terrain of wide level plains like those in the American heartland known as "tornado alley." But all the other factors necessary for the generation of tornadoes obviously do not come together nearly as often elsewhere.

Few of the world's socioeconomic disparities are quite as extreme as the world's distribution of tornadoes. But neither is the world's distribution of petroleum deposits, iron ore, earthquakes or navigable waterways at all egalitarian.[10] Summers bring drenching monsoon rains across much of southern Asia— and droughts across much of southern Europe at the same time, with some rivers there almost drying up, while people are experiencing flooding in southern Asia. Obviously the other factors with which summer interacts produce opposite rainfall results in these two continents, which are really one continuous landmass.

More than a parallel between nature's outcomes and human outcomes is involved, since human beings have lived and evolved over the centuries and millennia in very different geographic settings, some of which facilitate, and others impede, the development of both physical wealth and the human capital behind the creation of wealth and the evolution of societies.[11]

Multiethnic societies today have within them peoples with cultures that originated in very different geographic settings elsewhere, and developed in very different historical circumstances, quite aside from very different demographic and other factors between these groups in the society in which they all live today.

It might seem strange, for example, that during the nineteenth-century era of mass immigration from Europe to the United States, it was not uncommon to find Jewish and Italian neighborhoods in New York represented by Irish politicians— a situation that did not change until well into the early twentieth century.[12] But anyone familiar with the very different histories of these three groups in Europe would hardly be surprised that they did not all arrive in America with the same political skills and experience, just as they did not all have the same skills and experience in other endeavors.

Each of these groups exceeded the other two in some endeavor, not only in the United States but in other countries as well. Italians, for example, have been more prominent in wine-making than either Jews or the Irish, whether in the United States, Latin America or Australia, while Jews have been more prominent in the garment industry than the Italians or the Irish in those same countries. In other endeavors— agriculture, medicine, and labor union leadership, for example— each of these three groups also excelled the other two.

Nor is this pattern peculiar to these particular groups. Germans have produced the leading beers in America, as well as Tsingtao beer in China, in addition to being leading beer producers in Argentina and Australia. But German immigrants and their descendants have seldom become conspicuous as political leaders or leaders in high fashion or *haute cuisine* in either the United States or in other countries. Even groups that have lagged educationally and socioeconomically have nevertheless not merely held their own but excelled greatly, in particular endeavors not dependent on the factors that make for educational or socioeconomic success.[13] Various poverty-stricken mountain peoples around the world, for example, have produced exquisite handicrafts in great demand elsewhere.[14]

While such patterns of uneven distributions of outcomes by different groups in many endeavors have been common around the world, *what is harder to find in the real world are specific endeavors in which these or other groups' outcomes have been the same*. Even when different groups have similar incomes, those incomes have not necessarily been earned doing the same things.

Among nationally prominent, and even historic, figures in the world of business, Jews have been especially well represented in retailing, finance and garment production and sale, but by no means equally well represented in heavy industries, such as the production of steel or automobiles— again, whether in the United States or in other countries. Other groups have likewise been highly successful in particular sectors of the economy and virtually non-existent among the leaders in some other fields. Yet the equal outcomes *in specific endeavors* that are by no means pervasive in the real world have been taken as a social *norm*, deviations from which are regarded as weighty evidence of wrongdoing, urgently in need of correction.

"Disparate impact" statistics that carry much weight in courts of law, as evidence of biased discrimination, are collected not only from specific industries but more often from a particular firm within an industry. The more narrowly the specific endeavor is defined, the less likely is equal representation of groups to be found, and therefore the less likely are group statistics to be valid indicators of biased treatment.

If, for example, three different groups are roughly equally represented in professional occupations as a whole, that will not prevent one group from being far more prominent than the other two as lawyers, while one of the other two is most prominent as doctors and the third group most prominent as engineers. The more narrowly the endeavor is defined, the more "disparate impact" numbers are likely to be found.

Even in a narrowly defined endeavor like professional football, where blacks are greatly "over-represented," especially among the star players, blacks have for decades been almost non-existent among football players who kick punts and field goals. Only the fact that the same people who hire running backs and quarterbacks also hire kickers keeps racial discrimination lawsuits from being filed and won, as they could be if these different categories of football players were hired by different people. But there is no reason whatever to arbitrarily exclude the possibility that blacks themselves may prefer doing one thing rather than another— or that any number of other groups are simply better at doing particular things.

The seductive plausibility of the invincible fallacy makes it all the more important to subject it to critical scrutiny, instead of simply citing statistics on outcome differences and issuing denunciations. Nevertheless, assumptions of sameness are as common in social visions and their accompanying rhetoric as sharp differences are when examining empirical facts in the real world, whether examining the facts of nature or of human societies.

The very possibility that what different groups *want* to do, or have had a background to do, or are prepared to invest their efforts in doing, can affect their representation in different endeavors is ignored in assumptions as to how outcomes can differ so much in particular endeavors. As noted earlier, even among men who were all in the top one percent in IQs, there have been great disparities in their educational and career outcomes, which varied with the kind of families in which they were raised. Similar disparities have been found among siblings, depending on the order in which they were born.

Different social classes raise their children differently. In addition to studies showing that the children of parents in professional occupations hear far more words per hour than children in families on welfare,[15] empirical research has also shown that the *kinds* of words also differ greatly.

In families where parents have professional occupations, those parents used "more words and more different words of all kinds, more multiclause sentences, more past and future verb tenses." Such parents "also gave their children more affirmative feedback and responded to them more often each hour they were together." Moreover, they gave *less* "negative feedback to their children per hour" than other parents.[16] The ratio of affirmative words to negative words was six to one in families where the parents had professional occupations. By contrast, in families on welfare, negative or discouraging words outnumbered positive or encouraging words by more than two to one.[17] Negative responses included such words as "Don't," "Stop," "Quit" and "Shut up."[18]

Are we to believe that children raised in such very different ways— for many years before they reach an employer, a college admissions office or a crime scene— must be the same in orientation, capabilities and limitations when they eventually reach the sites at which statistical data are later collected?

All too often, there is an implicit assumption that the *cause* of some disparity is located where the statistics on that disparity were collected. Thus, for example, the under-representation of women in Silicon Valley is assumed to be caused by something that happens in Silicon Valley, and the higher prices charged by stores in many low-income neighborhoods are assumed to be caused by those who run those stores. This implicit assumption has been embedded in the law of the land by the Supreme Court of the United States, which has treated disparities in the employment, pay and promotions of people from different groups as evidence of discriminatory bias by employers under its "disparate impact" standard.

That approach ignores the very possibility that what happened to people *before* they reached an employer— or a college admissions office or a crime scene— may have had a "disparate impact" on the kinds of people they became and the kinds of skills, values, habits and limitations they bring with them to the places where statistics are later collected. The political system in the United States did not create differences in political skills and experience between the Irish, the Italians and the Jews. Those differences existed before they set foot on American soil, and persisted for generations after they arrived.

Similar implicit assumptions that where statistics are collected show where causation originated apply far beyond political or economic issues. Some hospitals may have higher death rates among their patients than other hospitals have, because those particular hospitals have much higher levels of medical skills and medical technology— and therefore treat patients with far more dire and dangerous conditions, such as conditions requiring brain surgery or heart transplants, rather than treating sprained ankles or digestive problems. Statistics showing disparate death rates in different hospitals can be grossly misleading without understanding the "disparate impact" of what happened to patients *before* they reached the hospitals where statistics were collected.

Nevertheless, fervent crusades and fierce denunciations abound over statistical disparities in outcomes between various social groups in matters large and small— whether "under-representation" of women in Silicon Valley, Hispanics in the Ivy League, blacks among Academy Award nominees or other groups in innumerable other endeavors. The "disparate impact" legal standards do not require even a single flesh-and-blood human being claiming to have been discriminated against, in order to launch a costly and time-consuming legal process that can go on for years. All that is needed is the implicit assumption that statistical disparities originated where the statistics were collected.

A related assumption is that people designated by the same word are the same in the factors relevant to the situation in which statistics are collected. When a study showed young male doctors earning very substantially higher incomes than young female doctors, that might signal sex discrimination to those who believe in the invincible fallacy. But when empirical data showed that young male doctors averaged 500 or more working hours annually than young female doctors worked,[19] that mattered to those who prefer hard facts to sweeping visions.

For those who think in terms of talking points, it may be sufficient to show that male airline employees in Britain are paid more than female airline employees. But, for those who are more interested in facts about the real world than about rhetorical successes in the world of words, it matters that far more pilots are male while most flight attendants are female— and you cannot make them be the same by calling both "airline employees."[20] Similar implicit assumptions of sameness among people described by the same words undermine many conclusions in comparing people of differing races or ethnicities.

The illogic of such verbal malpractice tells us nothing about what are the actual facts in any particular situation involving any particular group. The whole point here is that such verbal virtuosity serves as a *substitute* for empirical verification. Understanding the flaws in verbal vogues only highlights the importance of finding out what the actual facts are in the real world. Some crucial prevalent beliefs need to be re-examined or, in many cases, truly examined by some for the first time.

Social visions not only have assumptions and arguments addressed to others, they have their own internal prerequisites, if these visions are to succeed politically in getting their agendas adopted. Among these prerequisites is that the beneficiaries of the largesse to be distributed are not to be seen as causally— and hence morally— responsible for their own misfortunes. *There can only be external causality*, and hence external responsibility, according to many who promote this vision. Multiculturalism, with its bedrock premise that all cultures are equally deserving of respect, or at least that it is "blaming the victim" to say otherwise, is the logical corollary of the political or ideological prerequisite that causation be depicted as external.

The moral illegitimacy of the existing order— epitomized in such catchwords as "the system is rigged"— is likewise essential to the political success of the prevailing social vision. Violations of the moral or legal rules that apply to others by designated victim groups are therefore considered to be justified— or, at least, "understandable." Since the purpose of all this is a set of concrete policies, people who see the world differently are not to be engaged and debated, but instead discredited and silenced— even, or perhaps especially, on academic campuses.

There is, of course, a price to be paid for all this, in its human consequences.

HUMAN CONSEQUENCES

Even those of us who assume that the range of mental potential of human beings, at the moment of conception, is probably very similar across racial or other lines, must nevertheless concede that both geographic and demographic differences make equal developed capabilities, and outcomes based on developed capabilities, very unlikely. Even at this late date in history, with the scope of communications reaching farther than it has ever reached before, children born in isolated mountain villages are still unlikely to develop the same range of knowledge, skills and experiences as children born in major seaports around the world.

Geography still matters because isolation in general still matters, whether that isolation is geographic or social. Among various social subgroups of whites who have had average IQs similar to, or lower than, the average IQs of black Americans, the common factor has been isolation— whether it was isolation in the hills and mountains of Appalachia,[21] in the Hebrides islands off Scotland,[22] in canal boat communities in England,[23] or among various groups of immigrants from Europe, during the era before they became absorbed into the mainstream of American life.[24] Blacks have been socially isolated much longer.

Even native ability— the mental potential at birth— has already been affected by the environment in the womb, and expectant mothers from different social groups, or age groups, can differ in the extent to which they have nutritionally healthful diets, and in their intake of alcohol and drugs, among other behavioral differences that can affect the development of an unborn child.[25] Differences in how children are raised in different classes and cultures further reduces the probability of equal capabilities and outcomes as adults.

Against that background, the assumption that discriminatory bias can be automatically inferred when there are differences in socioeconomic outcomes— and that the source of that bias can be determined by where the statistics were collected— seems indefensible. Yet that seemingly invincible fallacy guides much of what is said and done in our educational institutions, in the media and in government policies.

None of this denies that discriminatory bias or genetic differences can have an effect. There would be no point in studying the costs of discrimination (in the sense of Discrimination II) if such discrimination had no effect.

Nor can genetics be proved to have no effect at all on outcomes. The plain and simple fact that pairs of identical twins have IQs more similar to each other than do pairs of fraternal twins is an undeniable effect of genetics, because the difference between these two kinds of twins is that fraternal twins have *some* identical genes, as other siblings do, but identical twins have *all* their genes identical. But to say that genetic differences can affect intellectual differences among individuals or families is not the same as saying that *all* intellectual differences between individuals or families must be caused by genetic differences. Systematic differences between the IQs of the first-born and their later siblings are an obvious example to the contrary.

In the case of whole races— each including innumerable families with their own different genetic makeups— there is even less reason to attribute all differences between races in developed capabilities, physical or mental, to genes. Nevertheless, leading genetic determinists of the early twentieth century went beyond assuming that average IQ differences among groups were genetically determined. They implicitly assumed that there was an intellectual "ceiling" for some racial or ethnic groups that was so low that it was imperative to impede or prevent their reproduction in various ways.[26]

Different races have wide dispersions of IQ scores within their own respective populations, and racial or ethnic groups with lower average IQs than others nevertheless have many people with IQs higher than the average IQ of higher-scoring groups. The idea that there would be black pilots flying fighter planes in the American air force during World War II,[27] or black doctors with international reputations in developing the use of blood plasma[28] or brain surgery[29] might have been considered inconceivable by many eugenicists, just a few decades before these things became realities.

By the second half of the twentieth century, even the leading proponent of the influence of genetic factors— Professor Arthur R. Jensen of the University of California at Berkeley— rejected the idea of a "ceiling" on the intellectual development of people in particular races. He also recognized that low IQs among children from a socially disadvantaged background did not necessarily indicate the same general disabilities as the same low IQs among children raised with the advantages of being from middle-class families.

"Lower-class children in the IQ range of about 60 to 80 do markedly *better* than middle-class children who are in this range of IQ," Professor Jensen said, citing various evidence from his own work and that of others.[30] Moreover, he asked, "why should anyone be surprised to find that there are Negro children having IQs of 115 or higher, or that they should be concentrated in the affluent integrated neighborhood in Los Angeles?"[31] The racial intelligence "ceiling" theory was now dead, even for the leading advocate of the influence of genetics on intelligence.

In short, no one who takes facts seriously today dismisses environment as a factor. The issue has narrowed to how much of a factor and what kinds of environments. Specialists can continue debating that issue among themselves, while the world goes on, without waiting for whatever indefinite time it may take for them to reach a definitive answer, if ever. Neither genes nor discrimination has been demonstrated to have the compelling influence claimed by many of their advocates.

The empirical case for deducing discriminatory bias from "under-representation" is as flawed as the theoretical case.

Is there a "glass ceiling" keeping down the proportion of white males in professional basketball, where most club owners are white males? Yet disparities in outcomes between the sexes are taken as automatic proof of a "glass ceiling." Innumerable empirical studies— often by female scholars— have shown how various factors account for sex differentials in income.[32] What emerges from these studies bears little relationship to the "glass ceiling" scenario. But such factual studies are seldom mentioned in much of the media or academia when outcome differences between women and men are discussed.

Statistical "under-representation" or "over-representation" of various groups is not peculiar to the United States or to our times. For centuries, there have been countries around the world where most members of various professions, and most business owners in whole industries, have been members of some subordinate minority— whether the overseas Chinese in Southeast Asia,[33] Jews in Eastern Europe,[34] Indians in East Africa,[35] Lebanese in West Africa,[36] Armenians in the Ottoman Empire,[37] Huguenots in France,[38] Germans in Brazil,[39] Japanese in Peru,[40] Chettiars in Burma,[41] Italians in Argentina,[42] and both Jains from India and Hasidic Jews in Antwerp's diamond industry,[43] among many others.

Nevertheless, there is a whole genre of words and phrases like "glass ceiling," "implicit bias" and "covert racism," which proclaim that statistical disparities show biased treatment— and that this conclusion must be believed without visible corroborating evidence (hence words like *glass*, *implicit* and *covert*), unless sheer insistent repetition is regarded as evidence.

In the real world, however, disparities in outcomes have been common in things extending far beyond socioeconomic differences. Homicide rates in Eastern Europe, for example, have been some multiple of homicide rates in Western Europe for centuries, and homicide rates in different regions of the United States have likewise differed by some multiple.[44] Where there are multiple prerequisites for particular outcomes, whether among people or in nature, skewed distributions of outcomes are not uncommon.

Median age differences among groups, varying by a decade or decades, are alone enough to preclude proportional representation in occupations requiring either long years of education and experience or the physical vitality of youth— even if all groups were absolutely identical in every other aspect besides age.

Age disparities exist among nations, as well as among particular social groups. There are more than twenty nations where the median age of the population is in the forties, and more than twenty other nations with median ages under twenty.[45] How rational is it to expect nations with such large and consequential differences in adult work experience to have equal, or even comparable, economic productivity? Among nations, as among individuals, age differences are just one difference among many.

Seekers of "social justice," in the sense of equal or comparable outcomes, proceed as if eliminating racial bias, sex bias or other group bias would produce some approximation of that ideal outcome. But what of the implications of the fact that a majority of the people in American prisons were raised with either one parent or no parent?[46] People in groups where many children grow up in single-parent homes do not have the same probability of being incarcerated as people who grow up in groups where single-parent homes are rare. But those who believe in the invincible fallacy may believe that the problem originated where the incarceration statistics were collected, in the criminal justice system.

Sometimes just a single inconspicuous difference in circumstances can make a huge, historic difference in human outcomes. One of the monumental natural catastrophes of the nineteenth century was the famine in Ireland that was due to the failure of the potato crop, at a time when potatoes were the principal food of the Irish. Deaths by starvation, and by diseases related to malnutrition, are estimated to have claimed a million lives in Ireland, a country of only 8.5 million people at the time.[47]

Nearly two million people are estimated to have fled that famine-stricken country between the mid-1840s and the mid-1850s,[48] a massive loss of population in a small country. Yet the very same variety of potato was grown in the United States— where Ireland's potatoes originated— with no crop failure.

The source of that crop failure has been traced to a fertilizer used in planting potatoes, on both sides of the Atlantic. That fertilizer contained a fungus which flourished in the mild and moist climate of Ireland, but not in the hot and dry summers of Idaho and other potato-growing areas of the United States.[49] That one difference meant millions of human tragedies and a massive loss of population.

Morally neutral factors such as crop failures, birth order, geographic settings, or demographic and cultural differences are among the many reasons why economic and social outcomes so often fail to fit the preconception of equal or comparable outcomes.

Yet morally neutral factors seem to attract far less attention than other causal factors which stir moral outrage, such as discrimination or exploitation. But our personal responses tell us nothing about the *causal* weight of different factors, however much those responses may shape political crusades and government policies.

Which causal factors predominate at a given place or time is ultimately an empirical question, independent of our emotions or inclinations. Nor is this simply a philosophical issue. The implications of a pervasive social vision can affect economic, educational and other social outcomes— including the shared norms that hold a society together.

A TOXIC VISION

Those who seem to be promising an end to existing group disparities, as a result of whatever policies they advocate, may be promising what cannot be delivered, regardless of those policies. Moreover, the clash between numerical goals, fervently pursued, and the repeatedly frustrated attempts to reach those goals is not without social consequences,

Among the dire consequences for society as a whole are widespread resentments, bitterness, disorder and violence on the part of those who have been told incessantly that they are "entitled" to a demographically defined "fair share" of what is produced, and that this "fair share" is being denied to them by others who are guilty of maliciously keeping them and their loved ones down.

When a *New York Times* headline depicts admissions standards for New York's elite high schools as a "moat" designed to keep the less fortunate out of institutions reserved for the socioeconomic elite,[50] that is a message widely proclaimed by others with the prevailing social vision, on both sides of the Atlantic— and it is applied far beyond the question of school admissions. That vision, however politically effective or ideologically satisfying, undermines the whole moral basis for shared social values that can hold a society together.

Adam Smith declared "the good temper and moderation of contending factions" to be "the most essential circumstance in the public morals of a free people."[51] But what good temper or moderation can be expected when a major segment of the population becomes convinced that "the system is rigged" against them and morality is just a giant fraud? That is when a society can fragment into mutually hostile groups and isolated individuals— something like Hobbes' war of each against all.

Such consequences of a toxic social vision tend to be especially dire for the less fortunate, who suffer most when social order breaks down and violence is unleashed amid heady crusades. Poverty did not do that. There was more poverty in the first half of the twentieth century than in the second half. But it was the second half, dominated by the triumphant new social vision, that saw what has aptly been called a "decivilizing" of a substantial segment of society, on both sides of the Atlantic. The actual consequences of a social vision cannot be assessed on the basis of its good intentions or even its plausibility. The real test is what has actually happened when that vision has been applied, and what the implications are of those social consequences.

Educational Implications

Education is just one of the venues where the implicit assumption that different groups tend to be similar in their aims and capabilities, so that disparities in outcomes imply their being treated differently by others, does not stand up well under scrutiny of the facts. Education is an area in which differences in values and behavior play havoc with policies based on an assumption of sameness.

There is no reason whatever to assume that education is valued equally by all individuals or groups. Not only are there differences among students from different groups in the amount of time they spend on their homework,[52] there are differences among groups in how their own higher-achieving members are regarded by other members of the same groups who are their classmates.

A survey of more than 90,000 black, white and Hispanic high school and junior high school students from 175 schools in 80 American communities found that those black students whose grade-point average reached 3.5 or higher had fewer friends of their own race than blacks with lower grade-point averages.[53] Such negative reactions by fellow black students to those among them who were higher achievers in school have been characterized as a rejection of those who were stigmatized as "acting white"— that is, behaving in ways that were equated with disloyalty to their race.

An empirical study published by the National Bureau of Economic Research found that having a higher percentage of black schoolmates had a strong *negative* effect on the educational achievements of black students— especially high-ability black students.[54] Another study, of ability-grouping in general, found that educating students among others of similar ability levels improved the academic performances of high-ability students— and especially high-ability *minority* students.[55]

Such patterns have by no means been confined to blacks or even to the United States. Among Hispanic American students, those with a grade-point average of 4.0 averaged 3 fewer friends of their own ethnicity than did white students with a 4.0 grade-point average.[56] Similar negative reactions to educational achievements among their peers have been found among Maoris in New Zealand, Burakumin in Japan and the white underclass in Britain.[57]

Clearly then, not all groups value education, or the behavior that leads to greater educational success, the same. Even students with the same potentialities or capabilities cannot be assumed to have the same educational outcomes, when they operate within an atmosphere of very different social responses from their peers, during a phase of life when peer responses tend to matter especially. Negative reactions within educationally lagging groups to those members of their group who choose to engage in the pursuit of educational achievement extend far beyond social ostracism. As Dr. Theodore Dalrymple described the situation among England's white underclass:

> If you don't mend your ways and join us, they were saying, we'll beat you up. This was no idle threat: I often meet people in their twenties and thirties in my hospital practice who gave up at school under such duress and subsequently realize that they have missed an opportunity which, had it been taken, would have changed the whole course of their lives much for the better. And those who attend the few schools in the city that maintain very high academic standards risk a beating if they venture to where the poor white stupids live. In the last year I have treated two boys in the emergency room after such a beating, and two others who have taken overdoses for fear of receiving one at the hands of their neighbors.[58]

Such things were not confined to boys:

> Many of my intelligent patients from the slums recount how, in school, they expressed a desire to learn, only to suffer mockery, excommunication, and in some instances outright violence from their peers. One intelligent child of fifteen, who had taken an overdose as a suicidal gesture, said she was subjected to constant teasing and abuse by her peers.[59]

While lower socioeconomic class school children who seek educational achievement have been seen as guilty of "class treachery"[60] in England, ghetto blacks who seek educational achievement in America are likewise often seen by some classmates as race traitors who are "acting white," and are often meted out similar ostracism, verbal abuse and/or physical violence.[61] In addition to such specific targeting of individuals, the general disorderly atmosphere in some schools in England has been described as being "on the knife-edge of anarchy."[62] This too is a pattern found on the other side of the Atlantic in similar American neighborhoods.[63]

In both Britain and the United States, one-sixth of the nation's children are classified as functionally illiterate.[64] This is a painful waste of mental potential, and the poor can afford it least of all.

Against this background, such policies as the "no child left behind" philosophy during the administration of President George W. Bush seem remote from reality. When a handful of disruptive or violent students can prevent a whole class from getting a decent education, such students must be separated— "left behind"— if the others are not to be denied an education, which may be their one chance for a better life.

In the subsequent administration of President Barack Obama, federal agencies went further in the same direction, pressuring and threatening schools where statistics showed a disciplining of minority male students at rates that were statistically disproportionate to the rate of disciplining of other students. It is as if black or Hispanic males cannot possibly have different behavior patterns than those of Asian females or other categories of students. The invincible fallacy in the background trumps even the most blatant and disastrous realities right in front of our eyes.[65]

The need to separate disruptive or violent children from others who are trying to learn is independent of whether or not there is any "solution" currently available, or on the horizon, for changing the behavior of disruptive and/or violent children. The alternative is to sacrifice the education of unending generations of poor and minority children until such indefinite time as a "solution" for their misbehaving and/or violent classmates can be found, created or faked.

For people enthralled by the prevailing social vision, with its invincible fallacy, all forms of sorting in schools are taboo, whether sorting by behavior, ability or other factors that can affect educational outcomes. It is as if schools exist to present a tableau that expresses a vision, rather than to educate all those who want to learn. None of this precludes trying to improve the behavior of problem students. It simply does not postpone the education of whole generations of other students until that project succeeds.

Political Implications

The most spectacularly successful political doctrine that swept into power in countries around the world in the twentieth century was Marxism, based on the implicit presumption that differences in wealth were due to capitalists growing rich by keeping the workers poor, through "exploitation."

This version of the invincible fallacy apparently seemed plausible to people in many different countries and cultures. But, if the wealth of rich capitalists comes from exploitation of poor workers, then we might expect to find that where there are larger concentrations of rich capitalists, we would find correspondingly larger concentrations of poverty. But the hard facts point in the opposite direction.

The United States has more than five times as many billionaires as there are in Africa and the Middle East put together.[66] Yet most Americans— including those living below the official poverty line— have a far higher standard of living than that of the populations of Africa and the Middle East. It would be difficult to find even a single country, ruled by Marxists, where the standard of living of working-class people has been as high as that of working-class people in a number of capitalist countries.

This is despite the fact that the first and largest of the avowedly Marxist countries, the Soviet Union, was one of the most richly endowed nations in the world, when it came to natural resources, if not *the* most richly endowed.[67] Yet the average standard of living of ordinary people in the Soviet Union was nowhere close to the average standard of living of ordinary people in most of Western Europe, or in the United States or Australia. But here, as elsewhere, hard facts have been repeatedly trumped by heady visions, such as that presented in *The Communist Manifesto*.

Other, non-Marxist, doctrines have been built on the same foundation of assumptions, and they too have had their sweeping political triumphs in the twentieth century, usually in the form of expansive welfare states in the second half of that century, with the 1960s being their pivotal, triumphant decade.

Hypothesis-testing has usually played a remarkably small role in these intellectual, legal and political developments. Indeed, scholars who have tested prevailing views against hard data, and found the prevailing views lacking, have often encountered hostility and demonization rather than counter-evidence or counter-arguments.[68] Riots to prevent their speaking have disgraced many of the most prestigious academic campuses in the United States— indeed, especially such campuses.[69]

Social Implications

If the clash of social visions were simply intramural contests among the intelligentsia, there might be little reason for others to be concerned about them. But social visions, and even the very catchwords and verbal style in which those visions are discussed, diffuse far beyond those intellectuals who create and elaborate social visions.

When treating imprisoned murderers in England, for example, physician Theodore Dalrymple found them using the same passive voice sentence constructions found among the intelligentsia when discussing social pathologies. Murderers discussing their crimes have said such things as, "the knife went in," instead of saying that they stabbed their victim.[70]

An echo of elite intellectuals even appeared in an old American musical, *West Side Story*, where a character says, "Hey, I'm depraved on account I'm deprived." Intellectuals say it more sophisticatedly, but they are nevertheless saying essentially the same thing. While what they are saying might be a plausible hypothesis to be tested empirically, it is too often treated as an established fact, requiring no such testing.

Yet neither in England nor in the United States was such depravity as rampant violence and other social pathology as common among low-income people in the first half of the twentieth century, when they were poorer, as in the second half, when the welfare state made them better off in material terms.

The importance of social visions goes far beyond the rhetoric they spawn. In a democratic nation, there can be no welfare state without a social vision first prevailing politically, a vision justifying the creation or expansion of a welfare state. Moreover, the triumph of that vision in

Western societies during the 1960s entailed far more than the welfare state itself.

With the prevailing social vision came a more non-judgmental approach to behavior, as well as multiculturalism, a de-emphasis of social rules and moral standards, as well as a de-emphasis of policing and punishments, and an emphasis on demographically based "fair shares" for all— along with a delegitimizing of both legal and moral standards. The reasons for all these beliefs have been elaborated in many ways by many individuals and groups. What has been elaborated far less often are empirical tests as to the validity of the new social vision, in terms of the results expected from following that vision versus what actually happened.

It is not simply that the social vision which greatly expanded the welfare state and undermined traditional moral values failed to achieve all its goals and fostered some negative consequences. What is particularly salient is that various social pathologies which had been *declining*— some for years, decades or even centuries— had a sudden resurgence, as these new and often self-congratulatory ideas triumphed politically and socially in the 1960s, on both sides of the Atlantic.

In the United States, homicide rates, rates of infection with venereal diseases and rates of teenage pregnancies were among the social pathologies whose steep declines over the preceding years were suddenly reversed in the 1960s, as all these pathologies soared to new and tragic heights.[71] After decades of declining homicide rates in the United States, that rate by the early 1960s was just under half of what it had been in the mid-1930s.[72] But homicide rates suddenly reversed and doubled from 1960 to 1980,[73] in the wake of the new vision and such consequences of that vision as newly imposed restrictions on law enforcement.

These trends, and reversals of trends, were not peculiar to the United States. A monumental treatise on the decline of violence in the world over the centuries— *The Better Angels of Our Nature* by Professor Steven Pinker of Harvard— pointed out that, in Europe, "rates of violence did a U-turn in the 1960s," including "a bounce in homicide rates that brought them back to levels they had said goodbye to a century before."[74]

Among the alarming increases in violence and disorder that were the most striking were those in places long known for law-abiding, orderly and polite behavior, England being a preeminent example. American economist J.K. Galbraith happened to be in London in May 1945, when a crowd estimated at "two or three hundred thousand"— and mostly young people— was gathered to celebrate the end of the war in Europe. He wrote to his wife: "Like all British crowds it was most orderly."[75]

Others who made similar observations at the time included internationally known British writer George Orwell, who in the 1940s referred to "the orderly behaviour of English crowds, the lack of pushing and quarrelling." He also observed:

> The manners of the English working class are not always very graceful, but they are extremely considerate. Great care is taken in showing a stranger the way, blind people can travel across London with the certainty that they will be helped on and off every bus and across every street.[76]

Shortly after the end of the Second World War, a young Asian man from Singapore named Lee Kuan Yew went to London to study, and was struck by the sight of a newspaper stand with no one attending it:

> He saw people stop and take a newspaper and then put their money in an old cardboard box next to the stall. He even saw people put in money notes and take out exactly the right change. Otherwise, no one interfered with or touched the money left uncovered and open to the world.[77]

Many years later, as an elderly man, Lee Kuan Yew— now a former Prime Minister of Singapore— writing his memoirs, recalled how postwar London had impressed him:

> I had seen a Britain scarred by war, yet whose people were not defeatist about the losses they had suffered, nor arrogant about the victory they had scored. Every bomb site in the City of London was

neatly tended, with bricks and rubble piled to one side, and often flowers and shrubs planted to soften the ruins. It was part of their understated pride and discipline.

    Their courtesy and politeness to each other and to foreigners were remarkable. Most impressive was the consideration motorists showed: you waved on the person with the right of way; he waved back to thank you. It was a very civilised society.[78]

In sports competition, British competitors were renowned for their sportsmanship. In a 1953 soccer match, for example, the team leading, with only two minutes to go, saw an opposing player snatch victory from them, scoring with only seconds left in the game— and members of the losing team stood up and applauded his spectacular performance. But, by the mid-1960s, such sportsmanship was gone, even in Britain's classic sportsmanlike game, cricket. Vulgar insults were now common among British players, and among players in British offshoot societies Australia and New Zealand.[79]

    English soccer fans especially became notorious for their hooligan behavior in other countries, where they went to attend international soccer matches involving their favorite teams against other countries' teams. In the year 2000, the British publication *The Economist* noted: "English fans have been intermittently terrorising towns overseas and attacking foreign rivals for three decades."[80] In Spain, for example, these hooligans were reported in the American magazine *Newsweek* as having attacked waiters, defecated in swimming pools and torn up hotel rooms. *Newsweek* asked: "why the upsurge of thuggery among a people renowned for civility?"[81] Poverty seems an unlikely reason, if they could afford to travel to other countries to engage in mob thuggery.

    Spain was by no means unique as a target of hooliganism by young Englishmen. The *New York Times* reported in 1988, for example: "With the European national soccer championships beginning Friday in Dusseldorf, the residents of West Germany and battalions of police are girding for the least-welcome tourists from Britain: English soccer hooligans." Nor was such hooliganism restricted to those visiting other countries. According to the *New York Times*, "the threat of violence at and around soccer matches every Saturday in England remains ever-present."[82]

The same social degeneration affected law-abiding behavior in general, during the same era. Writing in the 1940s, George Orwell could say that "except for certain well-defined areas in half a dozen big towns there is very little crime or violence."[83] Even in the next decade, in 1954, London had a total of just 12 armed robberies all year, at a time when anyone could buy a shotgun. But, in later years, armed robberies rose to 1,400 by 1981 and 1,600 in 1991,[84] despite increasingly severe restrictions on the purchase of firearms. Burglaries in 1964 were more than three times what they had been in 1938— and, in the early twenty-first century, burglaries were 30 times what they had been in 1938.[85] Other crimes likewise skyrocketed over the years.[86]

Contrary to beliefs that crime is caused by poverty, there is no evidence that there was more poverty in England in the second half of the twentieth century than in the first half. What had changed were the attitudes toward law and order in England, as in the United States and in other places where the new social vision took hold. Writing back in the 1940s, George Orwell observed: "The masses still more or less assume that 'against the law' is a synonym for 'wrong'." Unlike in some other countries, "An Englishman does not believe in his bones, as a Spanish or Italian peasant does, that the law is simply a racket."[87]

That would change, with the triumph of the new social vision in the 1960s, in which the whole moral order was depicted as a sham, rigged against ordinary people and in favor of the privileged. Nor was this delegitimization of moral and legal principles confined to demagogues on the fringes. It became pervasive among the intelligentsia, whether in the media or in academia.

By contrast with the orderly crowds that Galbraith, Orwell and others saw in earlier years, in 2011 urban riots spread through London, Manchester and other British cities, involving thousands of hoodlums and looters, who set fire to homes and businesses, as well as beating and robbing people on the streets and throwing gasoline bombs at police cars.[88]

The coarsening of life took other forms in England, during the era of the new social vision. It was not uncommon for men found stricken and unconscious on the streets, and taken to hospitals where the staff worked to revive them and treat their medical problems, to later speak insultingly and abusively to those who had taken care of them.[89] Insults and abuse of medical personnel became sufficiently widespread in England that the National Health Service posted signs in its facilities, warning that abusive and threatening behavior toward the staff would be prosecuted.[90]

In both Britain and the United States, the prevailing social vision— endlessly repeated and reinforced in the schools, the media and intellectual circles— depicted social pathology as caused by poverty and oppression. Yet in both countries— and others— after the welfare state produced higher living standards for low-income people, the social degeneracy that this was supposed to reduce, rose instead to far higher levels.

The same honesty that so impressed Lee Kuan Yew when he saw unattended money boxes on London's newsstands in the 1940s had counterparts in New York, in generations prior to the triumph of the 1960s vision:

> Self-service restaurants, called "cafeterias," were a novelty in New York City in the 1880s. The first on the scene was the Exchange Buffet, which opened its doors across the street from the New York Stock Exchange on September 4, 1885. . . Customers at the Exchange Buffet picked up their selections— sandwiches, salads, perhaps a slice of cake, and tea, coffee, or milk— from a buffet along the wall. . . Each customer bused his own dishes, tallied his own bill, and then told the cashier what he owed. This self-service operation based on the honor system was surprisingly successful, and over the next few years the Exchange Buffet opened thirty-five more cafeterias in Manhattan, Brooklyn, and Newark, New Jersey.[91]

The Exchange Buffet chain of restaurants lasted for 78 years. Then a *New York Times* headline reported: "Cafeterias Built On Honesty Fail."[92] They failed, not surprisingly, in the 1960s, after having endured for more than three-quarters of a century. The social degeneration in the wake of the new social vision did not take place all at once in all aspects of life. It took time to spread. But spread it did.

Among the areas in which social degeneration spread especially far were "public housing" projects— "public" being one of many euphemisms for government. These projects have now so long been cesspools of physical wreckage, social pathology, crime and violence— not only in the United States, but in Britain, France and elsewhere[93]— that many people today might be surprised to learn that it was not always like that. What is not surprising is that the big turnaround in public housing projects in the United States began in the 1960s. A 2009 retrospective article in the *New York Times* described the earlier years of public housing projects in New York:

> These were not the projects of idle, stinky elevators, of gang-controlled stairwells where drug deals go down. In the 1940s, '50s and '60s, when most of the city's public housing was built, a sense of pride and community permeated well-kept corridors, apartments and grounds.[94]

In the earlier decades, when not everyone could afford to buy a television set, some housing project families who had a television set would leave their apartment doors unlocked on Saturday mornings, so that their children's friends could readily come visiting to watch the children's programs on television that were broadcast then.[95]

Philadelphia's public housing projects were recalled in similar terms by economist Walter E. Williams, who grew up in one:

> Back in the '40s the Homes were not what they were to become— a location known for drugs, killings, and nighttime sounds of gunfire. One of the most noticeable differences back then compared to today was the makeup of the resident families. Most of the children we played with, unlike my sister and I, lived with both parents. More than likely, there were other single-parent households but I can recall none. Fathers worked, and the mothers often did as well. The buildings and yards were well kept.[96]

On hot summer nights, during an era when most people could not afford air conditioning, people in the project slept out on their balconies, and first-floor tenants slept in the yards. In the black neighborhood of which this project was part, old men could be seen sitting around a table, out on the streets at night, playing checkers or cards.[97] Such behavior was not peculiar to this project or community in these earlier times. Working-class people— whether black or white— often slept outside on hot summer nights, whether on fire escapes or rooftops or in parks. But, in later times, after the triumph of the new social vision, such behavior would have been far too dangerous, amid widespread violence in such neighborhoods.

Dr. Theodore Dalrymple's description of public housing projects in Britain during the later era would apply on both sides of the Atlantic: "The public spaces and elevators of all public housing blocks I know are so deeply impregnated with urine that the odor is ineradicable. And anything smashable has been smashed."[98]

While the welfare state helped raise the material standard of living of low-income people, the social vision that created the welfare state also featured an undermining of behavioral standards and moral values. In New York, for example, the earlier housing projects screened applicants and screened out people with a history of "alcoholism, irregular work history, single motherhood and lack of furniture."[99] In short, it was *judgmental* and *exclusive*— contrary to the taboos of the new social vision that began its triumph in the 1960s. The New York City Housing Authority, for example, "loosened its selectivity in 1968, under immense pressure from the federal government and social justice activists."[100]

In the world of words, the "social justice" vision has triumphed, far beyond New York or even the United States. But, in the world of reality, there have been consequences unlike anything envisioned by "social justice" advocates— and the consequences have extended far beyond public housing projects, which are only one of the many places where social degeneration became painfully visible. However commendable the intentions, the actual consequences of that vision have been toxic, and especially so for those who were expected to be its principal beneficiaries.

Earlier times were by no means idyllic. They had many problems. But common decency was still common.

SIDEBAR: A TALE OF TWO BLACKOUTS

In the United States, in addition to various statistics measuring social retrogressions and degeneration after the new social vision began to spread during the 1960s, two electrical blackouts— one in 1965 and one in 1977— dramatized that retrogression and degeneration.

On November 9, 1965, around 5:30 PM, a huge electric power failure blacked out most of New York state, and power was not restored until many hours later. Though there was a long night of darkness in New York City, the crime rate was *lower* than usual that night. There were many stories of strangers, caught in a common misfortune, behaving like friends or neighbors. Some "became volunteer cops and directed traffic." Others who had flashlights or candles led people out of the darkened office buildings in groups of people who "held hands with those they could not see."[101]

Such cooperation and even conviviality were widely reported in the press and later a movie was made about it.[102]

More than a decade later, in July 1977, another electric power outage struck the northeast, and New York City was again dark throughout the night. But now there was widespread looting and arson. When the lights went out in Harlem, "within minutes, the night was alight with fires, the pavement alive with looters, the music drowned out by whooping sirens and shattering glass. The pillaging ran until dawn, unchecked and unabashed."

Similar things happened in other parts of New York City, hundreds of police were injured, and jails were so filled that old, unused jails had to be reopened to handle the overflow of people arrested. The mayor of New York called it a "night of terror."[103] Several times as many arrests were made as during the 1965 blackout. "The good Samaritans of 1965 were not conspicuous last

Wednesday night," according to the *New York Times*,[104] and others likewise commented on the painful contrast between the earlier and the later blackout.[105] Clearly, there had been widespread social retrogressions and degeneration.

In addition to the reversals of declining social pathologies in America, other social pathologies, which had existed before, expanded to new magnitudes. These included fatherless children and urban riots. As of 1960, two-thirds of all black American children were living with both parents. That declined over the years, until only *one-third* were living with both parents in 1995. Fifty-two percent were living with their mother, 4 percent with their father and 11 percent with neither.[106] Among black families in poverty, 85 percent of the children had no father present.[107]

Although white American families did not have nearly as high a proportion of children living with one parent as black American families had in 1960, nevertheless the 1960s marked a sharp upturn in white children born to single mothers, to levels several times what they had been in the decades immediately preceding the 1960s. By 2008, nearly 30 percent of white American children were born to single mothers. Among white women with less than 12 years of education, more than 60 percent of their children were born to single mothers in the first decade of the twenty-first century.[108]

These social patterns were not peculiar to the United States, but were common in a number of Western societies. A study in England, for example, noted: "Births outside marriage were generally about four or five per cent of all births between 1900 and the early 1960s. They have now reached 40 per cent."[109] Countries where more than 40 percent of children were born to single mothers included France, Sweden, Norway, Denmark and Iceland.[110]

These have not been simply inevitable consequences of modernization. Modernized Asian countries such as Japan and South Korea have not succumbed to the Western nations' social vision, either as regards families or educational institutions. The net result has been that the proportion of children born to single mothers in these Asian nations has been a fraction of their proportions in Western nations. At the extremes, the proportion of children born to single mothers in Iceland has been two out of three, and in South Korea one out of sixty-six.[111]

Educationally, students from these modernized Asian nations have consistently scored higher on international tests than students in most Western nations.[112]

Post-1960 modern Western nations have not only fallen behind various modern Asian nations, they have in many ways also fallen far behind their own pre-1960 standards. Urban riots in America, which had been sporadic in some earlier years, spread in massive waves from coast to coast during the 1960s. Educational standards and performances in American schools began a decades' long decline in the 1960s, whether measured by test scores, by professors' assessments of incoming college students, by students' own reports of their time spent studying, or by employers' complaints about a lack of basic skills among the young people they hired.[113]

The factors on which those with the prevailing social vision relied for educational success— more spending for education in general and racial integration for blacks in particular— proved to be of little or no effectiveness.

Seldom does any era in human history have exclusively negative or exclusively positive trends. Perhaps the most often cited positive achievements of the 1960s in the United States were the civil rights laws and policies that put an end to racially discriminatory laws and policies in the South, especially the Civil Rights Act of 1964 and the Voting Rights Act of 1965. Although this has often been credited to the social vision of the political left, in reality a higher percentage of Congressional Republicans than of Congressional Democrats voted for these landmark laws.[114] But facts that do not fit the prevailing vision tend to be simply ignored in much of the media and academia.

However important civil rights laws and policies were for securing basic legal rights, they were not the basis for the economic rise of blacks. Poverty among blacks declined far more in the two decades *before* 1960 than in the two decades afterwards.[115]

Putting aside arbitrary changes in the official definition of poverty, and using instead a fixed definition of poverty-level real income in purchasing power terms, the proportion of the black American population living below the poverty line declined during the 1940s and 1950s, at a rate that *slackened* as the 1960s began and then temporarily *stopped* declining during the decade of the 1970s.[116]

Much of the economic progress among American blacks in the 1960s was a continuation of trends from earlier decades, usually at no increased rate and often at a lower rate.

In contrast with this *economic* progress among American blacks that continued, *social* retrogressions set in during the 1960s, in the form of massive urban riots that spread across the country. Many of the same kinds of social retrogressions took place among low-income whites in England during the second half of the twentieth century.[117]

Much of the social retrogression that took place on both sides of the Atlantic is traceable to the central tenet of the prevailing social vision, that unequal outcomes are due to adverse treatment of the less fortunate. This preconception became a fount of grievance-driven attitudes, emotions and actions— including what has been aptly called "decivilizing" behavior in many contexts.[118]

Despite what was, at best, a mixed record of outcomes from the new social vision, and the new laws and policies that followed from that vision, the image of the 1960s has been celebrated in the media, in politics and in academia, especially by those who took part in its social crusades. The response of one of the high-level American official participants in the 1960s crusades, upon meeting best-selling author Shelby Steele, who had expressed some skepticism about that era, was not atypical:

> "Look," he said irritably, "*only*— and I mean *only*— the government can get to that kind of poverty, that entrenched, deep poverty. And I don't care what you say. If this country was decent, it would let the government try again."[119]

Steele's attempt to focus on facts about the actual consequences of various government programs of the 1960s brought a heated response:

"Damn it, we *saved* this country!" he all but shouted. "This country was about to blow up. There were riots everywhere. You can stand there now in hindsight and criticize, but we had to keep the country together, my friend."[120]

That a high official of the Lyndon Johnson administration of the 1960s could believe things so completely counter to demonstrable facts was one sign of the power of a vision.

His claim that only government programs could effectively deal with deep poverty was contradicted by the plain fact that the black poverty rate declined from 87 percent in 1940 to 47 percent in 1960,[121] *prior* to the great expansion of the welfare state that began in the 1960s under the Johnson administration. There was a far more modest subsequent decline in the poverty rate among blacks after the Johnson administration's massive "war on poverty" programs began.

As for ghetto riots, these were never as numerous, nor of such magnitudes of violence, in the 1940s and 1950s, as they became in the 1960s, when the social vision behind the welfare state became triumphant in politics, in educational institutions and in the media. Nor were there similar numbers or magnitudes of violence in riots in the 1980s, during the eight years of the Reagan administration, in which that social vision was repudiated.

Much more is involved here than incorrect inferences from demonstrable facts by one man. His was a far too common example of the ability of a social vision to not only survive, but thrive, in defiance of empirical evidence— much of which never reaches the general public through the media, when those in the media share the same vision.

The prevailing social vision has become so pervasive that aspects of it have become part of the thinking— or at least the consciousness— of even some conservatives and libertarians who oppose most of that vision. One sign of that pervasiveness, and the sea change in social assumptions it represents, is that, back at the beginning of the twentieth century, even many socialists and religious people still endorsed the old saying, "He who does not work, neither shall he eat." But, by the beginning of the twenty-first century, even some conservatives and libertarians supported the idea that the government should automatically provide some level of basic subsistence for everyone.[122]

Generous as the idea might seem that no one should go hungry or lack shelter— in a society far more affluent than those of earlier times— there is nevertheless the question of what the human consequences are likely to be. This need not be a matter of pure speculation, since modern welfare states have already gone a considerable distance in that direction, and the track record of human consequences thus far is there to see.

However much the prevailing social vision may have aimed at creating a society that acts much as a family does in nurturing and protecting its members, what it has in fact done is replace the *reciprocal* obligations among members of a family with **unilateral** and unconditional subsidies of the welfare state that are a legal right and entitlement— freeing the recipient from reciprocal duties, even the duty of common decency.

We might imagine that freeing people from the burdens and pressures of having to continuously provide themselves and their dependents with food, shelter and other necessities would relieve them from much anxiety, and allow them to pursue other interests with their minds more at ease. But the actual track record of what has happened to people stripped of personal responsibility and purpose in their lives is very sobering, at best.[123]

Many of the beneficiaries of the welfare state have sought to fill the void with drugs, sex, violence and other self-indulgences, or joining in mob rampages over the grievance *du jour*. Far from an assurance of subsistence producing a relaxed sense of security and contentment, it seems instead to have produced a sense of inchoate grievance against a society that has left them adrift, with no intrinsically meaningful role in life, while others have both meaningful achievements and visibly higher standards of living than whatever is given to them as basic necessities— and all this amid unceasing emphasis on invidious comparisons and on how wrong it is that some have so much more than others.

Productivity is not the only concept that seems to have faded into the background among those with the prevailing social vision. While "rights" have proliferated, creating a sense of "entitlement" to what others have produced, duties have shrunk. A computer study of the frequency of the word "duty" in British and American books showed its frequency had shrunk to one-third of its frequency in earlier times.[124] Shame is another of the concepts that seems to have faded, as shameless behavior has flourished, and has even been celebrated as "liberation" in some quarters.

The widespread changes wrought in human behavior during the triumphant era of the welfare state *and its accompanying social vision* have included fear-filled people in a French public housing project where cars are "burned for fun";[125] fear-filled schools in Britain and America, where both children and their teachers have been targets of young thugs allowed to run amok;[126] single mothers on welfare in New Zealand saying, "If I don't have another baby, I'm going to have to go back to work";[127] and a woman in an American public housing project responding to an account of a brutal gang-rape of a woman in her own apartment with: "So a lady was raped. Big deal. There's too much other crime happening here."[128] We have already noted an international and centuries-long decline in homicides that suddenly reversed in the 1960s and shot up again, to levels not seen since the previous century.[129]

Replacing *reciprocal* social obligations with *unilateral* subsidies of self-indulgences does not sound promising, even in theory. In light of the social degeneration that has already taken place, the human consequences of the prevailing social vision hardly seem encouraging as an inducement to go further in that direction.

Chapter 7

Facts, Assumptions and Goals

*Things are what they are, and their consequences will
be what they will be. Why, then, should we deceive
ourselves?*

Winston Churchill

Many people may expect discussions of economic and social
disparities to end with "solutions"— usually something that
the government can create, institutionalize, staff and pay for with the
taxpayers' money.

The goal here is entirely different. There has never been a shortage
of people eager to draw up blueprints for running other people's lives.
But any "solution," however valid as of a given moment under given
conditions, is subject to obsolescence as time goes on and conditions
change.

The hope here is that clarification is less perishable, and can be
applied to both existing issues related to economic and social disparities
and to new issues, involving the same subject, that are sure to arise
with the passage of time. Given the limitations of prophecy, the point
here is to seek to provide enough clarification to enable others to make
up their own minds about the inevitable claims and counter-claims
sure to arise from those who are promoting their own notions or their
own interests.

What can we conclude from our survey of the many economic,
social and technological gaps of our times— and of other times and
places, going back for centuries? We have seen, in various ways, how
multiple prerequisites can produce skewed distributions of outcomes,

in no way resembling a normal bell curve, whether in human endeavors or in natural phenomena such as tornadoes or lightning.

To deny that a particular factor can be assumed *a priori* to be the cause of inequalities in outcomes is not to deny that the chances of achieving those outcomes have in fact been grossly unequal in societies around the world, and over thousands of years of recorded history. In a sense, life is a relay race, and each of us receives the baton at a time and place over which we have no control. Our parents, our birth order, our country and our surrounding culture have already been predetermined for us. Some of the prerequisites for achievement can be affected later by individual choices or social policies, but by no means 100 percent in most cases, much less in all cases. No human being and no human institution has either sufficient knowledge or sufficient power for that. More important, we have zero control over the past— and, as was said, long ago, "We do not live in the past, but the past in us."[1]

EQUALITY: MEANINGS AND PROSPECTS

Critics of disparities often either explicitly or implicitly call for some kind or approximation of equality. But when we speak of "equality" among human beings, what do we mean? We certainly cannot all sing like Pavarotti, think like Einstein or land a commercial airliner safely in the Hudson River like pilot "Sully" Sullenberger. Clearly we cannot all be equally capable of doing concrete things. In terms of specific capabilities in real life, a given man is not even equal to himself at different stages of life— sometimes not even on different days— much less equal to all others who are in varying stages of their own lives.

Even if we all had equal potential at birth, or at conception, too many factors are at work— and at work differently from one individual to another, even within the same family— for us to develop the same capabilities to the same degree. If we cannot have equality of capabilities, then we are left to define equality in some other way. These might include equality of rewards, though breaking the link between productivity and reward has had an unpromising track record in many times and places.[2] Rewarding people for their merit is another possibility, though not one free of pitfalls.

Merit versus Productivity

Much controversy about economic and other disparities center on whether what people get reflects their merit— that is, what they deserve as rewards, from a moral perspective, based on what they themselves have chosen to do, out of the particular possibilities open to them. But what they deserve morally is what we do not know and cannot know, for we have not "walked in their shoes." We can guess, surmise or imagine, but these are hardly sufficient bases for invoking the categorical compulsions of government.

Even if we were to concede that rewarding moral merit would be better, that raises the more fundamental question of our own competence to assess moral merit. Some college admissions officials, for example, implicitly seem to assume that they can assess applicants on the basis of how well an applicant has used the particular educational opportunities previously available to that applicant, rather than on the basis of how one applicant's record of educational accomplishments compares with another. But that turns the college admissions process into an attempt to assess merit in the past, rather than productivity in the future.

In general, judging merit seems far less likely to be within our competence than judging productivity. In the economy, what we are far more likely to be competent to judge for ourselves, individually, is whether whatever product or service someone offers us is worth what it costs. Judging *merit* in the sense of the moral worth that we could credit or blame an individual for, if we knew and understood all the myriad factors impinging on that particular individual's life, seems beyond the realm of human knowledge. But when we are forced to decide whether to part with our own money— that is, to forego other desirable uses of it— in order to purchase some product or service, that can concentrate our attention on demonstrable realities, with less distraction by heady words or sweeping visions.

Although productivity is far easier to assess than moral merit, productivity is often completely missing in discussions of socioeconomic disparities, especially by those promoting what is called "social justice." A classic example is a large *New York Times* article that began: "A Walmart employee earning the company's median salary of $19,177 would have to work for more than a thousand years to earn the $22.2 million that Doug McMillon, the company's chief executive, was awarded in 2017."[3] In this article, the subject of productivity was conspicuous by its absence.

Far from being a new approach, this *New York Times* article was in a long-standing tradition. As famed playwright and Fabian socialist George Bernard Shaw put it, in the early twentieth century:

> A division in which one woman gets a shilling and another three thousand shillings for an hour of work has no moral sense in it: it is just something that happens, and that ought not to happen. A child with an interesting face and pretty ways, and some talent for acting, may, by working for the films, earn a hundred times as much as its mother can earn by drudging at an ordinary trade.[4]

Here productivity is not simply missing, but implicitly repudiated, as a basis for income. The child movie star who is paid many times what her mother is paid is obviously being paid by someone who values her movie role more than anyone values her mother's work. In short, she is being paid for productivity— as judged by whoever pays her, who in turn is paid by vast numbers of other people, who pay for the enjoyment they get from watching her in the movies. It is *not* "just something that happens" and there is no basis on which a third-party observer can say that this voluntary transaction is something "that ought not to happen"— that his personal opinion should override other people's right to do as they choose with their own money or their own time.

This is about the power to preempt other people's decisions, even if it is called by the more appealing words "social justice." The very choice of targets for the wrath of "social justice" crusaders such as the *New York Times* is indicative. There are numerous professional athletes and entertainers who have been paid *some multiple* of what the chief executive of Walmart is paid.[5] But no one asks how many millennia someone who performs mundane tasks at a baseball park would have to work to earn as much as the team's star player is paid every year. No one asks how many millennia someone who performs such chores at a Hollywood studio would have to work, in order to earn as much as a movie star makes from one hit movie.

Why the difference behind the fierce cries of outrage at pay differentials in business, and the passing over in silence of far greater pay differentials in sports and entertainment? One possible explanation is that business owners and managers have roles in which they can be replaced by political decision-makers, who in turn can impose the kinds of policies preferred by those who imagine that their own superior wisdom or virtue entitles them to dictate to others. But professional athletes and entertainers have roles that obviously cannot be taken over by politicians or bureaucrats. So there would be no point in trying to discredit highly paid people in sports or entertainment, or to arouse public outrage against them.

In any event, the fundamental question is whether people should be paid according to what they produce or paid simply because of their presence. But productivity is an often ignored factor in much of the income disparity literature. Moreover, the question is seldom, if ever, raised as to how many thousands of years a low-level worker would have to work to *produce* as much wealth as was produced by Bill Gates' computer operating system that allowed billions of people around the world to operate an extremely complex mechanism that only a very few, highly technologically advanced people would be able to operate without such an intermediary system.

In much, if not most, of the literature on income and wealth disparities, the *production* of income and wealth is glided over, as something that just happens *somehow*, even though it happens to radically different degrees in different parts of the world and under different economic systems. Even a fraction of the wealth generated around the world by the Microsoft operating system that was received by Gates himself was enough to produce a gigantic fortune.

Contrary to fashionable rhetoric, this fortune was not some share of "the world's income" that Gates somehow "grabbed," "took" or "cornered." It was what billions of people around the world voluntarily paid for purchasing computers containing Gates' operating system— Microsoft Windows, something they judged individually would benefit themselves sufficiently to make the price worth paying. It was a share of the value *added*, as judged by the people who chose to spend their own money to get it.

None of this denies that there may well have been other people who were born with potentialities very much like those of Bill Gates, but who never had the same combination of prerequisites that Gates had. Bound up with issues involving moral merit is the reality of luck as a factor in socioeconomic outcomes, beginning with the luck involved in being born in one set of circumstances rather than another. But, although luck is beyond our control, we can nevertheless learn from examining what that luck consisted of. The luck of being an only child, or the first-born, can make us aware of the great importance of parental attention to all children in their earliest years of development, and lead to more attention to children in general, regardless of their particular birth order. Examining other lucky or unlucky influences can also provide clues to what kinds of behavior or policies to embrace or avoid.

If we could somehow determine what specifically are the prerequisites that can develop special individual potentialities into great achievements, that could benefit society as a whole in many ways, whether in technological advancements or by discovering cures or preventatives for devastating diseases. But our education system is too often oriented in the opposite direction, fiercely opposing differing levels and kinds of education for those individuals whose demonstrated capabilities exceed the demonstrated capabilities of others.

In many cases, educators verbally transmute higher capabilities into "privilege." Through the magic of words, and in the name of "social justice," such educators oppose using the schools to facilitate the development of special individual abilities that can benefit society as a whole, because that can cause an expansion of educational disparities and the economic disparities that follow. Many of those with this social vision not only proceed as if society is a zero-sum process, in which benefits to one segment necessarily come at the expense of other segments, they also often ignore, dismiss or demonize other ways of looking at the situation.

For others, whose thinking is not confined within the sealed bubble of the prevailing social vision, maximizing the productive potential of those with higher levels of capabilities benefits many others. The willingness of those others to pay for the fruits of those capabilities is what enables those with such capabilities to *earn* higher incomes through voluntary transactions— as distinguished from either seizing some pre-existing wealth or receiving whatever third-party surrogate decision-makers might deign to dole out to them in the name of "social justice."

Among the many dangers of surrogate decision-making is that such decision-makers cannot know the situation of millions of other people as well as those people know their own situations, which may not conform to the vision prevailing among the surrogates. Moreover, surrogate decision-makers often *pay no price for being wrong*, no matter how wrong or how catastrophic the consequences for those whose decisions they have preempted. Given the fallibility of all human beings, the chastening effect of facing the consequences of one's decisions can be dispensed with only at great peril.

Languages

Ignoring or downplaying productivity has many consequences, because any source of productivity can also be a source of disparities. That includes something as basic as language. Languages are not simply a means of personal communication, important as that is. Knowledge itself— from the most mundane to the most complex and valuable knowledge— is at the heart of productivity, *and different languages have stored vastly different amounts of knowledge* at different times and places. People with languages that have a spoken version, but no written version, have been forced to rely on the very limited capacity and fallibility of memory.

At one time, in centuries past, most of the higher level knowledge in Western civilization was stored in Latin, the language of the Romans who had long ruled, and created, much of Western civilization. Whether you went to a university in France or England, you were taught in Latin, because that is where the knowledge was stored, long after the Roman Empire was gone. Regardless of whatever great mental potential you might have been born with, if you did not understand Latin, you were not going to get that knowledge.

With the passing centuries, much of the knowledge once confined to writings in Latin was translated into the vernacular languages of Europe. But this took time, had high costs, and not all populations were either large enough or prosperous enough to cover the costs of having their particular language receive as much of that knowledge as others received. If you were a Czech child in the Habsburg Empire, you could not be taught in your own language beyond the elementary school level until 1848.[6] If you wanted to go on to the university level, it would be even longer before there were sufficient writings in your own language to make that possible. For much of Eastern Europe at that time, you had to learn German in order to get a university education. And millions of hard-working people had neither the time nor the money to do that.

There was nothing resembling equality of opportunity under these circumstances. At various times and places around the world, there have been many languages that had not yet developed written versions. Even within the same continent, the languages of Western Europe developed written versions centuries before the languages of Eastern Europe, and it took centuries more for the latter to catch up with the scope and variety of written material available in Western European languages. This was not a matter of genetics, discrimination or merit. It was simply a fact of life. And like other facts of life, it meant gross disparities in opportunities and outcomes.

Against that background, it is hardly surprising that differences in languages have polarized whole societies in various times and places,[7] leading even to violence and terrorism in Bohemia,[8] Canada[9] and India,[10] for example, and to outright civil war in Sri Lanka.[11] These have not been controversies about the qualities of the languages, as such, but about the socioeconomic consequences for people speaking different languages.

Controversies in contemporary America about whether Hispanic youngsters should be taught in English, or whether the particular variety of "black English" found in low-income ghettos should be used in schools, likewise affect what socioeconomic outcomes can be expected from following one policy rather than another. Here too, the issue is not about the particular qualities of the languages or dialects involved, as these might be judged by linguistic scholars. It is about how the future outcomes of these youngsters can be affected by their speech, and by their access to the knowledge stored in the language of the society around them.

Linguistic scholar John McWhorter, for example, has sought to justify using "black English" in schools to teach ghetto youngsters.[12] But where are the books on mathematics, science, engineering, medicine and innumerable other subjects that are written in "black English"? For Hispanic youngsters, there are books on these subjects in Spanish, but they are unlikely to be books found in American public schools and, even if they were, would the knowledge obtained be something that Hispanics could readily communicate to most of the Americans around them who do not speak Spanish? In both cases, the issue is the scope of the cultural universe available to youngsters living in an English-speaking country.

In an era of group-identity politics, various group spokesmen, activists or "leaders" may be preoccupied with languages as badges of cultural identity, but cultures exist to serve human beings. Human beings do not exist to preserve cultures, or to preserve a socially isolated constituency for the benefit of "leaders." Why create or perpetuate cultural handicaps for minority youngsters in today's America that were inescapable handicaps for minority youngsters in many other countries in earlier times with fewer and narrower options?

Where languages are seen as productive tools, rather than social symbols, the policies are very different. A Japanese-owned multinational company has decreed that English will be the sole language of the enterprise, wherever the company's branches are located around the world.[13] In other words, they recognized that English is the *lingua franca* of international commerce, as it is the language of international airline pilots communicating with airports around the world. Their decision was not based on the qualities of the English or Japanese languages, or their symbolic value, but on hard facts about the economics of doing business around the world.

In Singapore, with an overwhelmingly Asian population— whose languages spoken at home are Chinese, Malay or other— not only are all school children required to learn English, the language of instruction in other subjects is also English.[14] Singapore's productivity and prosperity as a major international port depends on its ability to communicate with many nations whose shipments pass through its harbor. English as a *lingua franca* is key to doing that.

In such cases, the choice of language is based on practical considerations for the welfare of people, rather than on symbolic or ideological issues. Despite how much some intellectuals may be drawn toward such issues in the world of words, symbolism is a luxury that the poor can afford least of all in the world of reality.

DISPARITIES RECONSIDERED

Much attention has been paid to possible reasons why some individuals and groups have traveled farther or faster on the road to achievements, but not nearly as much attention has been paid to the question of why others are not even on that road in the first place.

Ability no doubt plays a role in achievements, but large disparities in outcomes among men who were all in the top one percent in IQ suggest that ability may be necessary, but hardly sufficient, as an explanation. Indeed, the fact that two men, who failed to make the IQ cutoff of 140 for Professor Terman's landmark study, nevertheless won Nobel Prizes in physics suggests that other factors must have a large influence, since none of the hundreds of men who did make the 140 IQ cutoff won a Nobel Prize in anything.[15]

Before we can say who has failed, or who has succeeded, in some endeavor, we must first know who was trying to succeed in that endeavor in the first place. Those who are not trying are not likely to succeed, regardless of how much innate ability they may have, and regardless of how much opportunity may exist.

When all children are forced by law to go to school, for example, there is no basis for believing that they are all equally oriented toward getting an education. When, on both sides of the Atlantic, there are many children who not only do not put their own efforts into learning, but disrupt classrooms and harass, threaten and assault other children who do try to learn, surely the time is overdue to stop proceeding as if all educational deficiencies are due to external factors, or that the only internal factor that matters is genetic potential.

Education is just one of many areas where the seemingly invincible fallacy of presupposing a background probability of equality of outcomes defies both evidence and logic. Major demographic differences between different groups within nations, and between one nation and another— with median ages differing by a decade, or two decades or more— give an air of unreality to sweeping expectations of equal outcomes among groups or nations, and sweeping outrage when such expectations are not fulfilled.

Any serious empirical examinations of social groups, nations or races turn up major differences in their respective environments. Severe isolation has left some peoples centuries or even millennia behind others, whether these were Caucasians in the Canary Islands living at a Stone Age level during the Middle Ages[16] or black Australian aborigines still living as hunter-gatherers in the eighteenth century.[17] Progress is no more automatic than equality, whether for races, nations or other social groupings. We cannot argue as if good things happen automatically, and bad things are somebody's fault.

Illiteracy isolates people from thousands of years of accumulated knowledge, skills and insights from people around the world. After literacy, or even higher education, has been acquired, that does not make their benefits equally available to all who have acquired these things. Jews were known for centuries as "people of the book." But for most other people around the world, illiteracy remained common for most of those centuries, and higher education was the exception, rather than the rule, even in the twentieth century.

After most people in particular places had both literacy and education extending to the university level, those who were the first member of their family to achieve either of these things were not in the same position as those who came from a background where literacy and education had been common for generations— and common in the homes in which they grew up. During those generations and centuries intellectual interests, intellectual habits and intellectual standards and traditions could develop. Jewish boys, for example, faced an intellectual task when they reached the age for a Bar Mitzvah to mark their passage from the world of childhood onto the road to manhood.

In Eastern Europe during the years between the two World Wars, young people who were the first member of their families to become educated had no such tradition to prepare them for the world of higher education. Not surprisingly, such students lacked the intellectual background of Jewish students with whom they were in competition in universities, and students from such groups became prominent among members of anti-Semitic movements.[18]

In many less developed countries in the twentieth century— whether in Europe, Asia or Africa— where higher education was a new experience for many, those students whose cultural backgrounds provided no intellectual experience, traditions or norms as guidance, tended to study softer, more superficially attractive subjects in the "social sciences" or humanities rather than the hard sciences, engineering, medicine or other challenging subjects with major practical applications in the real world.

When Malaysian Prime Minister Mahathir bin Mohamad complained that Malay students admitted preferentially to the universities neglected their academic studies and were drawn toward politics,[19] he was in effect echoing what had been said of Romanian universities between the two World Wars, that they were "numerically swollen, academically rather lax, and politically overheated."[20] Most Romanians were illiterate at the beginning of the twentieth century. When there was a great expansion of the younger generation into higher education, Romanian students tended to choose the softer subjects to study, with only one percent studying medicine, for example.[21] There were similar patterns in Third World nations that gained their independence after the Second World War, such as Sri Lanka[22] and the African nations of Nigeria and Senegal.[23]

Why should we be surprised to see similar patterns among college students from groups lagging economically and educationally in American society today? Or surprised that such things are seldom even discussed in the politically correct monoculture of academia or in most of the media?

All of this merely scratches the surface of factors impeding equality of outcomes. Deliberate, biased suppressions of other people's opportunities are just one of the various other impediments to equal outcomes. But those things which offend our moral sense do not automatically have more *causal* weight than morally neutral factors such as demography, geography or language differences. Determining particular reasons for particular differences at particular times and places requires the hard work of examination and analysis, rather than heady rhetoric and sweeping presuppositions.

As a young scholar and the first black man to receive a Ph.D. from Harvard, W.E.B. Du Bois posed the question as to what would happen if all white people were to lose their racial prejudices overnight. He said that it would make little difference in the economic situation of most blacks. Although "some few would be promoted, some few would get new places" as a result of an end of racial discrimination, nevertheless "the mass would remain as they are" until the younger generation began to "try harder" and the race "lost the omnipresent excuse for failure: prejudice."[24]

Whether or not Du Bois' conclusion was justified, either at the time or more generally, his key point was that white racism— which he fiercely fought against all his life— was not *automatically* the main reason for racial disparities in outcomes.

We have seen in Chapter 2 that the actual *effects* of even undoubted and openly proclaimed racism, as in South Africa under apartheid, can depend greatly on the costs of discrimination to discriminators, in a variety of institutional settings. Similar factors and their consequences apply when there is bias against other groups, whether these are groups defined by sex, religion or other differences.

If injustices and persecutions were always causally paramount, Jews would be some of the poorest and least educated people in the world today. Few other groups can trace their victimhood back even half as many centuries or millennia as the Jews. There can be no doubt that a pervasive hostility to Jews often blighted their lives, impeded their progress and left many needlessly in poverty. At various times and places this hostility also made them targets of lethal violence. But the plain fact is that Jews today are by no stretch of the imagination among the poorest or least educated people.

Nor are a number of other groups who have played similar economic roles in countries around the world— and faced similar hostility, punctuated at times by outright mob violence and/or mass expulsions by governments. These other groups who played similar economic roles and faced similar hostility would include the overseas Chinese, sometimes called "the Jews of Southeast Asia," Parsees described as "the Jews of India" and Lebanese called "the Jews of West Africa," among others.

The violence unleashed against successful groups has often exceeded the violence unleashed against lagging groups disdained as "inferior." The number of overseas Chinese killed by mobs in Vietnam, in just one year, exceeded the number of lynchings of black Americans recorded in the history of the United States.[25] So did the number of Armenians killed in just one year by rampaging mobs in the Ottoman Empire,[26] and so has the number of Jews killed in a given year, at numerous times and places throughout history,[27] even before millions were murdered in the Holocaust.

In an era in which invidious gaps and disparities preoccupy so many people, it is necessary to point out that the purpose of making such comparisons here is *not* to praise, blame or rank different groups. The purpose is to try to get some sense of causation, and to apply whatever insights we can derive from that to human beings in general.

If nothing else, we can learn how dangerous it is, to a whole society, to incessantly depict outcome differences as evidence or proof of malevolent actions that need to be counter-attacked or avenged. Contrary to much that has been said, disparities in socioeconomic outcomes are neither improbable from a theoretical standpoint nor uncommon from an empirical standpoint. Among the real life corollaries of this is that taboos against discussing anything that might be considered negative in the individual behavior or social culture of lagging groups are counterproductive. Given the fallibility of *all* human beings— demonstrated innumerable times around the world and over thousands of years of recorded history— to exempt any group of people from criticism is not a blessing but a curse.

Against that background, calls for reducing either performance standards or behavioral standards in schools for young people from lagging groups may simply increase the number of members of such groups who develop *almost* all the prerequisites of success.

To have young people from lagging groups needlessly fail, because third parties preparing them decided not to hold them accountable for punctuality or standard English, or some other quality that their backgrounds may not have given them, is a personal misfortune and a social tragedy. There are few things more painfully frustrating than having done 90 percent of what is necessary for success, and yet failing nevertheless, despite all the efforts and sacrifices made.[28]

How can such unnecessary failures be avoided? Put bluntly, by paying more attention to facts than to assumptions or visions. Third parties whose lives have been quite different from the lives of those members of lagging groups whom they teach, advise or run programs for, may be forgiven for not understanding the situation *at the outset*. But vast amounts of evidence, accumulated over the years, show that the particular circumstances in which members of lagging groups have not only succeeded but excelled, have almost invariably been circumstances where there was no lowering of standards for them, and where ruthless competition was the norm for all.

Low-income and lagging groups in America— whether they were the Irish in the nineteenth century or blacks and Hispanics in the twentieth century— have often risen first and most spectacularly in sports and entertainment.[29] Both of these are fields of unsparing competition, in which even the stars of yesteryear are ruthlessly cast aside when their performances begin to fade.

In educational institutions as well, all-black Dunbar High School in Washington, D.C., during its 85 years of academic success from

1870 to 1955, had unsparing standards both for school work and for such behavioral qualities as punctuality and social demeanor.[30] The sheer volume of work required was also more than in most other public schools. Some parents of Dunbar students even protested to the Board of Education about the large amount of homework required.[31]

Today, in such highly successful charter schools as those of the KIPP school network and the Success Academy schools, standards have been at least as unsparing, with longer school days, longer school years, rigorous academic requirements and little tolerance for disruptive behavior, much less for the gross behavior so often overlooked or excused in other public schools.

The payoff to such uncompromising demands has been as dramatic in education as in sports or entertainment. As already noted in Chapter 3, black graduates of Dunbar High School were attending some of the most elite colleges in the country a hundred years ago, and graduating with honors, as well as going on to become the first blacks to have various career achievements in a number of fields. The academic achievements of low-income black and other minority students in many charter schools today have been similarly remarkable.

In school year 2016–2017, for example, the various Success Academy schools in New York City enrolled 14,000 students. On statewide tests given in 2017, the highest percentage of students in any of New York State's regular public school districts who passed the English Language Arts (ELA) test was 81 percent. In the Success Academy schools, 84 percent of the students passed the ELA test. In mathematics, the highest-scoring regular public school district in the state had 85 percent of its students pass. In the Success Academy schools, 95 percent passed.

This would be an outstanding record for Success Academy charter schools under normal circumstances. Under the actual circumstances— including the predominantly low-income black and Hispanic students who constitute the great majority in these schools, where students are admitted by lottery rather than ability— it is truly extraordinary, considering how poorly such students usually do in the regular public schools.

In New York State's regular public school district with the highest percentage of its students passing the math and English exams, 65 percent of those students were Asian and 29 percent were white. In fact, among the state's top five regular public school districts with the highest proportion of their students passing the statewide math and English exams, white-and-Asian majorities ranged from 86 percent to 94 percent. Black and Hispanic students, put together, were less than 10 percent of the students in each of these five highest-achieving regular public school districts.

By contrast, in the Success Academy schools, with even higher percentages of their students passing those same exams, 86 percent of the students were either black or Hispanic, and only 6 percent of the students were white and 3 percent Asian. The average family income of the children in the five highest-scoring regular public school districts in New York state ranged from four times the average family income of children in the Success Academy schools to more than nine times that of the Success Academy children's families.[32]

How many observers— of whatever race, class or political orientation— can honestly say that they expected such outcomes? Such results are a challenge, if not a devastating contradiction, to prevailing beliefs about either heredity or environment, as those terms are conventionally used. Neither the genes said by some to be a crippling intellectual handicap, nor the poverty said by others to blight minority children's educational prospects, turned out to be such insurmountable obstacles as many across the ideological spectrum believed.

Nevertheless, education is just one of the areas in which beliefs, arguments and policies are too often guided not by what has demonstrably worked but by what fits a prevailing vision. Racial "integration" in the schools, which the prevailing social vision proclaimed to be a prerequisite for equality of education— because, in the catchwords of Chief Justice Warren separate schools "are inherently unequal"— went from being a means to an end to becoming an end in itself. Accordingly, charter schools have been opposed by many minority "leaders," including the National Association for the Advancement of Colored People, which has advocated a ban on charter schools.[33]

Astonishing as such reactions might seem, Dunbar High School faced similar hostility in segments of the black population during the era of its academic excellence.[34] In many contexts around the world, egalitarianism as an abstract philosophy has often meant resentment of success as a social reality. More broadly, outstanding achievements of various sorts— whether educational, economic or other— have provoked hostile responses in many countries around the world and in many periods of history.

The time is long overdue to count the costs of runaway rhetoric and heedless accusations— especially since most of those costs, including the high social cost of a breakdown of law and order, are paid by vulnerable people for whose benefit such rhetoric and such accusations are ostensibly being made.

CULTURE

The impact of social visions and social policies, for good or ill, is not uniform across a society. Different groups with different cultures, faced with the same objective circumstances, can react in very different ways.

While the same welfare state benefits are available to Asian Americans as to other Americans, the culture and educational performances of Asian Americans provide them with far better options than a life on welfare. Similarly, to Scandinavians with some of the highest standards of living in the world, and some of the highest standards of honesty,* living on welfare may not be as attractive as to some members of lower-income groups in England or the United States.

---

* See, for example, Eric Felten, "Finders Keepers?" *Reader's Digest*, April 2001, pp. 102–107; "So Whom Can You Trust?" *The Economist*, June 22, 1996, p. 51; "Scandinavians Prove Their Honesty in European Lost-Wallet Experiment," *Deseret News*, June 20, 1996; Michael Booth, *The Almost Nearly Perfect People: Behind the Myth of the Scandinavian Utopia* (New York: Picador, 2014), p. 40.

The Scandinavian countries have so often been used as an example of welfare states which avoided some of the serious problems found in other welfare states that a closer look at Scandinavia may be useful, especially now that the situation in those countries has begun to evolve into circumstances much more like those in other welfare states.

Scandinavia

For most of their history, the Scandinavian countries have had populations especially homogeneous culturally, sparing them many of the internal conflicts complicating the welfare states of the United States and Britain. Homogeneous populations provide few opportunities for careers as polarizing ethnic "leaders" and activists promoting a sense of historic grievances behind differences in current outcomes.

In Sweden, for example, only about 1 percent of the Swedish population in 1940 was born outside of Sweden, and that rose over the years to just 7 percent by 1970. Moreover, back in that era, immigrants to Sweden came predominantly from Western European countries, and were typically well-educated, and often had higher labor force participation rates and lower unemployment rates than the native-born Swedes.[35] As late as 1970, 90 percent of foreign-born persons in Sweden had been born in Europe, including 60 percent from "Nordic" countries— that is, countries culturally similar to Sweden.

That all changed in the late twentieth century and early twenty-first century. By 2007, immigrants were 12 percent of the population of Sweden. Moreover, it was not simply the increasing numbers of immigrants, but the changed national and cultural *origins* of those immigrants that has been crucial.

Turmoil in the Middle East sent increasing numbers of people from that region of the world to Sweden, Denmark and Norway as refugees. As of 2012, there were more immigrants from Iraq than from any other country in these three Scandinavian nations.[36] Given the very small populations in the Scandinavian countries— only about 10 million people in all of Sweden— a relatively modest number of Middle Eastern refugees have had a major impact on Swedish society.

Moreover, this represented a drastic departure from the previous history of Sweden and of the immigrants who settled there.

The changing origins of immigrants to Sweden were reflected in changing behavior patterns within the Swedish welfare state. There was a sharply rising use of the government's "social assistance" programs by immigrants. Just 6.2 percent of the predominantly European immigrants in the pre-1976 era resorted to these "social assistance" programs, compared to 40.5 percent of the immigrants in the 1996–1999 period, when those immigrants were refugees predominantly from the Balkans and the Middle East.

The main difference was not in the times but in the people. Even in 1999, just 6.8 percent of the immigrants from Nordic countries received "social assistance" from the government, which was not very different from the 4.7 percent among native-born Swedes. But 44.3 percent of the immigrants from the Middle East received that same welfare state benefit.[37]

The non-judgmental aspects of the prevailing welfare state vision opened Sweden to an influx of people based on those people's status as asylum-seekers, rather than being based on the effect of this influx on the existing Swedish population and their social values. For example, more than half of the people accepted under Sweden's refugee policies lacked a high-school education.[38]

Among the consequences have been that unemployment among foreigners has become more than twice as high as among native Swedes. Moreover, "after 10 years in Sweden, only half of asylum seekers have a job."[39] Immigrants, who are now 16 percent of Sweden's small population, have become 51 percent of the long-term unemployed and 57 percent of the recipients of welfare payments.[40]

In Norway, the cost of supporting a single refugee in the manner prescribed by the country's many welfare state provisions has been calculated as $125,000, which would be enough to support a number of Syrian refugees in Jordan.[41] In Denmark, where the labor force participation rate is 76 percent for native Danes, it is less than 50 percent for immigrants from non-Western countries, ranging as low as 14 percent for immigrants from Somalia.[42]

As the ethnic and cultural homogeneity within Scandinavian countries has been changed by an influx of immigrants within recent decades— and especially immigrants admitted from non-Western nations— some of the same social problems as those in Britain and the United States have also begun to appear in Scandinavia.

In Sweden, immigrants from the Middle East show few signs of assimilating to the Swedish culture and many signs of transplanting their own culture to Sweden:

> There are stories— familiar in other parts of Europe where immigrants from the Muslim world have recently settled— of students harassing Jewish teachers and defacing textbooks that treat Jewish themes. Crime is high.[43]

There have been a "steady stream of 'honor killings'" among some Middle Eastern groups, usually involving "girls executed by their brothers or fathers for wearing short skirts or dating Swedish men."[44] The proportion of foreigners in Sweden's prisons is five times their proportion in Sweden's population.[45] For the more serious crimes, such as murder, rape and major drug dealing, about half the prison inmates are foreign-born.[46]

Among the implications of such patterns in Scandinavia is that the welfare state is an influence, rather than a predestination. Put differently, it is the *interaction* of the welfare state with differing existing cultures in the population which produces varying socioeconomic outcomes, whether within nations or between nations. But here, as in other contexts, the invincible fallacy often trumps the hardest facts, so that very different people are treated as if they were the same.

Immigration Issues

Neither sweeping attacks on immigrants in general nor sweeping defenses of immigrants in general make any sense, because there are no immigrants in general. Instead, there are very different behavior patterns— in education, employment and crimes, for example— among immigrants from different countries and cultures.

Verbal virtuosity can blur such distinctions and produce such wonderful-sounding generalities as judging each person as an individual, or declaring all cultures equally valid or valuable in some elusive and unverifiable sense. In this world of words, much controversy is based on assertions and counter-assertions, rather than on hard facts about such things as the educational levels, welfare state dependency, automobile accident rates, or crime rates of particular groups from particular countries or cultures. Rhetoric, visions and catchwords often serve as substitutes for such basic information.

Particular immigrant groups have greatly benefitted many societies, whether in Latin America, Southeast Asia or the United States. Whole industries have been created by immigrants in Argentina, Brazil and other South American countries,[47] as well as in Malaysia, Thailand and other Southeast Asian countries.[48] Even in advanced economies such as in Britain and the United States, there have been industries that did not exist before immigrants created them. The watch-making industry in Britain was created by Huguenot refugees from France,[49] and the first pianos in colonial America were built by German immigrants.[50]

Ironically, in some countries the immigrants who brought skills most lacking in the native population have been among the most resented and even hated. Often their predominance in particular industries has led to accusations that they have "taken over" those industries, even when the industries did not exist until the immigrants created them.

Not only countries, but also local communities most dependent upon outsiders to supply the economic skills most lacking in their own general population, tend to have the most resentment toward those who supply such skills and services, and who prosper by doing so.

In the 1992 ghetto riots in Los Angeles, for example, more than 2,000 stores owned by Koreans were burned and looted, creating $350 million worth of damage[51]— though Koreans had nothing to do with either the causes of that riot or with slavery or other calamities suffered by blacks. The prevailing social vision that blames "society" for disparities makes individuals and groups in that society targets, whether or not those individuals or groups had anything to do with the problems of lagging groups. This is not peculiar to the United

States. North African immigrants who attacked Chinese immigrants in France with knives said that it was because the Chinese had "nice clothes" and "big cars."[52]

Despite wide disparities among immigrant groups from different countries and cultures, empirical facts about such differences are seldom part of public debates about immigration policies. The very attempt to discuss such issues in factual terms has been treated as morally unworthy. Any concerns about a need to preserve a domestic culture that has produced a level of prosperity, order and freedom seldom found in some other cultures risks being dismissed as phobias or racism. It is as if the only morally legitimate way to discuss immigration issues is in terms of the prevailing social vision, based on the seemingly invincible fallacy of assuming a sameness of developed capabilities among both peoples and cultures.

PROCESS GOALS VERSUS OUTCOME GOALS

People with different visions of the world may have not only different goals but also different *kinds* of goals. Some kinds of goals are *process* goals, such as "free markets" or "a government of laws and not of men." Other goals are *outcome* goals, such as eliminating socioeconomic "gaps" or "disparities" between individuals or groups. Moreover, different kinds of institutions may be more suited to achieving these different kinds of goals.

Even those who seek to promote certain process goals recognize that outcomes are what ultimately matter. But the crucial question is: *Matter to whom?* In a free market, each individual transactor decides what particular outcomes that particular transactor wants, and at what cost, whether in money or in toil and sacrifice. Institutional structures that seek to maintain market processes leave individual decisions in the market to the particular individuals transacting directly with each other within the framework of that process.

By contrast, those who are seeking to have more women employed in Silicon Valley or more minority students admitted to Ivy League colleges are directly pursuing specific outcome goals chosen by third parties, to be imposed on others. Whatever the pros and cons of the particular goals, these pros and cons are not left to be weighed by those people directly affected, but by third-party surrogate decision-makers who may claim or assume superior knowledge, compassion or whatever.*

By contrast, those who are promoting *process* goals are seeking to have incremental *trade-offs* made by individuals directly experiencing both the benefits and the costs of their own decisions. Those who are promoting outcome goals are seeking to create categorical *priorities* chosen by third parties, and imposed by government compulsion on those who directly experience both the benefits and the costs.

Those who seek to establish priorities to eliminate gaps do not necessarily say that this is to be done "at all costs" or "by all means necessary." But, at the very least, the weighing of those costs and benefits is not left in the hands of those who will experience both. More important, the knowledge of all the costs— not only in money terms but in human terms as well— cannot possibly be known as well to distant surrogates as to the people who directly bear those costs.

Those surrogate decision-makers who have demolished whole neighborhoods, in order to replace these neighborhoods with new housing, planned and controlled by the government, not only destroy physical structures but also destroy an invisible web of valuable human connections that make a viable community. These include not only families related to each other who live nearby in the same community but also ties to particular neighbors, friends and connections with particular businesses and professionals known for years.

When all these people are scattered to the winds by the demolition of a neighborhood, they have to settle individually in whatever new

---

* Similar principles apply internationally. The principle of the "self-determination of peoples" announced by Woodrow Wilson during the First World War was in fact never *self*-determination. It was instead the determination of the fates of whole peoples by the triumvirate of President Wilson, French Premier Georges Clemenceau and British Prime Minister David Lloyd George— that is, by the victors in the war. Certainly there was no thought that the Irish in Ireland or the Germans in the newly created nation of Czechoslovakia would determine what sovereignty they would live under.

places they can find, where they have no such connections. For businesses that have lost their long-time customers and professionals who have lost long-time clients, these costs can be measured in dollars and cents, while other costs that cannot be quantified may be no less important to those who pay those human costs, despite how easily third-party surrogates can proceed as if those costs do not exist.

If the government had to pay people a price for their property sufficient to compensate them for voluntarily leaving the neighborhood, all those hidden costs would be included in that price. But by the use of compulsion, under the law of eminent domain, those hidden costs have no way of being expressed, as they would be in a free market. Even if the government pays the current market price for all the property it takes, that is clearly not sufficient compensation, for that price was already available to the current owners, and they obviously had not chosen to sell.

Similarly, those who want to see more women working in Silicon Valley cannot know what inescapable costs must be weighed by women contemplating the prospect of working there. These costs may be especially high for women who have young children to care for, and who know that not being there when their child happens to need them cannot be made up by arranging "quality time" after work, despite how much such glib rhetoric may sound good to others.

Women who are either mothers, or contemplating becoming mothers, also know that interrupting their career for a few years, due to child-rearing responsibilities— in a place like Silicon Valley, where fast-moving technological changes can leave them far behind when they later return to work— may not be a promising career prospect in the long run. In a freely competitive labor market, the amount of pay required to compensate some women for all such considerations might be well in excess of what it makes sense to pay anyone for the particular job to be done.

Even aside from the problems inherent in getting human costs, known only to those who have those costs, reflected when voluntary market transactions are replaced by compulsion from third-party surrogate decision-makers, there is the more fundamental question of why attempts to foster economic or other progress must take the form of eliminating "gaps" between groups. Is it of no consequence if everyone's income, education and life expectancy double over some span of time, even if that necessarily increases the gaps?

Why should eliminating gaps be the goal when different individuals and groups do not *want* the same things, or do not have the same priorities or urgencies about these gaps? Why should the gross "under-representation" of Asian Americans in professional basketball be a "gap" to be closed, if Asian Americans do not have nearly as much interest in that sport as black Americans have? Why should the "under-representation" of women in chess clubs or men in nursing be a gap to be closed? The process goal of preventing biased decision-making from arbitrarily closing off opportunities is an understandable goal. Creating a tableau to match the preconceptions of a vision is something very different.

People who depict markets as cold, impersonal institutions, and their own notions as humane and compassionate, have it directly backwards. It is when people make their own economic decisions, taking into account costs that matter to themselves, and known only to themselves, that this knowledge becomes part of the trade-offs they choose, whether as consumers or producers.

Much of the difference between those who promote process goals and those who promote outcome goals seems to reflect differences in how they conceive what knowledge is, and whether relevant knowledge is concentrated in a few or widely diffused among the many. Such knowledge includes knowledge of costs. Whatever the amount of socially consequential information that is known to surrogate decision-makers, no given decision-maker is likely to know more than a small fraction of what is necessary to know, in order to make the best decisions for a whole society. That can be a much more serious problem when prescribing outcome goals than when prescribing process goals.

John Stuart Mill saw this problem back in the nineteenth century, when he said, "even if a government were superior in intelligence and knowledge to any single individual in the nation, it must be inferior to all the individuals of the nation taken together."[53] In other words, Mill saw that the consequential knowledge and understanding relevant to making complex social trade-offs is too vast to be known and comprehended by any given individual or any manageably small set of individuals.

Process goals enable decisions incorporating that knowledge to be made through innumerable complex interactions among vast numbers of people who, in the aggregate, have far more consequential and highly specific knowledge than any given surrogate decision-maker, or any small group of surrogate decision-makers, can have.

Innumerable specific considerations which only those individuals involved could know are therefore mobilized in decisions made through complex market interactions linking innumerable transactors, most of whom are not in direct contact with most of the other transactors. But all those factors influence the innumerable transactions linked through prices across the market. "In general, 'the market' is smarter than the smartest of its individual participants," is the way *Wall Street Journal* editor Robert L. Bartley once put it.

To people who conceive of consequential knowledge as concentrated in a highly educated few with high IQs, specifying particular outcome goals for a whole society may seem far more doable than to people who see vast amounts of consequential knowledge as highly diffused among the people at large, in individually unimpressive fragments. It may be virtually impossible for any given individual, or any manageable number of surrogate decision-makers collectively, to take all the factors into account. But where decisions are made by vast numbers of individuals transacting in a marketplace, each with their own fragment of the necessary knowledge of factors to be considered, and all are forced to reach mutually compatible terms, that is when all the knowledge available to all those concerned affects the economic outcome.

Twentieth-century experience with economic central planning, which seemed so promising before it was tried, led ultimately to its being scaled back or abandoned, even by socialist and communist governments around the world, who eventually decided to allow more economic decisions to be made through market processes. In many countries, including notably India and China, the decision to allow freer markets led to significantly higher economic growth rates and striking reductions in poverty rates.[54]

This is a remarkable— almost impossible— outcome, if relevant knowledge is as concentrated as the prevailing social vision assumes. How could taking major economic decisions out of the hands of trained experts— armed with superior knowledge and vast amounts of data, and backed by the power of government— lead to higher economic growth rates when key economic decisions are transferred to millions of ordinary people lacking all these qualifications and competing in an uncontrolled market? Yet this result has been found in many other countries besides India and China.[55]

The clash of these very different kinds of goals is fought out on many fronts, involving a wide variety of issues. Controversies over whether minimum wage laws make the poor better off or worse off, for example, are meaningful only within the context of priorities set by third-party surrogates. During the Progressive era in the early twentieth century, Progressives who accepted the proposition that minimum wage laws priced low-skilled workers out of jobs were not at all deterred by that prospect, for the Progressives of that era specifically welcomed that outcome, especially when the low-skilled workers displaced were non-white.[56] That was what would fit the particular tableau they sought in that era.

If the costs and benefits of low-paying jobs were to be weighed by the low-skilled and inexperienced workers themselves, there would be no argument for having minimum wage laws in the first place. Similarly with other policies in which third parties specify outcomes, rather than promoting processes in which outcomes are systemic results of trade-offs made individually by those experiencing both benefits and costs within the framework of a process.

Given the fallibility of human beings in general, the role of feedback— that is, *consequential* feedback, as distinguished from simply information— can be crucial in any kind of decision-making process. The feedback from process goals is inescapable for those who directly experience the costs and benefits of their own decisions, while adverse experiences for those directly affected can be ignored, rationalized or obfuscated by third-party surrogates reluctant to admit it to others, and perhaps even to themselves, when their decisions have made matters worse.

In short, outcome-specific goals mean third-party preemption of other people's decisions about their own lives. What is remarkable is how seldom a basis for that preemption is specified. In an earlier era, the divine right of kings was cited as a justification for surrogate decision-making on issues ranging from work to religion. Today, the burden of justification is often put on those individuals whose desire to make decisions about their own lives is seen as claims for a special *exemption* from third-party supervision. As philosopher Thomas Nagel characterized this argument, the fact that one's socioeconomic benefits are not all due to one's own personal merits means that there is no "moral sanctity" about the current distribution of those benefits.[57]

In other words, because no individual was solely responsible for that individual's benefits, therefore politicians, bureaucrats and judges— that is, the government, Rawls' "society" which can "arrange" things— are to preempt decisions and redistribute benefits, presumably in a more moral way. But no burden of proof of either superior morality or superior efficiency in government is required for this preemption. The brazen non sequitur— that if "you didn't build that"[58] it is something the government is justified in taking over— is a fitting companion to the invincible fallacy that people tend to have comparable outcomes in the absence of biased treatment.

Take away both the invincible fallacy and the brazen non sequitur— and the prevailing social vision loses much, if not most, of its foundation. Such terms as "social justice" or "the common good" may be invoked by those with the prevailing vision, but it is not the common people who are to determine what is "the common good." That decision is reserved for third-party surrogates. Louis XIV said, "L'état c'est moi" (I am the state); today's income redistributionists say "social justice" or "the common good." But it all means essentially the same thing in decision-making terms— third-party compulsion to preempt individual choices.

Nor are the supposed beneficiaries of these supposedly more enlightened policies even to be presented with the choice as to how much of their own freedom they are prepared to give up in exchange for the presumed benefits of government policies. On the contrary, that trade-off itself is concealed by redefining words, so that the presumed benefits of government policies have been depicted as a "new freedom," verbally banishing consideration of the trade-off of freedom for government-promised benefits.

What is remarkable is not simply surrogates' preemption of other people's decisions about their own lives, by simply putting the burden of proof on those who wish to be exempted from this preemption, but that the prerogatives of the surrogates have no time limit nor revocation conditions, either explicit or implicit.

People who admit that race-based "affirmative action" has been counterproductive, for example, nevertheless advocate affirmative action based on poverty or some other socioeconomic criteria.[59] The fact that their policies have already inflicted decades of racial strife, polarization and lasting bitterness— among both the ostensible beneficiaries and those who resent the preferences given to the ostensible beneficiaries[60]— leaves those who orchestrated this policy undaunted in seeking to continue exercising their preemptive prerogatives. The boldness of their presumptions contrasts sharply with their suppression of relevant data[61] and the silencing and demonizing of those with different views, instead of answering their arguments.

"SOCIAL JUSTICE"

Much of what is said in the name of "social justice" implicitly assumes three things: (1) the seemingly invincible fallacy that various groups would be equally successful in the absence of biased treatment by others, (2) the cause of disparate outcomes can be determined by where statistics showing the unequal outcomes were collected, and (3) if the more fortunate people were not completely responsible for their own good fortune, then the government— politicians, bureaucrats and judges— will produce either efficiently better or morally superior outcomes by intervening.

When we look at facts in the real world, we repeatedly find skewed distributions of outcomes, whether among human beings or in nature. But, when we look at social visions or political agendas, we find equal outcomes to be the prevailing presumption, and the norm to be imposed by government policies when that presumption is not met. If some social categories of people are not equally represented in particular occupations, institutions or income brackets, that is regarded as someone's fault that the supposedly natural equality of outcomes has been thwarted. This is the seemingly invincible fallacy behind much that is said and done.

There is a fundamental asymmetry in burdens of proof. No matter how much empirical evidence of skewed distributions of outcomes is presented as evidence against the invincible fallacy, there is no corresponding burden of proof on the other side to present even a single example of the equal representation of various social groups in any given endeavor. In what country, or in what kind of endeavor, or in what century out of the vast millennia of human history, has there ever been a proportional representation of various groups in any activity where people have been free to compete? One can read reams of arguments that statistical disparities imply biased treatment without finding a single empirical example of the even distribution of social groups in any endeavor, in any country or in any period of history.

Equally missing in most "social justice" arguments for a redistribution of wealth is the question of the extent to which such a redistribution is actually possible, in any comprehensive, long-term sense. Certainly there have been many examples of times and places where money or other physical wealth has been confiscated by governments or looted by mobs. But physical wealth is a product of human capital— the knowledge, skills, talents and other qualities that exist inside the heads of people— *where it cannot be confiscated.*

Confiscating physical wealth for the purpose of redistribution is confiscating something that will be used up over time, and cannot be replaced without the human capital that created it. Nor is human capital itself easily created by third-party decision-makers. While it is possible to hire teachers and buy books, it is not possible to purchase a cultural past that will prepare and orient all people toward the acquisition of the skills, habits and attitudes that are decisive for human capital.

Over the centuries, many countries have confiscated the physical wealth created by the human capital of productive people. Where the confiscated physical wealth was owned by foreign investors, this process has often been called "nationalization" and celebrated as a patriotic triumph over foreign "exploitation." Where the confiscated physical capital belonged to productive domestic groups, similar rationales have been used, often leading to an exit of many such people from the country, whether fleeing from aroused mobs or as a result of adverse actions by governments— sometimes including mass expulsions.

In any case, the net result has often been such people's arrival as destitute refugees in some other country. Meanwhile, the consequences in their country of origin have often included economic decline after people with much human capital were gone. Examples would include the collapse of Uganda's economy after Asians were expelled in the 1970s and the economic rise of the Asian refugees in Britain, where many of them fled.[62] Refugees who fled Cuba after the Communist takeover in the mid-twentieth century likewise arrived in the United States destitute and survived by taking low-level, poorly paid jobs. But, in later years, the total revenue of Cuban-owned businesses in the United States exceeded the total revenue of the nation of Cuba.[63]

Variations on this theme can be found in many times and places. These would include the Jews expelled from Spain in the late fifteenth century, and forced to leave their physical wealth behind, but who rose again to prosperity in the Netherlands, contributing in the process to the economy of the Netherlands.[64] Huguenot refugees, fleeing France in the sixteenth and seventeenth centuries, made Switzerland the leading watch-making country in the world.[65] Expelling the vast majority of Germans from Czechoslovakia at the end of World War II left the Sudetenland region where they had been concentrated still economically stricken, decades later.[66] Similar or worse devastations followed the driving of white farmers out of Zimbabwe, in the late twentieth century.[67]

Despite how persuasive the words of John Rawls and other "social justice" advocates may be in the world of words, demonstrated facts in the world of reality raise the crucial question as to whether the redistribution of income or wealth can actually be done, in any comprehensive and sustainable sense. Where, instead, there is simply a humanitarian desire to see the less fortunate have better prospects for a better life, the "social justice" argument is both unnecessary and an impediment to joining forces toward that end with others who do not happen to share the implicit assumptions of that particular social vision.

The undeniable fact that *life* has never been remotely "fair"— in the sense of presenting equal likelihoods of achieving economic prosperity or other benefits— has led many people to conclude that *human* biases are the reason. There is no question that human biases have contributed to unfair prospects. But it is a complete non sequitur to say that human biases are the sole, or even primary, causes of unequal prospects, without hard evidence to support that conclusion.

When there are major disparities in outcomes among men who are all in the top one percent in IQ, and among siblings raised under the same roof, as well as discriminated-against minorities being more economically successful than those discriminating against them— as has happened in the Ottoman Empire, many Southeast Asian countries, and much of Eastern Europe, for example— the insistence on believing that human biases are the primary cause of disparities in outcomes ignores a vast range of evidence to the contrary.

This is not to say that nothing can be done to offer more people more opportunities. Much has already been done, and much can and will be done. But *how* it is done can be either helpful or harmful, depending on how well we understand and deal with the world as it is, rather than according to some vision that might seem more attractive, for whatever reason.

Despite the inability to confiscate and redistribute human capital, nevertheless human capital is— ironically— one of the few things that can be spread to others without those with it having any less remaining for themselves. But one of the biggest obstacles to this happening is the "social justice" vision, in which the fundamental problem of the less fortunate is not an absence of sufficient human capital, but the presence of other people's malevolence. For some, abandoning that vision would mean abandoning a moral melodrama, starring themselves as crusaders against the forces of evil. How many are prepared to give up all that— with all its psychic, political and other rewards— is an open question.

THE PAST AND THE FUTURE

Looking back over the centuries of human history, there is much to inspire and much to appall. As for the future, all that we can be certain of is that it is coming, whether we are well-prepared or ill-prepared for it.

Perhaps the most heartening things about the past are the innumerable examples of whole peoples who lagged far behind their contemporaries at a given time and yet, in later times, overtook them and moved to the forefront of human achievements.

These would include Britons, who were an illiterate tribal people in the ancient world, while the ancient Greeks and Romans were laying the intellectual and material foundations of Western civilization. Yet, more than a millennium later, it was the Britons who led the world into the industrial revolution.

At various times and places, China and the Islamic world were more advanced than Europe, and later fell behind, while Japan rose from poverty and backwardness in the middle of the nineteenth century to the forefront of economic and technological achievements in the twentieth century. Jews, who had played little or no role in the revolutionary emergence of science and technology in the early modern era, later produced a wholly disproportionate share of all the scientists who won Nobel Prizes in the twentieth century.

Among the many appalling things about the past, it is hard to know which was the worst, since there are all too many candidates, from around the world, for that designation. That something like the Holocaust could have happened, after thousands of years of civilization, and in one of the most advanced societies, is almost as incomprehensible intellectually as it is devastating morally and in terms of showing what depths of depravity are possible in *all* human beings. It is a painful reminder of a description of civilization as "a thin crust over a volcano."

If longevity and universality are criteria, then slavery must be among the leading candidates for the most appalling of all human institutions, for it existed around the world, for thousands of years, as far back as the history of the human species goes. Yet its full scope is often grossly under-estimated today, when slavery is so often discussed as if it were confined to one race enslaving another race, when in fact slavery existed virtually wherever it was feasible for some human beings to enslave other human beings— including in many, if not most, cases people of their own race.[68] This was as true in Europe and Asia as it was in Africa, or in the Western Hemisphere before Columbus' ships ever appeared on the horizon.

Despite how widely condemned slavery is today, the painful fact is that it reigned virtually unchallenged, prior to the eighteenth century, even though there were challenges to the abuse of slaves, or to the enslavement of particular peoples. But the institution itself was accepted as a fact of life— another disturbing reflection on human nature in all its branches— even among leading philosophers and religious leaders. Christian monasteries in Europe and Buddhist monasteries in Asia both had slaves.[69]

It was not until the eighteenth century that a serious movement arose to advocate abolishing the whole institution of slavery— and, at that point, this was a development solely within Western civilization and initially only among a minority there. Anti-slavery views remained largely confined to Western societies in the next century, and slaves continued to be bought and sold in the Ottoman Empire, among other places, after slavery had been abolished in all Western nations.

SIDEBAR: THE SCOPE AND DURATION OF SLAVERY

Many people may not be aware that the first century which began with slavery having already been abolished in most of the world was the *twentieth* century— and that remnants of slavery have remained, on into the twenty-first century.[70] Yet a well-known American economist called slavery America's "original sin" at its founding.[71] But there was nothing original about slavery in 1776, when Adam Smith wrote that Western Europe was the only place in the world where slavery had been completely abolished[72]— which of course did not prevent Western Europeans from owning slaves in the Western Hemisphere. Recognizing slavery as a virtually universal curse of the human race is very different from depicting it as more narrowly localized, in keeping with current visions and current agendas.

Europeans enslaved other Europeans for centuries before Europeans brought the first African slaves— most purchased from other Africans, who had enslaved them— to the Western Hemisphere. Nor was it unknown for Europeans to be enslaved by non-Europeans. Just one example were the European slaves brought to the coast of North Africa by Barbary Coast pirates. These European slaves were more numerous than the African slaves brought to the United States and to the American colonies from which it was formed.[73]

Other pirates made such widespread slave raids along the Mediterranean and Adriatic coasts of Europe that numerous watchtowers were built in those places, so that coastal peoples could be warned and flee when pirate ships were seen approaching. There were more than a hundred such watchtowers on the island of Sicily alone.[74]

The confining of discussions of slavery to that of blacks held in bondage by whites is just one of the many ways in which the agendas of the present distort our understanding of the past, forfeiting valuable lessons that an unfiltered knowledge of the past could teach. At a minimum, the worldwide history of slavery should be a grim warning for all people, and for all time, against giving any human beings unbridled power over other human beings, regardless of how attractively that unbridled power might be packaged rhetorically.

It was the twentieth century— the first century after slavery had been nearly eradicated around the world— that saw a new form of brutal human bondage arise, with the creation of totalitarian dictatorships that collectively killed tens of millions of their own people in peacetime during that century, and made life a nightmare for many who survived.

The last Western nation to end slavery (Brazil) did so in 1888, and the first totalitarian dictatorship arose in Russia in 1917. There was barely a generation between the suppression of one form of monumentally brutal subjugation of human beings and the creation of another. Yet these dehumanizing dictatorships were often founded on stirring rhetoric and lofty visions that resonated with many leading intellectuals in countries around the world. There could hardly be a clearer example of the need for the historic warning: "Eternal vigilance is the price of liberty."

As Edmund Burke said, more than two centuries ago, "In history a great volume is unrolled for our instruction, drawing the materials of future wisdom from past errors and infirmities of mankind." But he warned that the past could also be a means of "keeping alive, or reviving, dissensions and animosities."[75]

It is in this second sense that history is too often taught today,* under the banner of "social justice," and using the same toxic mixture of heady rhetoric and heedless visions that led to such monumental tragedies in the totalitarian dictatorships of the twentieth century.

After territorial irredentism has led nations to slaughter each other's people over land that might have little or no value in itself, simply because it once belonged in a different political jurisdiction, at a time beyond any living person's memory, what is to be expected from instilling the idea of *social* irredentism, growing out of historic wrongs done to people long dead?

Such wrongs abound in times and places around the world— inflicted on, and perpetrated by, people of virtually every race, creed and color. But what can any society today hope to gain by having newborn babies in that society enter the world as heirs to prepackaged

---

*   Any who doubt this can read Howard Zinn's *A People's History of the United States*, and reflect on the fact that it has been one of the most widely used textbooks in America— having sold more than two and a half million copies in North America as of 2015. Howard Zinn, *A People's History of the United States* (New York: Harper Perennial, 2015), p. xviii.

grievances against other babies born into that same society on the same day?

Nothing that we can do today can undo the many evils and catastrophes of the past, but we can at least learn from them, and not repeat the mistakes of the past, many of which began with lofty-sounding goals. Obvious as all this might seem, it is too often forgotten. Nothing that Germans can do today will in any way mitigate the staggering evils of what Hitler did in the past. Nor can apologies in America today for slavery in the past have any meaning, much less do any good, for either blacks or whites today. What can it mean for *A* to apologize for what *B* did, even among contemporaries, much less across the vast chasm between the living and the dead?

The only times over which we have any degree of influence at all are the present and the future— both of which can be made worse by attempts at symbolic restitution among the living for what happened among the dead, who are far beyond our power to help or punish or avenge. Galling as these restrictive facts may be, that does not stop them from being facts beyond our control. Pretending to have powers that we do not in fact have risks creating needless evils in the present, while claiming to deal with the evils of the past.

Any serious consideration of the world as it is around us today must tell us that maintaining common decency, much less peace and harmony, among living contemporaries is a major challenge, both among nations and within nations. To admit that we can do nothing about what happened among the dead is not to give up the struggle for a better world, but to concentrate our efforts where they have at least some hope of making things better for the living.

Acknowledgements

This late in human history, it is hard to imagine how anyone can write a book on any serious subject without standing on the shoulders of giants, whether giants of the present or of the distant past. In addition to the many writings cited in the footnotes and endnotes of this book, there have been many other writings and other sources of insights that provided a background of historical, geographic and economic knowledge, without which there would have been no basis for the particular research and analysis that enabled me to "cross-examine the facts," as the great economist Alfred Marshall defined the goal of economic analysis.

The importance of background knowledge especially needs emphasizing in an era when many educators argue that their students need not study mere facts, because facts can be looked up as needed, whether in reference books or on the Internet. But without a general background knowledge of such basic things as history, science and economics, students would have no basis for knowing which facts would be relevant to an issue at hand, and therefore necessary to look up.

Nothing seems more fundamental than the settings in which events took place— including the various times, places and circumstances in which the human species traveled the long road from the prehistoric world to the very different world of today. My interest in the particular kinds of geographic settings in which particular peoples evolved economically and culturally goes back several decades but my discovery of two scholars' monumental treatises on this subject was a special revelation that added new dimensions, going far beyond the technical facts found in textbooks for people studying to become geographers.

The oldest and most comprehensive of these landmark books was *Influences of Geographic Environment* by Ellen Churchill Semple. No one can read that sweeping, and yet finely detailed, book with its long chapters on economic and social patterns found among many island peoples around the world, and different patterns found among peoples in various kinds of mountain environments, coastal environments and others, and come away believing that nature provided equal opportunity for all. Nor can one read that 1911 book and accept the geographic determinism which was rampant during that era, and which Professor Semple both avoided and repudiated.[1] What she advanced— and documented extensively— were certain geographic and social patterns that existed "regardless of race or epoch."[2] The word "Influences" in the title was aptly chosen.[3]

A more geographically confined and differently organized series of monumental books by Professor N.J.G. Pounds bore the general title *An Historical Geography of Europe*, with each book in that series covering a different era in the development of that particular civilization— a civilization containing within itself many very different geographic settings and historical circumstances. It is an economic, as well as a geographic history. When Professor Pounds noted that "economic growth in Europe was a highly localised phenomenon"[4] and that fossil fuels "were notably absent from southern Europe,"[5] limiting where an industrial revolution was possible, such facts were yet another contrast with today's implicit assumptions that all would have equal outcomes if it were not for biased treatment or genetic deficiencies.

In addition to providing important context for understanding the unfolding of historic events, both worldwide geographic scholarship and scholarship concentrated on particular regions of the world— whether Western Europe, Southeast Asia or Latin America— are part of a background education sorely needed in our schools and colleges today. Many social "problems" and their "solutions" look very different when they are seen in terms of the inherent constraints of geographic or social circumstances, and the utter impossibility of changing the past.

There is something refreshing, and even redemptive, in the writings of old-fashioned scholars who devoted a lifetime to producing classic works on one aspect of the human condition, so that those who came after them would have some serious background of knowledge and understanding for proceeding to deal with particular issues of later times. Too much contemporary writing seems to start with a currently prevailing conclusion and working backward to seek evidence supporting that conclusion.

Among the conceptual landmark writings that formed the background for developing the particular analytical framework for *Discrimination and Disparities*, the work of Gary Becker on the economics of discrimination will be apparent to economists, though his insights and revelations have yet to become part of most current discussions and controversies on economic disparities. Many such discussions and controversies remain fruitless without Professor Becker's insights of more than half a century ago that remain still unknown to most of our contemporaries, groping in a world of words and visions.

Among factual studies, the pathbreaking research of sociologist E. Franklin Frazier, beginning with his studies of black ghettos in Chicago and New York in the first half of the twentieth century, is a model of the clarity, insights and honesty in discussions of racial issues that are all too rare among later writings on the subject.

Other examples of that kind of scholarship, clarity, insights and honesty can be found in the writings of Stephan and Abigail Thernstrom, especially in their landmark study, *America in Black and White*, from which much can still be learned— and needs to be learned— today, more than two decades after it was written. Their work cut through a jungle of misinformation and misconceptions by the intelligentsia, leaving a clearer path for those seeking knowledge and understanding, rather than politically correct rhetoric.

More recent writings that offer great insights into economic disparities, "social justice" visions and social degeneration in America include two landmark books that are not about America, but about similar developments in other countries— *Life at the Bottom* by Theodore Dalrymple (about England) and *The Welfare of Nations* by James Bartholomew (about welfare states in the Western world in general).

Dr. Dalrymple's deep insights, based on first-hand experience as a physician in a hospital in a low-income neighborhood in London, and as a physician serving prison inmates, are a truly masterful account of what he has learned, which goes so counter to much contemporary rhetoric and illusions. It is a compelling complement to the fact-filled empirical study of welfare states by James Bartholomew.

Reading either or both these books can be a liberation, as well as a revelation, for many Americans— especially those made uneasy by discussions of the same issues in the United States, where any mention of problems originating among the less fortunate themselves can be stigmatized as unconscious racism, when so many of the less fortunate are members of racial minorities. In Britain and various other Western nations, however, the underclass is predominantly white, and the very same social patterns seen there can be seen for what they are, without the distraction of the "white guilt" in America, so insightfully analyzed in the writings of Shelby Steele, beginning with his own landmark book, *The Content of Our Character*.

The parochialism of those educators who want to discuss contemporary American problems as if they were unique to America, and thus make the education of minority students be "relevant" to such students, forfeits vast amounts of evidence from around the world and across centuries of history that could be enlightening when we see ourselves as integral parts of the great and somber human tapestry.

One small but revealing episode that comes to mind in this regard involved a black student at Brandeis University, back in the 1960s, who came to my office to discuss some issues that he was wrestling with. I handed him an account of a brief but fierce encounter between Karl Marx and a young German Communist, back in the 1840s. After reading it, he exclaimed: "We had that same argument last week in the Black Students Union!" We can only hope that this helped open his mind to a wider world in general.

In a time when mind-opening writings are especially needed, if only to counter the mind-closing trends in so many academic institutions, the books, articles and syndicated columns of Professor Walter E. Williams of George Mason University are a treasure, and *Discrimination and Disparities* draws on some of those treasures, especially his fact-filled primer *Race and Economics* and his unique study of the economic forces at work under apartheid in South Africa, *South Africa's War Against Capitalism*.

Other mind-opening books, in a mind-closing time, that have been drawn upon in the writing of this book would include a monumental treatise on international trends in violence over the centuries, *The Better Angels of Our Nature* by Professor Steven Pinker of Harvard. His account of how centuries of progress in the reduction of violence suddenly reversed— internationally— in the 1960s is a painful contrast to many glib and sweeping celebrations of that decade.

Among people closer at hand whose help made this book possible are my wife Mary, whose critiques and suggestions— along with those of my friends Joseph Charney and Stephen Camarata— were valuable contributions. All three have both the insights and the candor essential to constructive commentaries. The whole enterprise would have been all but impossible, especially at my advanced age, without the dedicated work of my assistants of many years, Na Liu and Elizabeth Costa. The institutional support of the Hoover Institution and the Stanford University libraries has also been indispensable.

In the end, however, none of these can be held responsible for my conclusions or for any errors or shortcomings that may appear. For all these I must take sole responsibility.

Thomas Sowell
The Hoover Institution
Stanford University

Notes

PREFACE

1   Alan Greenspan, *The Age of Turbulence: Adventures in a New World* (New York: Penguin Press, 2007), p. 95.

EPIGRAPH

Fernand Braudel, *A History of Civilizations*, translated by Richard Mayne (New York: The Penguin Press, 1994), p. 17.

Chapter 1: DISPARITIES AND PREREQUISITES

1   A sharp reduction in the probability of success, when there are multiple factors required in a given endeavor, even when the prerequisites are few and common, is just one of the things making equality of outcomes less likely. Other factors may be influences without being prerequisites, and yet the increased multiplicity of factors— both prerequisites and other influences— increases the number of possible combinations and permutations affecting outcomes, thereby reducing the likelihood of equality of successful outcomes. A concrete example of an influence that is not a prerequisite is that being left-handed is an advantage for a baseball player who is playing first base. Even though there have been a number of right-handed first basemen who have been excellent fielders, nevertheless left-handers have tended to be over-represented among first basemen.

2   The chances of having one, two, three, four or five of the prerequisites may be normally distributed, as in a bell curve, but the outcomes will not be. If the distribution of outcomes is plotted on a graph, with the number of prerequisites measured on the horizontal axis and successful outcomes measured on the vertical axis, all those people with one, two, three and four of the prerequisites will have zero successes, represented by a line that coincides with the horizontal axis. At five prerequisites, this line will rise at right angles to the horizontal axis, representing various degrees of success. This is clearly nothing like a bell curve.

3   *World Illiteracy At Mid-Century: A Statistical Study* (Paris: United Nations Educational, Scientific and Cultural Organization, 1957), p. 15.

4   As of 1940, just under half of the women in the Terman group were employed full time. Lewis M. Terman, et al., *The Gifted Child Grows Up: Twenty-Five Years' Follow-Up of a Superior Group* (Stanford: Stanford University Press, 1947), p. 177.

5   Malcolm Gladwell, *Outliers: The Story of Success* (New York: Little, Brown and Company, 2008), p. 111.

6   Ibid., pp. 89–90. See also Joel N. Shurkin, *Terman's Kids: The Groundbreaking Study of How the Gifted Grow Up* (Boston: Little, Brown & Company, 1992), p. 35; Wolfgang Saxon "William B. Shockley, 79, Creator of Transistor and Theory on Race," *New York Times*, August 14, 1989, p. D9; J.Y. Smith; "Luis Alvarez, Nobel-Winning Atomic Physicist, Dies," *Washington Post*, September 3, 1988, p. B6.

7   Malcolm Gladwell, *Outliers*, pp. 111–112.

8   Ibid., p. 112.

9   Distinguished economist Richard Rosett was another example. See Thomas Sowell, *The Einstein Syndrome: Bright Children Who Talk Late* (New York: Basic Books, 2001), pp. 47–48. The best-selling author of *Hillbilly Elegy* was another. See J.D. Vance, *Hillbilly Elegy: A Memoir of a Family and Culture in Crisis* (New York: HarperCollins, 2016) pp. 2, 129–130, 205, 239.

10   Charles Murray, *Human Accomplishment: The Pursuit of Excellence in the Arts and Sciences, 800 B.C. to 1950* (New York: HarperCollins, 2003), pp. 98–99.

11   Ibid., p. 99.

12   James Corrigan, "Woods in the Mood to End His Major Drought," *The Daily Telegraph* (London), August 5, 2013, pp. 16–17.

13   Charles Murray, *Human Accomplishment*, p. 102.

14   Ibid., pp. 355–361.

15   John K. Fairbank and Edwin O. Reischauer, *China: Tradition & Transformation* (Boston: Houghton Mifflin, 1978), p. 17.

16   William D. Altus, "Birth Order and Its Sequelae," *Science*, Vol. 151 (January 7, 1966), p. 45.

17   Ibid.

18   Julia M. Rohrer, Boris Egloff, and Stefan C. Schmukle, "Examining the Effects of Birth Order on Personality," *Proceedings of the National Academy of Sciences*, Vol. 112, No. 46 (November 17, 2015), p. 14225. These differences in median IQs are not necessarily large. However, even modest differences in *median* IQs can translate into large disparities in the representation of different groups at IQs of 120 and above— which are the kinds of IQs found among people in elite occupations that attract major attention. Most observers are far less interested in what kinds of people qualify to work behind the counter of fast-food restaurants than they are in what kinds of people are qualified to work in chemistry labs or as engineers or physicians.

19   Lillian Belmont and Francis A. Marolla, "Birth Order, Family Size, and Intelligence," *Science*, Vol. 182, No. 4117 (December 14, 1973), p. 1098.

20   Sandra E. Black, Paul J. Devereux and Kjell G. Salvanes, "Older and Wiser? Birth Order and IQ of Young Men," *CESifo Economic Studies*, Vol. 57, 1/2011, pp. 103–120.

21   Lillian Belmont and Francis A. Marolla, "Birth Order, Family Size, and Intelligence," *Science*, Vol. 182, No. 4117 (December 14, 1973), pp. 1096–1097; Sandra E. Black, Paul J. Devereux and Kjell G. Salvanes, "Older and Wiser?

Birth Order and IQ of Young Men," *CESifo Economic Studies*, Vol. 57, 1/2011, p. 109.

22 Sidney Cobb and John R.P. French, Jr., "Birth Order Among Medical Students," *Journal of the American Medical Association*, Vol. 195, No. 4 (January 24, 1966), pp. 172–173.

23 William A. Layman and Andrew Saueracker, "Birth Order and Sibship Size of Medical School Applicants," *Social Psychiatry*, Vol. 13 (1978), pp. 117–123.

24 William D. Altus, "Birth Order and Its Sequelae," *Science*, Vol. 151 (January 7, 1966), pp. 44–49. See also Robert S. Albert, "The Achievement of Eminence: A Longitudinal Study of Exceptionally Gifted Boys and Their Families," *Beyond Terman: Contemporary Longitudinal Studies of Giftedness and Talent*, edited by Rena F. Subotnik and Karen D. Arnold (Norwood, New Jersey: Ablex Publishing Corporation, 1994), p. 293.

25 Alison L. Booth and Hiau Joo Kee, "Birth Order Matters: The Effect of Family Size and Birth Order on Educational Attainment," *Journal of Population Economics*, Vol. 22, No. 2 (April 2009), p. 377.

26 Robert J. Gary-Bobo, Ana Prieto and Natalie Picard, "Birth Order and Sibship Sex Composition as Instruments in the Study of Education and Earnings," Discussion Paper No. 5514 (February 2006), Centre for Economic Policy Research, London, p. 22.

27 Jere R. Behrman and Paul Taubman, "Birth Order, Schooling, and Earnings," *Journal of Labor Economics*, Vol. 4, No. 3, Part 2: The Family and the Distribution of Economic Rewards (July 1986), p. S136.

28 Philip S. Very and Richard W. Prull, "Birth Order, Personality Development, and the Choice of Law as a Profession," *Journal of Genetic Psychology*, Vol. 116, No. 2 (June 1, 1970), pp. 219–221.

29 Richard L. Zweigenhaft, "Birth Order, Approval-Seeking and Membership in Congress," *Journal of Individual Psychology*, Vol. 31, No. 2 (November 1975), p. 208.

30 *Astronauts and Cosmonauts: Biographical and Statistical Data*, Revised August 31, 1993, Report Prepared by the Congressional Research Service, Library of Congress, Transmitted to the Committee on Science, Space, and Technology, U.S. House of Representatives, One Hundred Third Congress, Second Session, March 1994 (Washington: U.S. Government Printing Office, 1994), p. 19.

31 Daniel S.P. Schubert, Mazie E. Wagner, and Herman J.P. Schubert, "Family Constellation and Creativity: Firstborn Predominance Among Classical Music Composers," *The Journal of Psychology*, Vol. 95, No. 1 (1977), pp. 147–149.

32 Arthur R. Jensen, *Genetics and Education* (New York: Harper & Row, 1972), p. 143.

33 R.G. Record, Thomas McKeown and J.H. Edwards, "An Investigation of the Difference in Measured Intelligence between Twins and Single Births," *Annals of Human Genetics*, Vol. 34, Issue 1 (July 1970), pp. 18, 19, 20.

34 "By age 3, the average child of a professional heard about 500,000 encouragements and 80,000 discouragements. For the welfare children, the situation was reversed: they heard, on average, about 75,000 encouragements and 200,000 discouragements." Paul Tough, "What it Takes to Make a Student," *New York Times Magazine*, November 26, 2006, p. 48. See also Betty Hart and Todd R. Risley, *Meaningful Differences in the Everyday Experience of Young American Children* (Baltimore: Paul H. Brookes Publishing Co., 1995), p. 253. See also Edward C. Banfield, *The Unheavenly City: The Nature and Future of Our Urban Crisis* (Boston: Little, Brown, 1970), pp. 224–229.

35 "Choose Your Parents Wisely," *The Economist*, July 26, 2014, p. 22.

36 See, for example, Kay S. Hymowitz, *Marriage and Caste in America: Separate and Unequal Families in a Post-Marital Age* (Chicago: Ivan R. Dee, 2006), pp. 78–82; Betty Hart and Todd R. Risley, *Meaningful Differences in the Everyday Experience of Young American Children*, p. 253; Edward C. Banfield, *The Unheavenly City*, pp. 224–229. It is painful to contemplate the prospects of a child born to a single mother on welfare who has failed to finish high school. Lacking the interactions of a father is not without consequences. "We find that after accounting for parental education, skills, and income, both a father's and a mother's time investment in the first five years of a child's life have a large effect on the child's completed education." George-Levi Gayle, Limor Golan, and Mrhmet A. Soytas, "Intergenerational Mobility and the Effects of Parental Education, Time Investment, and Income on Children's Educational Attainment," *Federal Reserve Bank of St. Louis Review*, Volume 100, No. 3 (Third Quarter 2018), p. 292.

37 For examples and a fuller discussion of social mobility see Thomas Sowell, *Wealth, Poverty and Politics*, revised and enlarged edition (New York: Basic Books, 2016), pp. 178–183, 360–375, 382–390.

38 Henry Thomas Buckle, *On Scotland and the Scotch Intellect* (Chicago: University of Chicago Press, 1970), p. 52.

39 Irokawa Daikichi, *The Culture of the Meiji Period*, translated and edited by Marius B. Jansen (Princeton: Princeton University Press, 1985), p. 7.

40 Joel Mokyr, *A Culture of Growth: The Origins of the Modern Economy* (Princeton: Princeton University Press, 2017), p. 256.

41 Steven Beller, "Big-City Jews: Jewish Big City— the Dialectics of Jewish Assimilation in Vienna, *c.* 1900," *The City in Central Europe: Culture and Society from 1800 to the Present*, edited by Malcolm Gee, Tim Kirk and Jill Steward (Brookfield, Vermont: Ashgate Publishing, Ltd., 1999), p. 150.

42 Charles Murray, *Human Accomplishment*, pp. 280, 282.

43 Charles O. Hucker, *China's Imperial Past: An Introduction to Chinese History and Culture* (Stanford: Stanford University Press, 1975), p. 65; Jacques Gernet, *A History of Chinese Civilization*, second edition, translated by J.R. Foster and Charles Hartman (New York: Cambridge University Press, 1996), p. 69.

44 David S. Landes, *The Wealth and Poverty of Nations: Why Some Are So Rich and Some So Poor* (New York: W.W. Norton & Company, 1998), pp. 93–95; William H. McNeill, *The Rise of the West: A History of the Human Community* (Chicago: University of Chicago Press, 1991), p. 526.

45 David S. Landes, *The Wealth and Poverty of Nations*, pp. 94–95.

46 See, for examples, Thomas Sowell, *Wealth, Poverty and Politics*, revised and enlarged edition, especially Part I; Ellen Churchill Semple, *Influences of Geographic Environment* (New York: Henry Holt and Company, 1911), pp. 144, 175, 397, 530, 531, 599, 600. By contrast, she refers to "the cosmopolitan civilization characteristic of coastal regions." Ibid., p. 347.

47 Andrew Tanzer, "The Bamboo Network," *Forbes*, July 18, 1994, pp. 138–144; "China: Seeds of Subversion," *The Economist*, May 28, 1994, p. 32.

48 Richard Rhodes, *The Making of the Atomic Bomb* (New York: Simon & Schuster, 1986), pp. 13, 106, 188–189, 305–314; Silvan S. Schweber, *Einstein and Oppenheimer: The Meaning of Genius* (Cambridge, Massachusetts: Harvard University Press, 2008), p. 138; Michio Kaku, *Einstein's Cosmos: How Albert Einstein's Vision Transformed Our Understanding of Space and Time* (New York: W.W. Norton, 2004), pp. 187–188; Howard M. Sachar, *A History of the Jews in America* (New York: Alfred A. Knopf, 1992), p. 527; American Jewish Historical Society, *American Jewish Desk Reference* (New York: Random House, 1999), p. 591.

49 Quoted in Bernard Lewis, *The Muslim Discovery of Europe* (New York: W.W. Norton, 1982), p. 139.

50 Giovanni Gavetti, Rebecca Henderson and Simona Giorgi, "Kodak and the Digital Revolution (A)," 9–705–448, Harvard Business School, November 2, 2005, pp. 3, 11.

51 "The Last Kodak Moment?" *The Economist*, January 14, 2012, pp. 63–64.

52 Mike Spector and Dana Mattioli, "Can Bankruptcy Filing Save Kodak?" *Wall Street Journal*, January 20, 2012, p. B1.

53 Henry C. Lucas, Jr., *Inside the Future: Surviving the Technology Revolution* (Westport, Connecticut: Praeger, 2008), p. 157.

54 Giovanni Gavetti, Rebecca Henderson and Simona Giorgi, "Kodak and the Digital Revolution (A)," 9–705–448, Harvard Business School, November 2, 2005, p. 4.

55 Ibid., p. 12.

56 More than half a century before the collapse of Eastman Kodak, economist J.A. Schumpeter pointed out that the most powerful economic competition is not that between producers of the same product, as so often assumed, but the competition between old and new technologies and methods of organization. In the case of Eastman Kodak, it was not the competition of Fuji film, but the competition of digital cameras, that was decisive. For Schumpeter, it was not the competition of firms producing the same products, as in economics textbooks, that was decisive. In Schumpeter's words, "it is not that kind of competition

which counts but the competition from the new commodity, the new technology, the new source of supply, the new type of organization (the largest-scale unit of control, for instance)— competition which commands a decisive cost or quality advantage and which strikes not at the margins of the profits and the outputs of the existing firms but at their foundations and their very lives." Joseph A. Schumpeter, *Capitalism, Socialism, and Democracy*, third edition (New York: Harper & Brothers, 1950), p. 84. Among other examples were the A&P chain of grocery stores that was for years the largest chain of retail stores of any kind, anywhere in the world. Eventually new competitors "competed against A&P not by doing better what A&P was the best company in the world at doing," but by organizing their businesses in very different ways that all but obliterated A&P. Richard S. Tedlow, *New and Improved: The Story of Mass Marketing in America* (New York: Basic Books, 1990), p. 246.

57   Darrell Hess, *McKnight's Physical Geography: A Landscape Appreciation*, eleventh edition (Upper Saddle River, New Jersey: Pearson Education, Inc., 2014), p. 200.

58   *Africa: Atlas of Our Changing Environment* (Nairobi, Kenya: United Nations Environment Programme, 2008), p. 29; Rachel I. Albrecht, Steven J. Goodman, Dennis E. Buechler, Richard J. Blakeslee and Hugh J. Christian, "Where Are the Lightning Hotspots on Earth?" *Bulletin of the American Meteorological Society*, November 2016, p. 2055; *The New Encyclopædia Britannica* (Chicago: Encyclopædia Britannica, Inc., 2005), Volume 3, p. 583.

59   Darrell Hess, *McKnight's Physical Geography*, eleventh edition, p. 198.

60   Alan H. Strahler, *Introducing Physical Geography*, sixth edition (Hoboken, New Jersey: Wiley, 2013), pp. 402–403.

61   Bradley C. Bennett, "Plants and People of the Amazonian Rainforests," *BioScience*, Vol. 42, No. 8 (September 1992), p. 599.

62   Ronald Fraser, "The Amazon," *Great Rivers of the World*, edited by Alexander Frater (Boston: Little, Brown and Company, 1984), p. 111.

63   Karen Kaplan, "Man, Chimp Separated by a Dab of DNA," *Los Angeles Times*, September 1, 2005, p. A12; Rick Weiss, "Scientists Complete Genetic Map of the Chimpanzee," *Washington Post*, September 1, 2005, p. A3; "A Creeping Success," *The Economist*, June 5, 1999, pp. 77–78.

64   David S. Landes, *The Wealth and Poverty of Nations*, p. 6.

65   A.H.M. Jones, *The Later Roman Empire 284–602: A Social and Administrative Survey* (Norman: University of Oklahoma Press, 1964), Volume 2, pp. 841–842.

66   Ellen Churchill Semple, *The Geography of the Mediterranean Region: Its Relation to Ancient History* (New York: Henry Holt and Company, 1931), p. 5.

67   Jack Chen, *The Chinese of America* (San Francisco: Harper & Row Publishers, 1980), pp. 65–66.

68   See, for example, Ellen Churchill Semple, *Influences of Geographic Environment*, pp. 20, 280, 281–282, 347, 521–531, 599, 600; Fernand Braudel, *The Mediterranean and the Mediterranean World in the Age of Philip II*, translated by

Siân Reynolds (Berkeley: University of California Press, 1995), Vol. I, pp. 34, 35; Thomas Sowell, *Wealth, Poverty and Politics*, revised and enlarged edition, pp. 45–54.

69   James S. Gardner, et al., "People in the Mountains," *Mountain Geography: Physical and Human Dimensions*, edited by Martin F. Price, et al (Berkeley: University of California Press, 2013), pp. 288–289; J.R. McNeill, *The Mountains of the Mediterranean World: An Environmental History* (New York: Cambridge University Press, 1992), pp. 223, 225–227; Ellen Churchill Semple, *Influences of Geographic Environment*, pp. 578–579.

70   See, for example, Frederick R. Troeh and Louis M. Thompson, *Soils and Soil Fertility*, sixth edition (Ames, Iowa: Blackwell, 2005), p. 330; Xiaobing Liu, et al., "Overview of Mollisols in the World: Distribution, Land Use and Management," *Canadian Journal of Soil Science*, Vol. 92 (2012), pp. 383–402; Darrel Hess, *McKnight's Physical Geography*, eleventh edition, pp. 362–363.

71   Andrew D. Mellinger, Jeffrey D. Sachs, and John L. Gallup, "Climate, Coastal Proximity, and Development," *The Oxford Handbook of Economic Geography*, edited by Gordon L. Clark, Maryann P. Feldman and Meric S. Gertler (Oxford: Oxford University Press, 2000), p. 169. Nearly a century earlier, a geographic treatise declared that, as a general rule, "the coasts of a country are the first part of it to develop." Ellen Churchill Semple, *Influences of Geographic Environment*, p. 280.

72   See, for documented examples, Thomas Sowell, *Wealth, Poverty and Politics*, revised and enlarged edition, Section I.   See also Ellen Churchill Semple, *Influences of Geographic Environment*,   especially chapters on coastal peoples (VIII), island peoples (XIII), peoples in river valleys (XI) and peoples in hills and mountains around the world (XV and XVI).

73   James S. Gardner, et al., "People in the Mountains," *Mountain Geography*, edited by Martin F. Price, et al., p. 268.

74   The world population in 2014 was 7.2 billion people. The population of the United States that year was 323 million people, while the population of Italy was 61 million people. The Economist, *Pocket World in Figures: 2017 edition* (London: Profile Books, 2016), pp. 14, 240.

75   Edward C. Banfield, *The Moral Basis of a Backward Society* (New York: The Free Press, 1958), pp. 35, 46–47.

76   Fernand Braudel, *A History of Civilizations*, translated by Richard Mayne (New York: The Penguin Press, 1994), p. 17.

77   Donald L. Horowitz, *Ethnic Groups in Conflict* (Berkeley: University of California Press, 1985), p. 677.

78   Myron Weiner, "The Pursuit of Ethnic Equality Through Preferential Policies: A Comparative Public Policy Perspective," *From Independence to Statehood*, edited by Robert B. Goldmann and A. Jeyaratnam Wilson (London: Frances Pinter, 1984), p. 64.

79   Cynthia H. Enloe, *Police, Military and Ethnicity: Foundations of State Power* (New Brunswick: Transaction Books, 1980), p. 143.

80   Angelo M. Codevilla, *The Character of Nations: How Politics Makes and Breaks Prosperity, Family, and Civility* (New York: Basic Books, 1997), p. 50.

81   Charles Murray, *Human Accomplishment*, p. 298.

82   Ibid., pp. 304, 305.

83   U.S. Bureau of the Census data show the median household income of people aged 45 to 54 to be double that of the median household income of people less than 25 years old. But white household income is less than double that of black household income. Kayla Fontenot, Jessica Semega and Melissa Kollar, "Income and Poverty in the United States: 2017," *Current Population Reports*, P60–263 (Washington: U.S. Census Bureau, 2018), Table 1, p. 2. So are median weekly earnings of full-time workers. "Usual Weekly Earnings of Wage and Salary Workers First Quarter 2017," U.S. Bureau of Labor Statistics, U.S. Department of Labor, April 18, 2017, Table 3.

84   See U.S. Census Bureau, S0201, Selected Population Profile in the United States, 2016 American Community Survey 1-Year Estimates, downloaded from the Census website on July 9, 2018: https://factfinder.census.gov/faces/tableservices/jsf/pages/productview.xhtml?pid=ACS_16_1YR_S0201&prodType=table.

85   For documented specifics, see Thomas Sowell, *Intellectuals and Race* (New York: Basic Books, 2013), Chapter 3.

86   Thomas C. Leonard, "Eugenics and Economics in the Progressive Era," *Journal of Economic Perspectives*, Vol. 19, No. 4 (Fall 2005), p. 216.

87   Sidney Webb, "Eugenics and the Poor Law: The Minority Report," *Eugenics Review*, Vol. II (April 1910-January 1911), p. 240; Thomas C. Leonard, "Eugenics and Economics in the Progressive Era," *Journal of Economic Perspectives*, Vol. 19, No. 4 (Fall 2005), p. 216; Richard Overy, *The Twilight Years: The Paradox of Britain Between the Wars* (New York: Viking, 2009), pp. 93, 105, 106, 107, 124–127; Donald MacKenzie, "Eugenics in Britain," *Social Studies of Science*, Vol. 6, No. 3–4 (September 1975), p. 518; Jakob Tanner, "Eugenics Before 1945," *Journal of Modern European History*, Vol. 10, No. 4 (2012), p. 465.

88   For documented specifics, see Thomas Sowell, *Intellectuals and Race*, pp. 29–35.

89   Leon J. Kamin, *The Science and Politics of I.Q.* (New York: John Wiley and Sons, 1974), p. 6.

90   Carl C. Brigham, *A Study of American Intelligence* (Princeton: Princeton University Press, 1923), p. 190.

91   *The World Almanac and Book of Facts: 2013* (New York: World Almanac Books, 2013), p. 335.

92   E.A. Pearce and C.G. Smith, *The Times Books World Weather Guide* (New York: Times Books, 1984), pp. 279, 380, 413.

93   Ibid., pp. 132, 376. In none of the winter months— from December through March— is the average daily low temperature in Washington warmer than in

London, and the lowest temperature ever recorded in Washington is lower for each of those winter months than in London.

94   For documented specifics, see Thomas Sowell, *Wealth, Poverty and Politics*, revised and enlarged edition, pp. 62–64.

95   Steven Pinker, *The Better Angels of Our Nature: Why Violence Has Declined* (New York: Viking, 2011), pp. 85–87.

96   "Solving Murder," *The Economist*, April 7, 2018, p. 9.

Chapter 2: DISCRIMINATION: MEANINGS AND COSTS

1   Harry J. Holzer, Steven Raphael, and Michael A. Stoll, "Perceived Criminality, Criminal Background Checks, and the Racial Hiring Practices of Employers," *Journal of Law and Economics*, Vol. 49, No. 2 (October 2006), pp. 452, 473. See also Gail L. Heriot, "Statement of Commissioner Gail Heriot in the U.S. Commission on Civil Rights' Report, "Assessing the Impact of Criminal Background Checks and the Equal Employment Opportunity Commission Conviction Records Policy," Legal Studies Research Paper Series, Research Paper No. 17–251 (San Diego: University of San Diego Law School, 2013); Jennifer L. Doleac and Benjamin Hansen, "The Unintended Consequences of 'Ban the Box': Statistical Discrimination and Employment Outcomes When Criminal Histories Are Hidden," Social Science Research Network, last revised August 22, 2018.

2   See, for example, Zy Weinberg, "No Place to Shop: Food Access Lacking in the Inner City," *Race, Poverty & the Environment*, Vol. 7, No. 2 (Winter 2000), pp. 22–24; Michael E. Porter, "The Competitive Advantage of the Inner City," *Harvard Business Review*, May-June 1995, pp. 63–64; James M. MacDonald and Paul E. Nelson, Jr., "Do the Poor Still Pay More? Food Price Variations in Large Metropolitan Areas," *Journal of Urban Economics*, Vol. 30 (1991), pp. 349, 350, 357; Donald R. Marion, "Toward Revitalizing Inner-City Food Retailing," *National Food Review*, Summer 1982, pp. 22, 23, 24.

3   David Caplovitz, *The Poor Pay More: Consumer Practices of Low-Income Families* (New York: The Free Press, 1967), p. xvi.

4   See, for example, "Democrats Score A.&P. Over Prices," *New York Times*, July 18, 1963, p. 11; Elizabeth Shelton, "Prices Are Never Right," *Washington Post*, December 4, 1964, p. C3; "Gouging the Poor," *New York Times*, August 13, 1966, p. 41; "Overpricing of Food in Slums Is Alleged at House Hearing," *New York Times*, October 13, 1967, p. 20; "Ghetto Cheats Blamed for Urban Riots," *Chicago Tribune*, February 18, 1968, p. 8; "Business Leaders Urge Actions to Help Poor," *Los Angeles Times*, April 11, 1968, p. C13; Frederick D. Sturdivant and Walter T. Wilhelm, "Poverty, Minorities, and Consumer Exploitation," *Social Science Quarterly*, Vol. 49, No. 3 (December 1968), p. 650.

5   Donald R. Marion, "Toward Revitalizing Inner-City Food Retailing," *National Food Review*, Summer 1982, pp. 23–24. "Sales in urban stores are 13 percent lower by volume, and operating costs are 9 percent higher. Profits, before taxes, are less than half of the suburban stores. Labor costs are higher, shrinkage costs are greater, sales per customer are lower, insurance and repair costs are higher, and losses due to crime are more than doubled in the inner-city stores." *Hearings Before the Subcommittee on Agricultural Production, Marketing, and Stabilization of Prices of the Committee on Agriculture and Forestry*, United States Senate, Ninety-Fourth Congress, Second Session, June 23 and 25, 1976 (Washington: U.S. Government Printing Office, 1976), p. 57. See also pp. 116, 124–125.

6   Dorothy Height, "A Woman's Word," *New York Amsterdam News*, July 24, 1965, p. 34.

7   Ray Cooklis, "Lowering the High Cost of Being Poor," *Cincinnati Enquirer*, May 28, 2009, p. A7.

8   Jonathan Gill, *Harlem: The Four Hundred Year History from Dutch Village to Capital of Black America* (New York: Grove Press, 2011), p. 119.

9   See U.S. Census Bureau, S0201, Selected Population Profile in the United States, 2016 American Community Survey 1-Year Estimates, downloaded from the Census website on July 9, 2018: https://factfinder.census.gov/faces/tableservices/jsf/pages/productview.xhtml?pid=ACS_16_1YR_S0201&prodType=table.

10   "Choose Your Parents Wisely," *The Economist*, July 26, 2014, p. 22. "We find that after accounting for parental education, skills, and income, both a father's and a mother' time investment in the first five years of a child's life have a large effect on the child's completed education." George-Levi Gayle, Limor Golan, and Mehmet A. Soytas, "Intergenerational Mobility and the Effects of Parental Education, Time Investment and Income on Children's Educational Attainment," *Federal Reserve Bank of St. Louis Review*, Volume 100, No. 3 (Third Quarter 2018), pp. 291–292.

11   *The Chronicle of Higher Education: Almanac 2017–2018*, August 18, 2017, p. 46.

12   Karl Marx and Frederick Engels, *Selected Correspondence 1846–1895*, translated by Dona Torr (New York: International Publishers, 1942), p. 476.

13   Adam Smith, *An Inquiry into the Nature and Causes of the Wealth of Nations* (New York: Modern Library, 1937), p. 423.

14   Adam Smith denounced "the mean rapacity, the monopolizing spirit of merchants and manufacturers" and "the clamour and sophistry of merchants and manufacturers," whom he characterized as people who "seldom meet together, even for merriment and diversion, but the conversation ends in a conspiracy against the public." As for policies recommended by such people, Smith said: "The proposal of any new law or regulation of commerce which comes from this order, ought always to be listened to with great precaution, and ought never to be adopted till after having been long and carefully examined, not only with the most scrupulous, but with the most suspicious attention. It comes from an order of men, whose interest is never exactly the same with that of the public, who

have generally an interest to deceive and even to oppress the public, and who accordingly have, upon many occasions, both deceived and oppressed it." Adam Smith, *An Inquiry into the Nature and Causes of the Wealth of Nations*, pp. 128, 250, 460. Karl Marx wrote, in the preface to the first volume of *Capital*: "I paint the capitalist and the landlord in no sense *couleur de rose*. But here individuals are dealt with only in so far as they are the personifications of economic categories, embodiments of particular class-relations and class-interests. My stand-point, from which the evolution of the economic formation of society is viewed as a process of natural history, can less than any other make the individual responsible for relations whose creature he socially remains, however much he may subjectively raise himself above them." In Chapter X, Marx made dire predictions about the fate of workers, but not as a result of subjective moral deficiencies of the capitalist, for Marx said: "As capitalist, he is only capital personified" and "all this does not, indeed, depend on the good or ill will of the individual capitalist." Karl Marx, *Capital: A Critique of Political Economy* (Chicago: Charles H. Kerr & Company, 1909), Vol. I, pp. 15, 257, 297.

15 William Julius Wilson, *The Declining Significance of Race: Blacks and Changing American Institutions*, third edition (Chicago: University of Chicago Press, 2012), pp. 52–53, 54–55, 59.

16 Robert Higgs, *Competition and Coercion: Blacks in the American Economy 1865–1914* (New York: Cambridge University Press, 1977), pp. 47–49, 130–131.

17 In many cases, they did not have to literally *go* anywhere because, in an era where many blacks in the rural South had no access to either public or private transportation, white landlords or employers either went, or sent an emissary, to where black workers were congregated, and announced what work was available and on what terms. Even in some urban settings today, similar recruitment patterns occur in the hiring of casual day laborers.

18 Robert Higgs, *Competition and Coercion*, pp. 102, 144–146.

19 Ibid., p. 117.

20 Walter E. Williams, *South Africa's War Against Capitalism* (New York: Praeger, 1989), pp. 101, 102, 103, 104, 105. See also Brian Lapping, *Apartheid: A History* (New York: G. Braziller, 1987), p. 164; Merle Lipton, *Capitalism and Apartheid: South Africa, 1910–1984* (Aldershot, Hants, England: Gower, 1985), pp. 152, 153.

21 The book that resulted from this research was Walter E. Williams, *South Africa's War Against Capitalism*.

22 Ibid., pp. 112, 113.

23 See, for example, Thomas Sowell, *Applied Economics: Thinking Beyond Stage One*, revised and enlarged edition (New York: Basic Books, 2009), Chapter 7; Thomas Sowell, *Economic Facts and Fallacies* (New York: Basic Books, 2008), pp. 73–75, 123, 170–172.

24 Jennifer Roback, "The Political Economy of Segregation: The Case of Segregated Streetcars," *Journal of Economic History*, Vol. 46, No. 4 (December 1986), pp. 893–917.

25 Ibid., pp. 894, 899–901, 903, 904, 912, 916.

26 Kermit L. Hall and John J. Patrick, *The Pursuit of Justice: Supreme Court Decisions that Shaped America* (New York: Oxford University Press, 2006), pp. 59–64; Michael J. Klarman, *From Jim Crow to Civil Rights: The Supreme Court and the Struggle for Racial Equality* (Oxford: Oxford University Press, 2004), p. 8.

27 Bernard E. Anderson, *Negro Employment in Public Utilities: A Study of Racial Policies in the Electric Power, Gas, and Telephone Industries* (Philadelphia: University of Pennsylvania Press, 1970), pp. 73, 80.

28 Ibid., pp. 93–95.

29 Venus Green, *Race on the Line: Gender, Labor, and Technology in the Bell System, 1880–1980* (Durham: Duke University Press, 2001), p. 210.

30 Bernard E. Anderson, *Negro Employment in Public Utilities*, pp. 84–87, 150, 152.

31 Ibid., pp. 150, 152. During the 1950s, the percentage of male employees in the telecommunications industry who were black actually fell in such Southern states as Alabama, Arkansas, Florida, Georgia, Kentucky, Louisiana, Mississippi, North Carolina, South Carolina, Tennessee, Texas and Virginia. Ibid., pp. 84–87.

32 Ibid., pp. 114, 139.

33 Michael R. Winston, "Through the Back Door: Academic Racism and the Negro Scholar in Historical Perspective," *Daedalus*, Vol. 100, No. 3 (Summer 1971), pp. 695, 705.

34 Milton & Rose D. Friedman, *Two Lucky People: Memoirs* (Chicago: University of Chicago Press, 1998), pp. 91–92, 94–95, 105–106, 153–154.

35 Greg Robinson, "Davis, Allison," *Encyclopedia of African-American Culture and History*, edited by Colin A. Palmer (Detroit: Thomson-Gale, 2006), Volume C–F, p. 583; "The Talented Black Scholars Whom No White University Would Hire," *Journal of Blacks in Higher Education*, No. 58 (Winter 2007/2008), p. 81.

36 George J. Stigler, "The Economics of Minimum Wage Legislation," *American Economic Review*, Vol. 36, No. 3 (June 1946), p. 358.

37 Walter E. Williams, *Race & Economics: How Much Can Be Blamed on Discrimination* (Stanford: Hoover Institution Press, 2011), pp. 42–43.

38 Ibid.; Edward C. Banfield, *The Unheavenly City: The Nature and Future of Our Urban Crisis* (Boston: Little, Brown, 1970), p. 98.

39 Charles Murray, *Losing Ground: American Social Policy, 1950–1980* (New York: Basic Books, 1984), p. 77; Walter E. Williams, *Race & Economics*, p. 44.

40 Chas Alamo and Brian Uhler, *California's Housing Costs: Causes and Consequences* (Sacramento: Legislative Analyst's Office, 2015), pp. 9, 11–12, 14.

41 Sandra Fleishman, "High Prices? Cheaper Here Than Elsewhere," *Washington Post*, January 8, 2005, p. F1; Jason B. Johnson, "Making Ends Meet: Struggling in Middle Class," *San Francisco Chronicle*, October 16, 2005, p. A11.

42   Stephen Coyle, "Palo Alto: A Far Cry from *Euclid*," *Land Use and Housing on
      the San Francisco Peninsula*, edited by Thomas M. Hagler (Stanford: Stanford
      Environmental Law Society, 1983), pp. 85, 89.
43   Leslie Fulbright, "S.F. Moves to Stem African American Exodus," *San Francisco
      Chronicle*, April 9, 2007, p. A1.
44   Bureau of the Census, *1990 Census of Population: General Population
      Characteristics California*, 1990 CP–1–6, Section 1 of 3, pp. 27, 28, 31; U.S.
      Census Bureau, *Profiles of General Demographic Characteristics 2000: 2000 Census
      of Population and Housing, California*, Table DP–1, pp. 2, 20, 42.
45   Gilbert Osofsky, *Harlem: The Making of a Ghetto, Negro New York 1890–1930*
      (New York: Harper & Row, 1966), pp. 106–110; Jonathan Gill, *Harlem*,
      pp. 180–184.
46   Gilbert Osofsky, *Harlem*, p. 110.

Chapter 3: SORTING AND UNSORTING PEOPLE

1   Joses C. Moya, *Cousins and Strangers: Spanish Immigrants in Buenos Aires,
      1850–1930* (Berkeley: University of California Press, 1998), pp. 119, 145–146.
      Similarly, most of the Italian immigrants to Australia, between 1881 and 1899,
      came from places containing only 10 percent of the population of Italy. Helen
      Ware, *A Profile of the Italian Community in Australia* (Melbourne: Australian
      Institute of Multicultural Affairs and Co.As.It Italian Assistance Association,
      1981), p. 12.
2   Australia's eminent historian of immigration, Professor Charles A. Price, pointed
      out long ago that "immigrants rarely come in equal proportions from all parts of
      the country of origin, but rather in bunches from a few districts here and there.
      One of the main reasons for this is chain migration, the process whereby one
      member of a family, village, or township successfully establishes himself abroad
      and then writes to one or two friends and relatives at home encouraging them to
      come and join him, frequently helping with housing, jobs, and passage expenses.
      The few who join him then write home in their turn, so setting off a 'chain'
      system of migration that may send hundreds of persons from one small district
      of origin to one relatively confined area in the country of settlement." Charles A.
      Price, *Jewish Settlers in Australia* (Canberra: The Australian National University,
      1964), p. 21.
3   Jonathan Gill, *Harlem: The Four Hundred Year History from Dutch Village to
      Capital of Black America* (New York: Grove Press, 2011), p. 140; Charles A.
      Price, *Southern Europeans in Australia* (Melbourne: Oxford University Press,
      1963), p. 162; Philip Taylor, *The Distant Magnet: European Emigration to the
      USA* (New York: Harper & Row, 1971), pp. 210, 211; Dino Cinel, *From Italy
      to San Francisco: The Immigrant Experience* (Stanford: Stanford University Press,
      1982), pp. 28, 117–120; Samuel L. Baily, "The Adjustment of Italian Immigrants

in Buenos Aires and New York, 1870–1914," *American Historical Review*, April 1983, p. 291; John E. Zucchi, *Italians in Toronto: Development of a National Identity, 1875–1935* (Kingston, Ontario: McGill-Queen's University Press, 1988), pp. 41, 53–55, 58.

4   Moses Rischin, *The Promised City: New York's Jews 1870–1914* (Cambridge, Massachusetts: Harvard University Press, 1962), pp. 76, 85–108, 238–239.

5   Annie Polland and Daniel Soyer, *Emerging Metropolis: New York Jews in the Age of Immigration, 1840–1920* (New York: New York University Press, 2012), p. 31; Tyler Anbinder, *City of Dreams: The 400-Year Epic History of Immigrant New York* (Boston: Houghton Mifflin Harcourt, 2016), pp. 174–175, 178, 356, 358; Stephen Birmingham, *"The Rest of Us": The Rise of America's Eastern European Jews* (Boston: Little, Brown, 1984), pp. 12–24.

6   Louis Wirth, *The Ghetto* (Chicago: University of Chicago Press, 1956), pp. 182–184; Irving Cutler, "The Jews of Chicago: From Shetl to Suburb," *Ethnic Chicago: A Multicultural Portrait*, fourth edition, edited by Melvin G. Holli and Peter d'A. Jones (Grand Rapids, Michigan: William B. Eerdmans Publishing Company, 1995), pp. 127–129, 134–135, 143–144.

7   Fred Rosenbaum, *Visions of Reform: Congregation Emanu-El and the Jews of San Francisco, 1849–1999* (Berkeley: Judah L. Magnes Museum, 2000), pp. 59–60, 184.

8   William A. Braverman "The Emergence of a Unified Community, 1880–1917," *The Jews of Boston*, edited by Jonathan D. Sarna, Ellen Smith and Scott-Martin Kosofsky (New Haven: Yale University Press, 2005), p. 66. Both the German Jews and the Polish Jews moved out when the Russian Jews moved in. The Polish Jews in this case were from German-ruled areas, there being no Poland at the time, and were apparently more culturally like German Jews than like Russian Jews.

9   Daniel J. Elazar and Peter Medding, *Jewish Communities in Frontier Societies: Argentina, Australia, and South Africa* (New York: Holmes & Meier, 1983), pp. 263–264, 332–334; Hilary L. Rubinstein, *The Jews in Victoria: 1835–1985* (Sydney: Allen & Unwin, 1986), Chapters 10–12. One sign of these internal differences was a saying among Australian Jews that Sydney was a warm city with cold Jews, while Melbourne was a cold city with warm Jews. Hilary Rubinstein, *Chosen: The Jews in Australia* (Sydney: Allen & Unwin, 1987), p. 220.

10   H.L. van der Laan, *The Lebanese Traders in Sierra Leone* (The Hague: Mouton & Co., 1975), pp. 237–240; Louise L'Estrange Fawcett, "Lebanese, Palestinians and Syrians in Colombia," *The Lebanese in the World: A Century of Emigration*, edited by Albert Hourani and Nadim Shehadi (London: The Centre for Lebanese Studies, 1992), p. 368.

11   Tyler Anbinder, *City of Dreams*, pp. 176–177.

12   Teiiti Suzuki, *The Japanese Immigrant in Brazil: Narrative Part* (Tokyo: University of Tokyo Press, 1969), p. 109.

13   Tyler Anbinder, *City of Dreams*, p. 185.
14   Charles A. Price, *The Methods and Statistics of 'Southern Europeans in Australia'* (Canberra: The Australian National University, 1963), p. 45.
15   E. Franklin Frazier, "The Negro Family in Chicago," *E. Franklin Frazier on Race Relations: Selected Writings*, edited by G. Franklin Edwards (Chicago: University of Chicago Press, 1968), pp. 122–126.
16   E. Franklin Frazier, "The Impact of Urban Civilization Upon Negro Family Life," *American Sociological Review*, Vol. 2, No. 5 (October 1937), p. 615.
17   David M. Katzman, *Before the Ghetto: Black Detroit in the Nineteenth Century* (Urbana: University of Illinois Press, 1973), p. 27.
18   Kenneth L. Kusmer, *A Ghetto Takes Shape: Black Cleveland, 1870–1930* (Urbana: University of Illinois Press, 1978), p. 209.
19   Jonathan Gill, *Harlem*, p. 284.
20   Andrew F. Brimmer, "The Labor Market and the Distribution of Income," *Reflections of America: Commemorating the Statistical Abstract Centennial*, edited by Norman Cousins (Washington: U.S. Department of Commerce, Bureau of the Census, 1980), pp. 102–103.
21   Rakesh Kochhar and Anthony Cilluffo, *Income Inequality in the U.S. Is Rising Most Rapidly Among Asians* (Washington: Pew Research Center, 2018), p. 4. See also William Julius Wilson, *When Work Disappears: The World of the New Urban Poor* (New York: Alfred A. Knopf, 1996), p. 195.
22   Horace Mann Bond, *A Study of Factors Involved in the Identification and Encouragement of Unusual Academic Talent among Underprivileged Populations* (U.S. Department of Health, Education, and Welfare, January 1967), p. 147. [Contract No. SAE 8028, Project No. 5–0859].
23   Ibid.
24   See, for example, Willard B. Gatewood, *Aristocrats of Color: The Black Elite, 1880–1920* (Bloomington: Indiana University Press, 1990), pp. 188–189, 247; David M. Katzman, *Before the Ghetto*, Chapter V; Theodore Hershberg and Henry Williams, "Mulattoes and Blacks: Intra-Group Differences and Social Stratification in Nineteenth-Century Philadelphia," *Philadelphia: Work, Space, Family, and Group Experience in the Nineteenth Century*, edited by Theodore Hershberg (Oxford: Oxford University Press, 1981), pp. 392–434.
25   Stephen Birmingham, *Certain People: America's Black Elite* (Boston: Little, Brown and Company, 1977), pp. 196–197. As a personal note, I delivered groceries to people in that building during my teenage years, entering through the service entrance in the basement, rather than through the canopied front entrance with its uniformed doorman and ornate lobby. My own home was in a tenement apartment some distance away.
26   St. Clair Drake and Horace R. Cayton, *Black Metropolis: A Study of Negro Life in a Northern City*, revised and enlarged edition (Chicago: University of Chicago Press, 1993), pp. 73–74; James R. Grossman, "African-American Migration to Chicago," *Ethnic Chicago*, fourth edition, edited by Melvin G. Holli and Peter

d'A. Jones, pp. 323, 332, 333–334; Henri Florette, *Black Migration: Movement North, 1900–1920* (Garden City, New York: Anchor Press, 1975), pp. 96–97; Allan H. Spear, *Black Chicago: The Making of a Negro Ghetto, 1890–1920* (Chicago: University of Chicago Press, 1967), p. 168.

27 James R. Grossman, "African-American Migration to Chicago," *Ethnic Chicago*, fourth edition, edited by Melvin G. Holli and Peter d'A. Jones, pp. 323, 330, 332, 333–334; Willard B. Gatewood, *Aristocrats of Color*, pp. 186–187, 332; Allan H. Spear, *Black Chicago*, p. 168; E. Franklin Frazier, *The Negro in the United States*, revised edition (New York: Macmillan, 1957), p. 284; Henri Florette, *Black Migration*, pp. 96–97; Gilbert Osofsky, *Harlem: The Making of a Ghetto, Negro New York 1890–1930* (New York: Harper & Row, 1966), pp. 43–44; Ivan H. Light, *Ethnic Enterprise in America: Business and Welfare Among Chinese, Japanese, and Blacks* (Berkeley: University of California Press, 1972), Figure 1 (after p. 100); W.E.B. Du Bois, *The Black North in 1901: A Social Study* (New York: Arno Press, 1969), p. 25.

28 James R. Grossman, "African-American Migration to Chicago," *Ethnic Chicago*, fourth edition, edited by Melvin G. Holli and Peter d'A. Jones, p. 331. See also Ethan Michaeli, *The Defender: How the Legendary Black Newspaper Changed America* (Boston: Houghton Mifflin Harcourt, 2016), p. 84.

29 Willard B. Gatewood, *Aristocrats of Color*, pp. 186–187; James R. Grossman, "African-American Migration to Chicago," *Ethnic Chicago*, fourth edition, edited by Melvin G. Holli and Peter d'A. Jones, pp. 323, 330; St. Clair Drake and Horace R. Cayton, *Black Metropolis*, revised and enlarged edition, pp. 73–74.

30 E. Franklin Frazier, *The Negro in the United States*, revised edition, p. 643.

31 According to Professor Steven Pinker, "the North-South difference is not a by-product of the white-black difference. Southern whites are more violent than northern whites, and southern blacks are more violent than northern blacks." Steven Pinker, *The Better Angels of Our Nature: Why Violence Has Declined* (New York: Viking, 2011), p. 94.

32 Davison M. Douglas, *Jim Crow Moves North: The Battle over Northern School Segregation, 1865–1954* (Cambridge: Cambridge University Press, 2005), pp. 2–5, 61–62; Willard B. Gatewood, *Aristocrats of Color*, p. 250; E. Franklin Frazier, *The Negro in the United States*, revised edition, p. 441.

33 Willard B. Gatewood, *Aristocrats of Color*, pp. 64, 65, 300–301; E. Franklin Frazier, *The Negro in the United States*, revised edition, pp. 250–251.

34 Davison M. Douglas, *Jim Crow Moves North*, pp. 128, 129; Kenneth L. Kusmer, *A Ghetto Takes Shape*, pp. 57, 64–65, 75–76, 80, 178–179. In St. Louis and Chicago, the number of restrictive covenants skyrocketed during the great migrations at around the time of the First World War. Michael Jones-Correa, "The Origins and Diffusion of Racial Restrictive Covenants," *Political Science Quarterly*, Vol. 115, No. 4 (Winter 2000–2001), p. 558.

35 Davison M. Douglas, *Jim Crow Moves North*, pp. 130–131; Willard B. Gatewood, *Aristocrats of Color*, p. 147.

36   James N. Gregory, *The Southern Diaspora: How the Great Migrations of Black and White Southerners Transformed America* (Chapel Hill: University of North Carolina Press, 2005), p. 123; Isabel Wilkerson, *The Warmth of Other Suns: The Epic Story of America's Great Migration* (New York: Random House, 2010), p. 291; Carl Wittke, *The Irish in America* (New York: Russell & Russell, 1970), pp. 101–102; Oscar Handlin, *Boston's Immigrants* (New York: Atheneum, 1970), pp. 169–170; Jay P. Dolan, *The Irish Americans: A History* (New York: Bloomsbury Press, 2008), pp. 118–119; Irving Howe, *World of Our Fathers: The Journey of the East European Jews to America and the Life They Found and Made* (New York: Harcourt Brace Jovanovich, 1976), pp. 229–230.

37   Daniel J. Elazar and Peter Medding, *Jewish Communities in Frontier Societies*, pp. 282–283.

38   Marilynn S. Johnson, *The Second Gold Rush: Oakland and the East Bay in World War II* (Berkeley: University of California Press, 1993), p. 198.

39   Douglas Henry Daniels, *Pioneer Urbanites: A Social and Cultural History of Black San Francisco* (Philadelphia: Temple University Press, 1980), pp. 50, 75, 77, 97.

40   Marilynn S. Johnson, *The Second Gold Rush*, p. 52.

41   Ibid., p. 55.

42   Douglas Henry Daniels, *Pioneer Urbanites*, p. 165.

43   Marilynn S. Johnson, *The Second Gold Rush*, pp. 95–96, 152, 170; E. Franklin Frazier, *The Negro in the United States*, revised edition, p. 270; Douglas Henry Daniels, *Pioneer Urbanites*, pp. 171–175.

44   E. Franklin Frazier, *The Negro in the United States*, revised edition, p. 270.

45   Gunnar Myrdal, *An American Dilemma: The Negro Problem and Modern Democracy* (New York: Harper & Brothers, 1944), p. 965.

46   Arthur R. Jensen, *Genetics and Education* (New York: Harper & Row, 1972), pp. 106–107, 129–130.

47   Mya Frazier, "After the Walmart Is Gone," *Bloomberg Businessweek*, October 16, 2017, p. 59.

48   William Julius Wilson, *More Than Just Race: Being Black and Poor in the Inner City* (New York: W.W. Norton & Company, 2009), pp. 1–2.

49   Walter E. Williams, *Race & Economics: How Much Can Be Blamed on Discrimination* (Stanford: Hoover Institution Press, 2011), p. 117.

50   So did Paul R. Williams in the early twentieth century, when he decided to become an architect, at a time when such a career seemed all but impossible for a black man. He said: "White Americans have a reasonable basis for their prejudice against the Negro race, and if that prejudice is ever to be overcome it must be through the efforts of individual Negroes to rise above the average cultural level of their kind. Therefore, I owe it to myself and to my people to accept this challenge." He went on to have a highly successful career as an architect, designing everything from banks and churches to mansions for Hollywood movie stars. See Karen E. Hudson, *Paul R. Williams, Architect: A Legacy of Style* (New York: Rizzoli International Publications, 1993), p. 12.

51   See, for example, Christopher Silver, "The Racial Origins of Zoning in American Cities," *Urban Planning and the African American Community: In the Shadows*, edited by June Manning Thomas and Marsha Ritzdorf (Thousand Oaks: Sage Publications, 1997), pp. 23–42; Michael Jones-Correa, "The Origins and Diffusion of Racial Restrictive Covenants," *Political Science Quarterly*, Vol. 115, No. 4 (Winter 2000–2001), pp. 541–568.

52   See Abbot Emerson Smith, *Colonists in Bondage: White Servitude and Convict Labor in America 1607–1776* (Gloucester, Massachusetts: Peter Smith, 1965), pp. 3–4.

53   E. Franklin Frazier, *The Negro in the United States*, revised edition, pp. 22–26; John Hope Franklin, *From Slavery to Freedom: A History of American Negroes*, second edition (New York: Alfred A. Knopf, 1947), pp. 70–72.

54   St. Clair Drake and Horace R. Cayton, *Black Metropolis*, revised and enlarged edition, pp. 44–45.

55   David M. Katzman, *Before the Ghetto*, pp. 35, 69, 102, 200.

56   Ibid., p. 160; Willard B. Gatewood, *Aristocrats of Color*, p. 125.

57   W.E.B. Du Bois, *The Philadelphia Negro: A Social Study* (New York: Schocken Books, 1967), pp. 7, 41–42, 305–306.

58   Jacob Riis, *How the Other Half Lives: Studies among the Tenements of New York* (Cambridge, Massachusetts: Harvard University Press, 1970), p. 99; David M. Katzman, *Before the Ghetto*, pp. 35, 37, 138, 139, 160; St. Clair Drake and Horace R. Cayton, *Black Metropolis*, revised and enlarged edition, pp. 44–45; Willard B. Gatewood, *Aristocrats of Color*, p. 125.

59   Davison M. Douglas, *Jim Crow Moves North*, p. 3.

60   Jacob Riis, *How the Other Half Lives*, p. 99.

61   Davison M. Douglas, *Jim Crow Moves North*, p. 3.

62   Ibid., pp. 155–156.

63   Ibid., pp. 154.

64   For documentation, see Thomas C. Leonard, *Illiberal Reformers: Race, Eugenics & American Economics in the Progressive Era* (Princeton: Princeton University Press, 2016), pp. 119–124; Thomas Sowell, *Intellectuals and Race* (New York: Basic Books, 2013), pp. 24–43.

65   See, for example, Jacqueline A. Stefkovich and Terrence Leas, "A Legal History of Desegregation in Higher Education," *Journal of Negro Education*, Vol. 63, No. 3 (Summer 1994), pp. 409–410.

66   *Brown v. Board of Education of Topeka*, 347 U.S. 483 (1954), at 495.

67   Ibid., at 494.

68   T. Rees Shapiro, "Vanished Glory of an All-Black High School," *Washington Post*, January 19, 2014, p. B6. "The year the Supreme Court decisions came down, Dunbar sent 80 percent of its graduates to college, the highest percentage of any Washington school, white or Negro. That same year it had the highest percentage attending college on scholarship: one in four." Alison Stewart, *First*

Class: The Legacy of Dunbar, America's First Black Public High School (Chicago: Lawrence Hill Books, 2013), p. 173.

69 Henry S. Robinson, "The M Street High School, 1891–1916," *Records of the Columbia Historical Society*, Washington, D.C., Vol. LI (1984), p. 122; *Report of the Board of Trustees of Public Schools of the District of Columbia to the Commissioners of the District of Columbia: 1898–99* (Washington: Government Printing Office, 1900), pp. 7, 11.

70 Mary Gibson Hundley, *The Dunbar Story: 1870–1955* (New York: Vantage Press, 1965), p. 75.

71 Ibid., p. 78. Mary Church Terrell, "History of the High School for Negroes in Washington," *Journal of Negro History*, Vol. 2, No. 3 (July 1917), p. 262.

72 Louise Daniel Hutchison, *Anna J. Cooper: A Voice from the South* (Washington: The Smithsonian Institution Press, 1981), p. 62; Jervis Anderson, "A Very Special Monument," *The New Yorker*, March 20, 1978, p. 100; Alison Stewart, *First Class*, p. 99; "The Talented Black Scholars Whom No White University Would Hire," *Journal of Blacks in Higher Education*, No. 58 (Winter 2007/2008), p. 81.

73 Tucker Carlson, "From Ivy League to NBA," *Policy Review*, Spring 1993, p. 36.

74 See "Success Academy: #1 in New York," downloaded from the website of Success Academy Charter Schools: http://www.successacademies.org/app/uploads/2017/08/sa_1_in_new_york.pdf. See also "New York Attacks Success," *Wall Street Journal*, August 23, 2017, p. A14; Katie Taylor, "Struggling City Schools Improve Their Test Scores, but Not All Are Safe," *New York Times*, August 23, 2017, p. A16.

75 See, for example, Alex Kotlowitz, "Where Is Everyone Going?" *Chicago Tribune*, March 10, 2002; Mary Mitchell, "Middle-Class Neighborhood Fighting to Keep Integrity," *Chicago Sun-Times*, November 10, 2005, p. 14; Jessica Garrison and Ted Rohrlich, "A Not-So-Welcome Mat," *Los Angeles Times*, June 17, 2007, p. A1; Paul Elias, "Influx of Black Renters Raises Tension in Bay Area," *The Associated Press*, December 31, 2008; Mick Dumke, "Unease in Chatham, But Who's at Fault?" *New York Times*, April 29, 2011, p. A23; James Bovard, "Raising Hell in Subsidized Housing," *Wall Street Journal*, August 18, 2011, p. A15; Frank Main, "Crime Felt from CHA Relocations," *Chicago Sun-Times*, April 5, 2012, p. 18.

76 Alex Kotlowitz, "Where Is Everyone Going?" *Chicago Tribune*, March 10, 2002.

77 Mary Mitchell, "Middle-Class Neighborhood Fighting to Keep Integrity," *Chicago Sun-Times*, November 10, 2005, p. 14.

78 Mick Dumke, "Unease in Chatham, But Who's at Fault?" *New York Times*, April 29, 2011, p. A23.

79 Gary Gilbert, "People Must Get Involved in Section 8 Reform," *Contra Costa Times*, November 18, 2006, p. F4.

80   Geetha Suresh and Gennaro F. Vito, "Homicide Patterns and Public Housing: The Case of Louisville, KY (1989–2007), *Homicide Studies*, Vol. 13, No. 4 (November 2009), pp. 411–433.

81   Alex Kotlowitz, "Where Is Everyone Going?" *Chicago Tribune*, March 10, 2002.

82   Ibid.

83   J.D. Vance, *Hillbilly Elegy: A Memoir of a Family and Culture in Crisis* (New York: HarperCollins, 2016), p. 140.

84   Ibid., p. 141.

85   Lisa Sanbonmatsu, Jeffrey R. Kling, Greg J. Duncan and Jeanne Brooks-Gunn, "Neighborhoods and Academic Achievement: Results from the Moving to Opportunity Experiment," *The Journal of Human Resources*, Vol. 41, No. 4 (Fall, 2006), p. 682.

86   Jens Ludwig, et al., "What Can We Learn about Neighborhood Effects from the Moving to Opportunity Experiment?" *American Journal of Sociology*, Vol. 114, No. 1 (July 2008), p. 148.

87   Jeffrey R. Kling, et al., "Experimental Analysis of Neighborhood Effects," *Econometrica*, Vol. 75, No. 1 (January 2007), p. 99.

88   Jens Ludwig, et al., "Long-Term Neighborhood Effects on Low-Income Families: Evidence from Moving to Opportunity," *American Economic Review*, Vol. 103, No. 3 (May 2013), p. 227.

89   Lawrence F. Katz, Jeffrey R. Kling, and Jeffrey B. Liebman, "Moving to Opportunity in Boston: Early Results of a Randomized Mobility Experiment," *Quarterly Journal of Economics*, Vol. 116, No. 2 (May 2001), p. 648.

90   *Moving To Opportunity for Fair Housing Demonstration Program: Final Impacts Evaluation, Summary* (Washington: U.S. Department of Housing and Urban Development, November 2011), p. 3.

91   "HUD's Plan to Diversify Suburbs," *Investor's Business Daily*, July 23, 2013, p. A12.

92   Ibid.

93   During the Great Depression of the 1930s, for example, the Secretary of the Treasury, Henry Morgenthau, was appalled by a program run by the Secretary of Agriculture, Henry Wallace, who was trying to get farmers to produce less, and to dispose of existing surpluses at a time when, in Morgenthau's words, "there's people going hungry in America, all over America." Morgenthau's plan to give more of the surplus to people who were hungry was vetoed by presidential advisor Harry Hopkins. According to Morgenthau's diary: "The minute I turned my back Harry went to Wallace and said they couldn't do it because that is admitting everything you have done is wrong. . . . If we feed the undernourished the surplus food stuffs, that was admitting the plan was a flop, and we'd better not do it." Wallace in turn told Morgenthau that giving more surplus food to the hungry would be "bad politics." Janet Poppendieck, *Breadlines Knee-Deep in Wheat: Food Assistance in the Great Depression*, updated and expanded (Berkeley: University of California Press, 2014), pp. 238, 239–240.

94   See, for example, Raj Chetty, Nathaniel Hendren, and Lawrence F. Katz, "The Effects of Exposure to Better Neighborhoods on Children: New Evidence from the Moving to Opportunity Experiment," *American Economic Review*, Vol. 106, No. 4 (April 2016), pp. 857, 899; Lawrence F. Katz, Jeffrey R. Kling, and Jeffrey B. Liebman, "Moving to Opportunity in Boston: Early Results of a Randomized Mobility Experiment," *Quarterly Journal of Economics*, Vol. 116, No. 2 (May 2001), pp. 607, 611–612, 648.

95   *Equal Employment Opportunity Commission v. Sears, Roebuck & Company*, 839 F.2d 302 at 311, 360; Peter Brimelow, "Spiral of Silence," *Forbes*, May 25, 1992, p. 77.

96   Paul Sperry, "Background Checks Are Racist?" *Investor's Business Daily*, March 28, 2014, p. A1.

97   Harry J. Holzer, Steven Raphael, and Michael A. Stoll, "Perceived Criminality, Criminal Background Checks, and the Racial Hiring Practices of Employers," *Journal of Law and Economics*, Vol. 49, No. 2 (October 2006), pp. 451–480.

98   Jason L. Riley, "Jobless Blacks Should Cheer Background Checks," *Wall Street Journal*, August 23, 2013, p. A11; Paul Sperry, "Background Checks Are Racist?" *Investor's Business Daily*, March 28, 2014, p. A1.

99   Douglas P. Woodward, "Locational Determinants of Japanese Manufacturing Start-ups in the United States," *Southern Economic Journal*, Vol. 58, Issue 3 (January 1992), pp. 700, 706; Robert E. Cole and Donald R. Deskins, Jr., "Racial Factors in Site Location and Employment Patterns of Japanese Auto Firms in America," *California Management Review*, Fall 1988, pp. 17–18.

100 Philip S. Foner, "The Rise of the Black Industrial Working Class, 1915–1918," *African Americans in the U.S. Economy*, edited by Cecilia A. Conrad, et al (Lanham, Maryland: Rowman and Littlefield, 2005), pp. 38–43; Leo Alilunas, "Statutory Means of Impeding Emigration of the Negro," *Journal of Negro History*, Vol. 22, No. 2 (April 1937), pp. 148–162; Carole Marks, "Lines of Communication, Recruitment Mechanisms, and the Great Migration of 1916–1918," *Social Problems*, Vol. 31, No. 1 (October 1983), pp. 73–83; Theodore Kornweibel, Jr., *Railroads in the African American Experience: A Photographic Journey* (Baltimore: Johns Hopkins University Press, 2010), pp. 174–180; Peter Gottlieb, *Making Their Own Way: Southern Blacks' Migration to Pittsburgh, 1916–1930* (Urbana: University of Illinois Press, 1987), pp. 55–59; Sean Dennis Cashman, *America in the Twenties and Thirties: The Olympian Age of Franklin Delano Roosevelt* (New York: New York University Press, 1989), p. 267.

101 August Meier and Elliott Rudwick, *Black Detroit and the Rise of the UAW* (New York: Oxford University Press, 1979), pp. 9–11; Milton C. Sernett, *Bound for the Promised Land: African American Religion and the Great Migration* (Durham: Duke University Press, 1997), pp. 148–149.

Chapter 4: THE WORLD OF NUMBERS

Epigraph

Mark Twain, *Mark Twain's Autobiography* (New York: Harper & Brothers, 1924), Volume I, p. 246.

1   United States Commission on Civil Rights, *Civil Rights and the Mortgage Crisis* (Washington: U.S. Commission on Civil Rights, 2009), p. 53.

2   Ibid. See also page 61; Robert B. Avery and Glenn B. Canner, "New Information Reported under HMDA and Its Application in Fair Lending Enforcement," *Federal Reserve Bulletin, Summer 2005*, p. 379; Wilhelmina A. Leigh and Danielle Huff, "African Americans and Homeownership: The Subprime Lending Experience, 1995 to 2007," *Joint Center for Political and Economic Studies*, November 2007, p. 5.

3   Jim Wooten, "Answers to Credit Woes are Not in Black and White," *Atlanta Journal-Constitution*, November 6, 2007, p. 12A.

4   Harold A. Black, M. Cary Collins and Ken B. Cyree, "Do Black-Owned Banks Discriminate Against Black Borrowers?" *Journal of Financial Services Research*, Vol. 11, Issue 1–2 (February 1997), pp. 189–204. Here, as elsewhere, it should not be assumed that two unexamined samples are equal in the relevant variables. In this case, there is no reason to assume that those blacks who applied to black banks were the same as those blacks who applied to white banks.

5   Robert Rector and Rea S. Hederman, "Two Americas: One Rich, One Poor? Understanding Income Inequality in the United States," Heritage Foundation *Backgrounder*, No. 1791 (August 24, 2004), pp. 7, 8.

6   The number of people in the various quintiles in 2015 was computed by multiplying the number of "consumer units" in each quintile by the average number of people per consumer unit. See Table 1 in Veri Crain and Taylor J. Wilson, "Use with Caution: Interpreting Consumer Expenditure Income Group Data," *Beyond the Numbers* (Washington: U.S. Bureau of Labor Statistics, May 2017), p. 3.

7   Ibid.

8   U.S. Census Bureau, "Table HINC–05. Percent Distribution of Households, by Selected Characteristics within Income Quintile and Top 5 Percent in 2016," from the Current Population Survey, downloaded on July 11, 2018: https://www.census.gov/data/tables/time-series/demo/income-poverty/cps-hinc/hinc-05.html

9   Herman P. Miller, *Income Distribution in the United States* (Washington: U.S. Department of Commerce, Bureau of the Census, 1966), p. 7.

10   Rose M. Kreider and Diana B. Elliott, "America's Family and Living Arrangements: 2007," *Current Population Reports*, P20–561 (Washington: U.S. Bureau of the Census, 2009), p. 5.

11   W. Michael Cox and Richard Alm, "By Our Own Bootstraps: Economic Opportunity & the Dynamics of Income Distribution," *Annual Report, 1995*, Federal Reserve Bank of Dallas, p. 8.

12   Richard V. Reeves, "Stop Pretending You're Not Rich," *New York Times*, June 11, 2017, Sunday Review section, p. 5.

13   Mark Robert Rank, Thomas A. Hirschl and Kirk A. Foster, *Chasing the American Dream: Understanding What Shapes Our Fortunes* (Oxford: Oxford University Press, 2014), p. 105.

14   U.S. Department of the Treasury, "Income Mobility in the U.S. from 1996 to 2005," November 13, 2007, pp. 2, 4, 7.

15   Peter Saunders, *Poor Statistics: Getting the Facts Right About Poverty in Australia* (St. Leonards, Australia: Centre for Independent Studies, 2002), pp. 1–12; David Green, *Poverty and Benefit Dependency* (Wellington: New Zealand Business Roundtable, 2001), pp. 32, 33; Jason Clemens and Joel Emes, "Time Reveals the Truth about Low Income," *Fraser Forum*, September 2001, The Fraser Institute in Vancouver, Canada, pp. 24–26; Niels Veldhuis, et al., "The 'Poor' Are Getting Richer," *Fraser Forum*, January/February 2013, p. 25.

16   U.S. Department of the Treasury, "Income Mobility in the U.S. from 1996 to 2005," November 13, 2007, p. 4.

17   Danny Dorling, "Inequality in Advanced Economies," *The New Oxford Handbook of Economic Geography*, edited by Gordon L. Clark, et al (Oxford: Oxford University Press, 2018), p. 41.

18   Thomas A. Hirschl and Mark R. Rank, "The Life Course Dynamics of Affluence," *PLoS ONE*, January 28, 2015, p. 1.

19   U.S. Department of the Treasury, "Income Mobility in the U.S. from 1996 to 2005," November 13, 2007, pp. 2, 4; Internal Revenue Service, "The 400 Individual Income Tax Returns Reporting the Highest Adjusted Gross Incomes Each Year, 1992–2000," *Statistics of Income Bulletin*, Spring 2003, Publication 1136 (Revised 6–03), p. 7.

20   Heather Mac Donald, *Are Cops Racist? How the War Against the Police Harms Black Americans* (Chicago: Ivan R. Dee, 2003), pp. 28, 31, 32. The original report was: James E. Lange, Ph.D., et al., *Speed Violation Survey of the New Jersey Turnpike: Final Report* (Calverton, Maryland: Public Services Research Institute, 2001). It was submitted to the Office of the State Attorney General in Trenton, New Jersey.

21   Heather Mac Donald, *Are Cops Racist?*, pp. 28–34.

22

GROUPS	MEDIAN AGE
Black	33.9
Cambodian	32.9
Chinese	38.1
Cuban	40.7
Japanese	50.6
Mexican	27.0
Puerto Rican	29.9
White	40.6
TOTAL POPULATION	37.9

SOURCE: U.S. Census Bureau, S0201, Selected Population Profile in the United States, 2016 American Community Survey 1-Year Estimates.

23 Heather Mac Donald, *Are Cops Racist?*, p. 29.

24 Heather Mac Donald, *The War on Cops: How the New Attack on Law and Order Makes Everyone Less Safe* (New York: Encounter Books, 2016), pp. 56–57, 69–71.

25 Sterling A. Brown, *A Son's Return: Selected Essays of Sterling A. Brown*, edited by Mark A. Sanders (Boston: Northeastern University Press, 1996), p. 73.

26 Mark Robert Rank, Thomas A. Hirschl and Kirk A. Foster, *Chasing the American Dream*, p. 97.

27 Internal Revenue Service, "The 400 Individual Income Tax Returns Reporting the Highest Adjusted Gross Incomes Each Year, 1992–2000," *Statistics of Income Bulletin*, Spring 2003, Publication 1136 (Revised 6–03), p. 7.

28 Internal Revenue Service, Statistics of Income Division, "The 400 Individual Income Tax Returns Reporting the Largest Adjusted Gross Incomes Each Year, 1992-2014," December 2016, p. 17.

29 Devon Pendleton and Jack Witzig, "The World's Richest People Got Poorer This Year," *Bloomberg.com*, December 28, 2015; Devon Pendleton and Jack Witzig, "World's Wealthiest Saw Red Ink," *Montreal Gazette*, January 2, 2016, p. B8.

30 "Billionaires," *Forbes*, March 21, 2016, p. 10.

31 With nine people who are transients in the higher bracket for just one year out of a decade, that means that 90 transients will be in that bracket during that decade. The one person who is in that higher income bracket in every year of the decade brings the total number of people in the income bracket at some point during the decade to 91. The transients' total income for that decade, which was $12.6

million for the initial 9 transients, adds up to $126 million for all 90 transients who spent a year each in the higher bracket. When the $5 million earned by the one person who was in the higher bracket for all ten years of the decade is added, that makes $131 million for all 91 people who were in the higher bracket at some point during the course of the decade. These 91 people thus have an average annual income of $143,956.04— which is less than three times the average annual income of the 10 people who earned $50,000 a year.

32 See data and documentation in Thomas Sowell, *Wealth, Poverty and Politics*, revised and enlarged edition (New York: Basic Books, 2016), pp. 321–322.

33 William Julius Wilson, *When Work Disappears: The World of the New Urban Poor* (New York: Alfred A. Knopf, 1996), p. xix.

34 Ibid., p. 67.

35 Ibid., p. 140.

36 Ibid., pp. 178, 179.

37 David Caplovitz, *The Poor Pay More: Consumer Practices of Low-Income Families* (New York: The Free Press, 1967), pp. 94–95.

38 John U. Ogbu, *Black American Students in an Affluent Suburb: A Study of Academic Disengagement* (Mahwah, New Jersey: Lawrence Erlbaum Associates, 2003), pp. 15, 17, 21, 28, 240.

39 Thomas D. Snyder, Cristobal de Brey and Sally A. Dillow, *Digest of Education Statistics: 2015*, 51st edition (Washington: U.S. Department of Education, National Center for Education Statistics, 2016), pp. 328, 329. See also Valerie A. Ramey, "Is There a Tiger Mother Effect? Time Use Across Ethnic Groups," *Economics in Action*, Issue 4 (May 3, 2011).

40 Richard Lynn, *The Global Bell Curve: Race, IQ, and Inequality Worldwide* (Augusta, Georgia: Washington Summit Publishers, 2008), p. 51.

41 James Bartholomew, *The Welfare of Nations* (Washington: The Cato Institute, 2016), pp. 104–106; *PISA 2015: Results in Focus* (Paris: OECD, 2018), p. 5.

42 Robert A. Margo, "Race, Educational Attainment, and the 1940 Census," *Journal of Economic History*, Vol. 46, No. 1 (March 1986), pp. 196–197.

43 Ibid., p. 197.

44 Abigail Thernstrom and Stephen Thernstrom, *No Excuses: Closing the Racial Gap in Learning* (New York: Simon & Schuster, 2004), p. 13.

45 Stephan Thernstrom and Abigail Thernstrom, *America in Black and White: One Nation, Indivisible* (New York: Simon & Schuster, 1997), p. 446; Richard J. Herrnstein and Charles Murray, *The Bell Curve: Intelligence and Class Structure in American Life* (New York: The Free Press, 1994), pp. 321–323; William R. Johnson and Derek Neal, "Basic Skills and the Black-White Earnings Gap," *The Black-White Test Score Gap*, edited by Christopher Jencks and Meredith Phillips (Washington: Brookings Institution Press, 1998), pp. 480–497. Similar results have been found where the data permit qualitative comparisons of other factors. See, for example, Richard B. Freeman, *Black Elite: The New Market for Highly Educated Black Americans* (New York: McGraw-Hill, 1976), pp. 207, 209.

46   See, for example, Richard B. Freeman, *Black Elite*, pp. 206–207; Thomas Sowell, *Education: Assumptions Versus History* (Stanford: Hoover Institution Press, 1986), pp. 82–89.

47   See data in Thomas Sowell, *Education*, pp. 83–88. See also Richard B. Freeman, *Black Elite*, pp. 208–209.

48   Thomas Sowell, *Education*, p. 96.

49   U.S. Department of Labor, Bureau of Labor Statistics, *Characteristics of Minimum Wage Workers: 2017* (Washington: Department of Labor, Bureau of Labor Statistics, 2018), p. 1 and tables 1 and 7.

50   Michael A. Fletcher and Jonathan Weisman, "Bush Supports Democrats' Minimum Wage Hike Plan," *Washington Post*, December 21, 2006, p. A14.

51   "Labours Lost," *The Economist*, July 15, 2000, pp. 64–65; Robert W. Van Giezen, "Occupational Wages in the Fast-Food Restaurant Industry," *Monthly Labor Review*, August 1994, pp. 24–30.

52   Professor William Julius Wilson is one of those who have done this, in various books of his: *The Declining Significance of Race: Blacks and Changing American Institutions*, third edition (Chicago: University of Chicago Press, 2012), pp. 16, 95, 165; *The Truly Disadvantaged: The Inner City, the Underclass, and Public Policy*, second edition (Chicago: University of Chicago Press, 2012), p. 177; *When Work Disappears*, p. 25.

53   "Labours Lost," *The Economist*, July 15, 2000, pp. 64–65.

54   Richard A. Lester, "Shortcomings of Marginal Analysis for Wage-Employment Problems," *American Economic Review*, Vol. 36, No. 1 (March 1946), pp. 63–82.

55   David Card and Alan B. Krueger, "Minimum Wages and Employment: A Case Study of the Fast-Food Industry in New Jersey and Pennsylvania," *American Economic Review*, Vol. 84, No. 4 (September 1994), pp. 772–793; David Card and Alan B. Krueger, *Myth and Measurement: The New Economics of the Minimum Wage* (Princeton: Princeton University Press, 1995); Douglas K. Adie, Book Review, "Myth and Measurement: The New Economics of the Minimum Wage," *Cato Journal*, Vol. 15, No. 1 (Spring/Summer 1995), pp. 137–140; Bill Resnick, "Studies Refute Argument Wage Increase Costs Jobs," *The Oregonian* (Portland), August 25, 1995, p. B7.

56   Richard B. Berman, "Dog Bites Man: Minimum Wage Hikes Still Hurt," *Wall Street Journal*, March 29, 1995, p. A12; "Testimony of Richard B. Berman," *Evidence Against a Higher Minimum Wage*, Hearing Before the Joint Economic Committee, Congress of the United States, One Hundred Fourth Congress, first session, April 5, 1995, Part II, pp. 12–13; Gary S. Becker, "It's Simple: Hike the Minimum Wage, and You Put People Out of Work," *BusinessWeek*, March 6, 1995, p. 22; Paul Craig Roberts, "A Minimum-Wage Study with Minimum Credibility," *BusinessWeek*, April 24, 1995, p. 22; David Neumark and William L. Wascher, *Minimum Wages* (Cambridge, Massachusetts: MIT Press, 2008), pp. 63–65, 71–78.

57 Professor George J. Stigler, in a critique of Professor Lester's survey research, not long after World War II, pointed out that "by parallel logic it can be shown by a current inquiry of health of veterans in 1940 and 1946 that no soldier was fatally wounded." George J. Stigler, "Professor Lester and the Marginalists," *American Economic Review*, Vol. 37, No. 1 (March 1947), p. 157.

58 Dara Lee Luca and Michael Luca, "Survival of the Fittest: The Impact of the Minimum Wage on Firm Exit," Harvard Business School, Working Paper 17–088, April 2017, pp. 1, 2, 3, 10.

59 Don Watkins and Yaron Brook, *Equal Is Unfair: America's Misguided Fight Against Income Inequality* (New York: St. Martin's Press, 2016), p. 125.

60 Ekaterina Jardim, et al., "Minimum Wage Increases, Wages, and Low-Wage Employment: Evidence from Seattle," Working Paper Number 23532, "Abstract" (Cambridge, Massachusetts: National Bureau of Economic Research, June 2017).

61 "Economic and Financial Indicators," *The Economist*, March 15, 2003, p. 100.

62 "Economic and Financial Indicators," *The Economist*, March 2, 2013, p. 88.

63 "Economic and Financial Indicators," *The Economist*, September 7, 2013, p. 92.

64 "Hong Kong's Jobless Rate Falls," *Wall Street Journal*, January 16, 1991, p. C16.

65 U. S. Bureau of the Census, *Historical Statistics of the United States: Colonial Times to 1970* (Washington: Government Printing Office, 1975), Part 1, p. 126.

66 Steven Pinker, *Enlightenment Now: The Case for Reason, Science, Humanism, and Progress* (New York: Viking, 2018), p. 99.

67 Thomas Piketty, *Capital in the Twenty-First Century* (Cambridge, Massachusetts: Harvard University Press, 2014), p. 252.

68 Thomas A. Hirschl and Mark R. Rank, "The Life Course Dynamics of Affluence," *PLoS ONE*, January 28, 2015, p. 5.

69 Thomas Piketty, *Capital in the Twenty-First Century*, p. 278.

70 Robert Arnott, William Bernstein, and Lillian Wu, "The Myth of Dynastic Wealth: The Rich Get Poorer," *Cato Journal*, Fall 2015, p. 461.

71 "Spare a Dime," a special report on the rich, *The Economist*, April 4, 2009, p. 4.

72 See, for example, Phil Gramm and John F. Early, "The Myth of American Inequality," *Wall Street Journal*, August 10, 2018, p. A15. See also Thomas Sowell, *Basic Economics: A Common Sense Guide to the Economy*, fifth edition (New York: Basic Books, 2015), pp. 426–427, 428.

73 Gene Smiley and Richard Keehn, "Federal Personal Income Tax Policy in the 1920s," *Journal of Economic History*, Vol. 55, No. 2 (June 1995), p. 286; Benjamin G. Rader, "Federal Taxation in the 1920s," *The Historian*, Vol. 33, No. 3 (May 1971), p. 432; Burton W. Fulsom, Jr., *The Myth of the Robber Barons: A New Look at the Rise of Big Business in America*, sixth edition (Herndon, Virginia: Young America's Foundation, 2010), pp. 108, 115, 116.

74 Burton W. Fulsom, Jr., *The Myth of the Robber Barons*, sixth edition, p. 109.

75   Andrew W. Mellon, *Taxation: The People's Business* (New York: The Macmillan Company, 1924), p. 170.

76   Gene Smiley and Richard Keehn, "Federal Personal Income Tax Policy in the 1920s," *Journal of Economic History*, Vol. 55, No. 2 (June 1995), p. 289.

77   Burton W. Fulsom, Jr., *The Myth of the Robber Barons*, sixth edition, p. 116. The share of income tax *revenues* paid by people with incomes up to $50,000 a year *fell*, and the share of income tax revenues paid by people with incomes of $100,000 and up *increased*. At the extremes, taxpayers in the lowest income bracket paid 13 percent of all income tax revenues in 1921, but less than half of one percent of all income taxes in 1929, while taxpayers with incomes of a million dollars a year and up saw their share of income taxes paid rise from less than 5 percent to just over 19 percent. Gene Smiley and Richard Keehn, "Federal Personal Income Tax Policy in the 1920s," *Journal of Economic History*, Vol. 55, No. 2 (June 1995), p. 295; Benjamin G. Rader, "Federal Taxation in the 1920s," *The Historian*, Vol. 33, No. 3 (May 1971), pp. 432–434.

78   Alan Reynolds, "Why 70% Tax Rates Won't Work," *Wall Street Journal*, June 16, 2011, p. A19; Stephen Moore, "Real Tax Cuts Have Curves," *Wall Street Journal*, June 13, 2005, p. A13. Professor Joseph E. Stiglitz argued that the tax rate cuts during the Reagan administration failed: "In fact, Reagan had promised that the incentive effects of his tax cuts would be so powerful that tax revenues would *increase*. And yet, the only thing that increased was the deficit." Joseph E. Stiglitz, *The Price of Inequality* (New York: W.W. Norton, 2012), p. 89. However, the tax revenues collected by the federal government during every year of the Reagan administration exceeded the tax revenues collected in any previous administration in the history of the country. *Economic Report of the President: 2018* (Washington: Government Printing Office, 2018), p. 552; U. S. Bureau of the Census, *Historical Statistics of the United States*, Part 2, pp. 1104–1105. The deficit reflected the fact that there is no amount of money that Congress cannot outspend.

79   Edmund L. Andrews, "Surprising Jump in Tax Revenues Curbs U.S. Deficit," *New York Times*, July 9, 2006, p. A1.

80   James Gwartney and Richard Stroup, "Tax Cuts: Who Shoulders the Burden?" *Federal Reserve Bank of Atlanta Economic Review*, March 1982, pp. 19–27; Benjamin G. Rader, "Federal Taxation in the 1920s: A Re-examination," *Historian*, Vol. 33, No. 3, p. 432; Burton W. Folsom, Jr., *The Myth of the Robber Barons*, sixth edition, p. 116; Robert L. Bartley, *The Seven Fat Years: And How to Do It Again* (New York: The Free Press, 1992), pp. 71–74; Alan Reynolds, "Why 70% Tax Rates Won't Work," *Wall Street Journal*, June 16, 2011, p. A19; Stephen Moore, "Real Tax Cuts Have Curves," *Wall Street Journal*, June 13, 2005, p. A13; *Economic Report of the President: 2017* (Washington: Government Printing Office, 2017), p. 586. See also United States Internal Revenue Service, *Statistics of Income 1920–1929* (Washington: Government Printing Office, 1922–1932).

81   Alan S. Blinder, "Why Now Is the Wrong Time to Increase the Deficit," *Wall Street Journal*, January 31, 2018, p. A15.

82   The national debt, which was a little over $24 billion in 1920— the last year of President Woodrow Wilson's administration— was reduced to less than $18 billion in 1928, the last year of President Calvin Coolidge's administration. U. S. Bureau of the Census, *Historical Statistics of the United States*, Part 2, p. 1104. See also David Greenberg, *Calvin Coolidge* (New York: Times Books, 2006), p. 67.

83   David Greenberg, *Calvin Coolidge*, p. 72.

Chapter 5: THE WORLD OF WORDS

Epigraph

Thomas Hobbes, *Leviathan* (London: J.M. Dent, 1928), p. 16.

1   William Julius Wilson, *More Than Just Race: Being Poor and Black in the Inner City* (New York: W.W. Norton, 2009), pp. 152–153.

2   U.S. Census Bureau, "Table 4. Poverty Status of Families, by Type of Family, Presence of Related Children, Race, and Hispanic Origin: 1959 to 2016," Downloaded from the website of the Census Bureau: https://www.census.gov/data/tables/time-series/demo/income-poverty/historical-poverty-people.html.

3   Ibid.; Jessica L. Semega, Kayla R. Fontenot, and Melissa A. Kollar, "Income and Poverty in the United States: 2016," *Current Population Reports*, P60–259 (Washington: U.S. Census Bureau, 2017), pp. 45, 47.

4   U.S. Census Bureau, "Table 4. Poverty Status of Families, by Type of Family, Presence of Related Children, Race, and Hispanic Origin: 1959 to 2016," Downloaded from the website of the Census Bureau: https://www.census.gov/data/tables/time-series/demo/income-poverty/historical-poverty-people.html; Jessica L. Semega, Kayla R. Fontenot, and Melissa A. Kollar, "Income and Poverty in the United States: 2016," *Current Population Reports*, P60–259 (Washington: U.S. Census Bureau, 2017), pp. 45, 47.

5   Richard B. Freeman, *Black Elite: The New Market for Highly Educated Black Americans* (New York: McGraw-Hill, 1976), pp. 97–98, 102.

6   Daniel Bergner, "Class Warfare," *New York Times Magazine*, September 7, 2014, p. 62. See also "Success Academy: #1 in New York," downloaded from the website of Success Academy Charter Schools: http://www.successacademies.org/app/uploads/2017/08/sa_1_in_new_york.pdf; "New York Attacks Success," *Wall Street Journal*, August 23, 2017, p. A14; Molly Peterson, "Good to Great Hits Grade School," *Bloomberg BusinessWeek*, February 15, 2010, p. 56; *KIPP: 2014 Report Card* (San Francisco: KIPP Foundation, 2014), pp. 10, 19; Jay Mathews, "KIPP Continues to Break the Mold and Garner Excellent Results," *Washington Post*, February 3, 2014, p. B2.

7   William Julius Wilson, *The Truly Disadvantaged: The Inner City, the Underclass, and Public Policy* (Chicago: University of Chicago Press, 1987), p. 3.

8   Ibid.

9   See, for example, David Levering Lewis, *When Harlem Was in Vogue* (New York: Penguin Books, 1997), pp. 182–183; Jervis Anderson, *This Was Harlem: A Cultural Portrait, 1900–1950* (New York: Farrar Straus Giroux, 1982), pp. 138–139; Milton & Rose D. Friedman, *Two Lucky People: Memoirs* (Chicago: University of Chicago Press, 1998), p. 48. A Lithuanian child who ended up in a refugee camp run by the U.S. Army at the end of World War II, later wrote a memoir that gave a glimpse of how he and other children in that camp—and in other camps—found black soldiers more sympathetic to them than white soldiers. Leo L. Algminas, *Samogitia Mea Patria: Autobiographical Remembrances* (2015), pp. 124–125.

10   Nicholas Eberstadt, *Men Without Work: America's Invisible Crisis* (West Conshohocken, Pennsylvania: Templeton Press, 2016) p. 72.

11   Andrea Flynn, Susan Holmberg, Dorian T. Warren and Felicia J. Wong, *The Hidden Rules of Race: Barriers to an Inclusive Economy* (New York: Cambridge University Press, 2017), pp. 1–3.

12   "Devils and Enemies," *Far Eastern Economic Review*, July 7, 1994, p. 53.

13   Paul Mojzes, *Balkan Genocides: Holocaust and Ethnic Cleansing in the Twentieth Century* (Lanham, Maryland: Rowman & Littlefield, 2011), p. 2.

14   As a Sri Lankan scholar described the situation: "In striking contrast to other parts of South Asia (including Burma), Sri Lanka in 1948 was an oasis of stability, peace and order. The transfer of power was smooth and peaceful, a reflection of the moderate tone of the dominant strand in the country's nationalist movement. More important, one saw very little of the divisions and bitterness which were tearing at the recent independence of the South Asian countries. In general, the situation in the country seemed to provide an impressive basis for a solid start in nation-building and national regeneration." K.M. de Silva, "Historical Survey," *Sri Lanka: A Survey*, edited by K.M. de Silva (Honolulu: The University Press of Hawaii, 1977), p. 84. "Sri Lanka had better prospects than most new states when independence came in 1948." Donald L. Horowitz, "A Splitting Headache," *The New Republic*, February 23, 1987, p. 33. See also Robert N. Kearney, *Communalism and Language in the Politics of Ceylon* (Durham: Duke University Press, 1967), p. 27.

15   See, for example, Steven R. Weisman, "Sri Lanka: A Nation Disintegrates," *New York Times*, December 13, 1987, pp. SM 34ff; A.R.M. Imtiyaz and Ben Stavis, "Ethno-Political Conflict in Sri Lanka," *Journal of Third World Studies*, Vol. XXV, No. 2 (Fall 2008), pp. 135–152; Robert Draper, "Fragile Peace," *National Geographic*, November 2016, pp. 108–129.

16   Amy L. Freedman, "The Effect of Government Policy and Institutions on Chinese Overseas Acculturation: The Case of Malaysia," *Modern Asian Studies*, Vol. 35, No. 2 (May 2001), p. 416.

17   Donald R. Snodgrass, *Inequality and Economic Development in Malaysia* (Kuala Lumpur: Oxford University Press, 1980), p. 4.

18   According to former prime minister Mahathir bin Mohamad, Malay students given preferential admissions and scholarships "don't seem to appreciate the opportunities that they get. They become more interested in other things, politics in particular, to the detriment of their studies." Mahathir bin Mohamad, "Not One But Two New Malay Dilemmas," *Straits Times* (Singapore), August 1, 2002. Dr. Mahathir declared: "I feel disappointed because I achieved too little of my principal task of making my race a successful race, a race that is respected." Michael Shari, "Mahathir's Change of Heart?" *BusinessWeek,* International-Asia edition, July 29, 2002, p. 20.

19   Donald Harman Akenson, "Diaspora, the Irish and Irish Nationalism," *The Call of the Homeland: Diaspora Nationalisms, Past and Present,* edited by Allon Gal, et al (Leiden: Brill, 2010), pp. 190–191; Mei Luo, "Asian Pacific Americans," *Encyclopedia of Educational Leadership and Administration,* edited by Fenwick W. English (Thousand Oaks, California: SAGE Publications, 2006), Volume 1, pp. 53–56; Nana Oishi, "Pacific: Japan, Australia, New Zealand," *The New Americans: A Guide to Immigration Since 1965,* edited by Mary C. Waters and Reed Ueda (Cambridge, Massachusetts: Harvard University Press, 2007), p. 546; "Affirmative Non-Action," *Boston Globe,* January 14, 1985, p. 10.

20   Karyn R. Lacy, *Blue-Chip Black: Race, Class, and Status in the New Black Middle Class* (Berkeley: University of California Press, 2007), pp. 66–68, 77; Mary Pattillo-McCoy, *Black Picket Fences: Privilege and Peril Among the Black Middle Class* (Chicago: University of Chicago Press, 1999), p. 12.

21   Joseph E. Stiglitz, *The Great Divide: Unequal Societies and What We Can Do About Them* (New York: W.W. Norton & Company, 2015), p. 74.

22   Angus Deaton, *The Great Escape: Health, Wealth, and the Origins of Inequality* (New York: Penguin Books, 2013), p. 207.

23   Kay S. Hymowitz, "Brooklyn's Chinese Pioneers," *City Journal,* Spring 2014, pp. 21–29.

24   "A New Kind of Ghetto," *The Economist,* November 9, 2013, Special Report on Britain, p. 10.

25   Theodore Dalrymple, *Life at the Bottom: The Worldview That Makes the Underclass* (Chicago: Ivan R. Dee, 2001), p. 114.

26   See, for example, Joseph Stiglitz, "Equal Opportunity, Our National Myth," *New York Times,* February 17, 2013, Sunday Review, p. 4; Bob Herbert, "The Mobility Myth," *New York Times,* June 6, 2005, p. A19; Michael W. Weinstein, "America's Rags-to-Riches Myth," *New York Times,* February 18, 2000, p. A28.

27   Isabel V. Sawhill, "Overview," Julia B. Isaacs, Isabel V. Sawhill and Ron Haskins, *Getting Ahead or Losing Ground: Economic Mobility in America* (Washington: Economic Mobility Project, an initiative of The Pew Charitable Trusts, 2008), p. 6.

28   Joseph E. Stiglitz, *The Great Divide,* p. 159.

29   Theodore Dalrymple, *Life at the Bottom*, p. 70.
30   "A New Kind of Ghetto," *The Economist*, November 9, 2013, Special Report on Britain, p. 10.
31   Theodore Dalrymple, *Life at the Bottom*, p. 69.
32   Ibid., p. 68.
33   Theodore Dalrymple, "The Barbarians Inside Britain's Gates," *Wall Street Journal*, August 15, 2011, p. A13.
34   Natalie Perera and Mike Treadway, *Education in England: Annual Report 2016* (London: Centre Forum, 2016), p. 7.
35   Jason L. Riley, *Please Stop Helping Us: How Liberals Make It Harder for Blacks to Succeed* (New York: Encounter Books, 2014), p. 49.
36   Maria Newman, "Cortines Has Plan to Coach Minorities into Top Schools," *New York Times*, March 18, 1995, p. 1; Fernanda Santos, "Black at Stuy," *New York Times*, February 26, 2012, Metropolitan Desk, p. 6.
37   Sharon Otterman, "Diversity Debate Convulses Elite High School," *New York Times*, August 5, 2010, p. A1.
38   Valerie A. Ramey, "Is There a Tiger Mother Effect? Time Use Across Ethnic Groups," *Economics in Action*, Issue 4 (May 3, 2011).
39   Kenneth Clark, "Behind the Harlem Riots— Two Views," *New York Herald-Tribune*, July 20, 1964, p. 7.
40   Newton Garver, "What Violence Is," *The Nation*, June 24, 1968, p. 822.
41   National Committee of Negro Churchmen, "'Black Power,'" *New York Times*, July 31, 1966, p. E5.
42   Joseph A. Hill, "Some Results of the 1920 Population Census," *Journal of the American Statistical Association*, Vol. 18, No. 139 (September 1922), p. 353.
43   Stanley Lebergott, *Pursuing Happiness: American Consumers in the Twentieth Century* (Princeton: Princeton University Press, 1993), pp. 40, 120.
44   Allan Nevins and Henry Steele Commager, *A Short History of the United States*, fifth edition (New York: Alfred A. Knopf, 1966), p. 469. Frederick Lewis Allen, *Only Yesterday: An Informal History of the 1920s* (New York: Harper Perennial Classics, 2010), p. 142.
45   Stanley Lebergott, *The American Economy: Income, Wealth, and Want* (Princeton: Princeton University Press, 1976), p. 287.
46   Stanley Lebergott, *Pursuing Happiness*, p. 130.
47   David A. Shannon, *Between the Wars: America, 1919–1941* (Boston: Houghton Mifflin Company, 1965), p. 95.
48   Roger E. Bilstein, *Flight in America: From the Wrights to the Astronauts*, revised edition (Baltimore: Johns Hopkins Press, 1994), p. 57.
49   U.S. Bureau of the Census, *Historical Statistics of the United States: Colonial Times to 1970* (Washington: Government Printing Office, 1975), Part 1, p. 400.
50   Ibid.
51   Chris Willis, *The Man Who Built the National Football League: Joe F. Carr* (Lanham, Maryland: Scarecrow Press, 2010), p. 268.

52 The number of Sears department stores rose from 8 in 1925 to 319 by 1929. The three largest chains of grocery retailers all had the number of their stores increase severalfold from 1920 to 1929, with the largest of the grocery retailers— A&P— having the number of its stores rising from 4,600 in 1920 to 15,400 in 1929. Richard S. Tedlow, *New and Improved: The Story of Mass Marketing in America* (New York: Basic Books, 1990), pp. 195, 290.

53 Ibid., pp. 198–199, 200, 202, 203, 204, 213. See also David Delbert Kruger, "'It Pays to Shop at Penny's': A National Department Store on the Main Streets of Arkansas," *Arkansas Historical Quarterly*, Vol. 71, No. 4 (Winter 2012), pp. 348, 353, 354.

54 Henry Steele Commager and Richard Brandon Morris, "Editors' Introduction," John D. Hicks, *Republican Ascendancy: 1921–1933* (New York: Harper & Brothers, 1960), p. xi.

55 Edward Alsworth Ross, *Seventy Years of It: An Autobiography* (New York: D. Appleton-Century Company, 1936), p. 98.

56 Arthur M. Schlesinger, Jr., *The Age of Roosevelt*, Vol. I: *The Crisis of the Old Order 1919–1933* (Boston: Houghton-Mifflin, 1957), p. 68. See also James Truslow Adams, *The Epic of America* (Boston: Little, Brown and Company, 1934), p. 400.

57 Arthur M. Schlesinger, Jr., *The Age of Roosevelt*, Vol. I: *The Crisis of the Old Order*, p. 68.

58 David A. Shannon, *Between the Wars: America, 1919–1941*, p. 86.

59 "Text of President's Speech Elaborating His Views," *Washington Post*, February 13, 1924, p. 4. See also Burton W. Fulsom, Jr., *The Myth of the Robber Barons: A New Look at the Rise of Big Business in America*, sixth edition (Herndon, Virginia: Young America's Foundation, 2010), p. 116; James Gwartney and Richard Stroup, "Tax Cuts: Who Shoulders the Burden?" *Federal Reserve Bank of Atlanta Economic Review*, March 1982, p. 25; Benjamin G. Rader, "Federal Taxation in the 1920s: A Re-examination," *Historian*, Vol. 33, No. 3, pp. 432–433.

60 U. S. Bureau of the Census, *Historical Statistics of the United States: Colonial Times to 1970*, Part 1, p. 126.

61 Allan Nevins and Henry Steele Commager, *A Short History of the United States*, fifth edition, p. 463.

62 See, for example, Thomas E. Woods, Jr., "Warren Harding and the Forgotten Depression of 1920," *Intercollegiate Review*, Fall 2009, p. 23; Herbert Hoover, *The Memoirs of Herbert Hoover: The Great Depression 1929–1941* (New York: The Macmillan Company, 1952), Chapters 5–18.

63 James A. Smith, *The Idea Brokers: Think Tanks and the Rise of the New Policy Elite* (New York: The Free Press, 1991), p. 76.

64 Richard Vedder and Lowell Gallaway, *Out of Work: Unemployment and Government in Twentieth-Century America* (New York: Holmes & Meier, 1993), p. 77.

65 Ibid.

66   U. S. Bureau of the Census, *Historical Statistics of the United States: Colonial Times to 1970,* Part 1, p. 126; Richard Vedder and Lowell Gallaway, *Out of Work,* p. 77.

67   Richard Vedder and Lowell Gallaway, *Out of Work,* p. 77.

68   See, for example, Janet Poppendieck, *Breadlines Knee-Deep in Wheat: Food Assistance in the Great Depression,* updated and expanded (Berkeley: University of California Press, 2014), pp. 26–27; "The Misery of Garbage," *Social Service Review,* Vol. 6, No. 4 (December 1932), pp. 637–642; Edmund Wilson, *The American Earthquake: A Documentary of the Twenties and Thirties* (New York: Octagon Books, 1975), pp. 462–463; William E. Leuchtenburg, *Franklin D. Roosevelt and the New Deal, 1932–1940* (New York: Harper & Row, 1963), p. 249; Harvey Levenstein, *Paradox of Plenty: A Social History of Eating in Modern America,* revised edition (Berkeley: University of California Press, 2003), pp. 3, 4; "Ravages of Crisis in Cleveland Told," *New York Times,* December 27, 1939, p. 14; Samuel Lubell and Walter Everett, "The Breakdown of Relief," *The Nation,* August 20, 1938, p. 171; "Capone Feeds 3,000 a Day in Soup Kitchen," *New York Times,* November 15, 1930, p. 4; "First Bread Line Starts in Boston," *Daily Boston Globe,* October 12, 1931, p. 1.

69   Harold L. Cole and Lee E. Ohanian, "New Deal Policies and the Persistence of the Great Depression: A General Equilibrium Analysis," *Journal of Political Economy,* Vol. 112, No. 4 (August 2004), pp. 779–816. Back in 1935, a Brookings Institution study concluded that FDR's National Industrial Recovery Act "on the whole retarded recovery." Leverett S. Lyon, et al., *The National Recovery Administration: An Analysis and Appraisal* (Washington: Brookings Institution, 1935), pp. 873, 874. In a 1933 open letter to President Roosevelt, published in the *New York Times,* John Maynard Keynes said, "I cannot detect any material aid to recovery" in the National Industrial Recovery Act. John Maynard Keynes, "From Keynes to Roosevelt: Our Recovery Plan Assayed," *New York Times,* December 31, 1933, p. XX2. In 1939, FDR's own Secretary of the Treasury said to some Congressional Democrats: "We have tried spending money. We are spending more than we have ever spent before and it does not work. And I have just one interest, and if I am wrong. . . somebody else can have my job. I want to see this country prosperous. I want to see people get a job. I want to see people get enough to eat. We have never made good on our promises. . ." Burton Folsom, Jr., *New Deal or Raw Deal? How FDR's Economic Legacy Has Damaged America* (New York: Threshold Editions, 2008), p. 2.

70   J.A. Schumpeter, *History of Economic Analysis* (New York: Oxford University Press, 1954), p. 90.

71   See, for example, Paul Krugman, "Inequality Is a Drag," *New York Times,* August 8, 2014, p. A23; Paul Krugman, "Obama's Trickle-Up Economics," *New York Times,* September 16, 2016, p. A27; Joseph E. Stiglitz, *The Great Divide,* pp. 136, 145, 147; Alan Blinder, "Almost Everything Is Wrong With the New Tax Law," *Wall Street Journal,* December 28, 2017, p. A15. Like many others

who denounce what they call "trickle-down" economics, Professor Stiglitz, refers to "giving" high-income people something when, in fact, the reduction of the top tax rate from 73 percent to 24 percent led to *taking* more tax revenue from them as this lower tax rate drew investments out of tax shelters— which was the whole point, as Secretary of the Treasury Andrew Mellon spelled out beforehand. Compare Joseph E. Stiglitz, *The Price of Inequality: How Today's Divided Society Endangers Our Future* (New York: W.W. Norton and Company, 2012), p. 6 and Andrew W. Mellon, *Taxation: The People's Business* (New York: The Macmillan Company, 1924), pp. 72, 79, 152, 158, 160, 170.

72   See, for example, B.L. Mungekar, "State, Market and the Dalits: Analytics of the New Economic Policy," *Dalits in Modern India,* edited by S.M. Michael (New Delhi: Vistaar, 1999), p. 288.

73   *Public Papers of the Presidents of the United States: John F. Kennedy, 1962* (Washington: U.S. Government Printing Office, 1963), p. 626; *Public Papers of the Presidents of the United States: John F. Kennedy, 1963* (Washington: U.S. Government Printing Office, 1964), p. 762.

74   John Maynard Keynes, *The Means to Prosperity* (New York: Harcourt, Brace and Company, 1933), p. 5.

75   Woodrow Wilson, *The Hope of the World* (New York: Harper & Brothers, 1920), pp. 185–186. See also *Annual Report of the Secretary of the Treasury on the State of the Finances for the Fiscal Year Ended June 30, 1919* (Washington: Government Printing Office, 1920), p. 24; *Annual Report of the Secretary of the Treasury on the State of the Finances for the Fiscal Year Ended June 30, 1920* (Washington: Government Printing Office, 1921), pp. 36–37.

76   United States Internal Revenue, Treasury Department, *Statistics of Income from Returns of Net Income For 1920* (Washington: Government Printing Office, 1922), p. 5; Bureau of Internal Revenue, U.S. Treasury Department, *Statistics of Income For 1929* (Washington: Government Printing Office, 1931), p. 5. At the extremes, people with incomes of a million dollars a year or more paid less than 5 percent of all income taxes in 1920, when the highest income tax rate was 73 percent, while people with incomes of $5,000 or less paid 15 percent. After the tax rate cuts of the 1920s brought the highest tax rate down to 24 percent, people with an income of a million dollars or more paid 19 percent of all income taxes, while people with incomes of $5,000 or less paid less than half of one percent of all income taxes.

77   Robert L. Bartley, *The Seven Fat Years: And How to Do It Again* (New York: The Free Press, 1992), pp. 71–74; James Gwartney and Richard L. Stroup, "As Reagan Promised, the Rich Pay More," *New York Times,* March 31, 1985, p. F2; "How to Raise Revenue," *Wall Street Journal,* August 24, 2007, p. A14.

78   Oliver Wendell Holmes, *Collected Legal Papers* (New York: Peter Smith, 1952), pp. 230–231.

79   John M. Blum, et al., *The National Experience: A History of the United States,* eighth edition (New York: Harcourt, Brace and Jovanovich, 1991), p. 640.

80   Andrew W. Mellon, *Taxation*, pp. 9, 54–57, 61–62, 94.

81   Ibid., pp. 13, 79–80, 94, 127–128. Secretary Mellon also quoted President Calvin Coolidge as making essentially the same argument. Ibid., pp. 132–133, 220–221.

82   Ibid., pp. 106–107.

83   Ibid., Chapter VIII.

84   Ibid., p. 13.

85   Ibid., p. 167. See also Ibid., pp. 79–80, 141–142, 171–172.

86   Ibid., p. 170.

87   Ibid., p. 94.

88   Ibid., p. 79.

89   Ibid., p. 160.

90   Thomas A. Bailey, David M. Kennedy and Lizabeth Cohen, *The American Pageant: A History of the Republic,* eleventh edition (Boston: Houghton-Mifflin, 1998), p. 768. Later editions expressed similar conclusions, saying that Andrew Mellon sought to "succor the 'poor' rich people." David M. Kenney and Lizabeth Cohen, *The American Pageant: A History of the American People,* sixteenth edition (Boston: Engage Learning, 2016), p. 717.

91   United States Internal Revenue, Treasury Department, *Statistics of Income from Returns of Net Income For 1920,* p. 5; Bureau of Internal Revenue, U.S. Treasury Department, *Statistics of Income For 1929,* p. 5.

92   [Daniel Patrick Moynihan], *The Negro Family: The Case for National Action* (Washington: Government Printing Office, 1965), p. 18. The statistics cited were for "nonwhite" children, but before the immigration laws were changed in 1965, "nonwhite" Americans were overwhelmingly black before the immigration laws were changed that year, leading to great increases in the immigration of people from Asia and Latin America.

93   For example, the *New York Amsterdam News,* a Harlem newspaper, carried a column calling the Moynihan Report "the most serious threat to the ultimate freedom of American Negroes to appear in print in recent memory." James Farmer, "The Controversial Moynihan Report," *New York Amsterdam News,* December 18, 1965, p. 36.

94   "The Negro Family: Visceral Reaction," *Newsweek,* December 6, 1965, p. 39.

95   [Daniel Patrick Moynihan], *The Negro Family,* p. 17.

96   Godfrey Hodgson, *The Gentleman from New York: Daniel Patrick Moynihan* (Boston: Houghton Mifflin, 2000), pp. 31, 32; Steven R. Weisman, "Introduction," *Daniel Patrick Moynihan: A Portrait in Letters of an American Visionary,* edited by Steven R. Weisman (New York: Public Affairs, 2010), p. 1.

97   Godfrey Hodgson, *The Gentleman from New York,* p. 31.

98   Steven R. Weisman, "Introduction," *Daniel Patrick Moynihan,* p. 1; Douglas Schoen, *Pat: A Biography of Daniel Patrick Moynihan* (New York: Harper & Row, 1979), pp. 17–18.

99 Stephan Thernstrom and Abigail Thernstrom, *America in Black and White: One Nation, Indivisible* (New York: Simon & Schuster, 1997), pp. 237, 238; U.S. Census Bureau, *Statistical Abstract of the United States: 2010* (Washington: Government Printing Office, 2009), p. 59; Proquest, *Statistical Abstract of the United States: 2017* (Lanham, Maryland: Bernam Press, 2016), p. 53.

100 For example, in the most controversial of his books, *The Bell Curve*, co-authored with the late Richard Herrnstein, the following statement appears, with all the words italicized: *That a trait is genetically transmitted in individuals does not mean that group differences in that trait are also genetic in origin.* Richard J. Herrnstein and Charles Murray, *The Bell Curve: Intelligence and Class Structure in American Life* (New York: The Free Press, 1994), p. 298.

101 Associated Press, "Scholar of Race, Class Looks Ahead," *Telegram & Gazette* (Massachusetts), December 29, 2015, p. 14.

102 Timothy M. Phelps and Helen Winternitz, *Capitol Games: The Inside Story of Clarence Thomas, Anita Hill, and a Supreme Court Nomination* (New York: HarperPerennial, 1993), p. xii.

103 Lanny Ebenstein, *Chicagonomics: The Evolution of Chicago Free Market Economics* (New York: St. Martins's Press, 2015), p. 200.

104 See, for example, Thomas Sowell, *A Man of Letters* (New York: Encounter Books, 2007), pp. 118–119, 305–306.

105 Joseph E. Stiglitz, *The Great Divide*, p. 153; "The Tax Bill That Inequality Created," *New York Times*, December 17, 2017, Sunday Review section, p. 10.

106 "Remarks by the President on Economic Mobility," December 4, 2013, downloaded from the Obama White House archives: https://obamawhitehouse.archives.gov/the-press-office/2013/12/04/remarks-president-economic-mobility.

107 Danny Dorling, "Inequality in Advanced Economies," *The New Oxford Handbook of Economic Geography*, edited by Gordon L. Clark, et al (Oxford: Oxford University Press, 2018), pp. 40, 42, 43, 52.

108 [Anonymous], *An Inquiry Into Those Principles Respecting the Nature of Demand and the Necessity of Consumption Lately Advocated by Mr. Malthus* (London: R. Hunter, 1821), p. 110.

109 John Rawls, *A Theory of Justice* (Cambridge, Massachusetts: Harvard University Press, 1971), pp. 43, 60, 61, 265, 302.

110 Woodrow Wilson, *The New Freedom: A Call for the Emancipation of the Energies of a People* (New York: Doubleday, Page & Company, 1913).

111 Robert A. Dahl and Charles E. Lindblom, *Politics, Economics, and Welfare: Planning and Politico-Economic Systems Resolved into Basic Social Processes* (Chicago: University of Chicago Press, 1976), p. 49.

112 Ibid., p. 425.

113 Angus Deaton, *The Great Escape*, p. 2.

114 Thomas Hobbes, *Leviathan*, p. 16. Writing about one of the doctrines of his own time, Adam Smith said, "they who first taught it were by no means such

fools as they who believed it." Adam Smith, *An Inquiry into the Nature and Causes of the Wealth of Nations* (New York: Modern Library, 1937), p. 461.

Chapter 6: SOCIAL VISIONS AND HUMAN CONSEQUENCES

Epigraph

Joseph A. Schumpeter, Review of Keynes' General Theory, *Journal of the American Statistical Association*, Vol. 31, No. 196 (December 1936), p. 795.

1   See Thomas Sowell, *The Einstein Syndrome: Bright Children Who Talk Late* (New York: Basic Books, 2001); Stephen M. Camarata, *Late-Talking Children: A Symptom or a Stage?* (Cambridge, Massachusetts: MIT Press, 2014).

2   See, for example, Thomas Sowell, *Intellectuals and Race* (New York: Basic Books, 2013), pp. 24–43; Thomas C. Leonard, *Illiberal Reformers: Race, Eugenics & American Economics in the Progressive Era* (Princeton: Princeton University Press, 2016), pp. 119–124.

3   Oliver Wendell Holmes, *Collected Legal Papers* (New York: Peter Smith, 1952), p. 293.

4   Jean-Jacques Rousseau, *A Discourse on Inequality*, translated by Maurice Cranston (New York: Penguin Books, 1984), p. 57.

5   William S. Maltby, *The Rise and Fall of the Spanish Empire* (New York: Palgrave Macmillan, 2009), p. 18; Peter Pierson, *The History of Spain* (Westport, Connecticut: Greenwood Press, 1999), pp. 7–8. Geographer Ellen Churchill Semple described the Canary Islanders as offshoots of "their parent stock of northern Africa." Ellen Churchill Semple, *Influences of Geographic Environment* (New York: Henry Holt and Company, 1911), p. 411. However, she pointed out that the white race existed in Europe, Asia and Africa (Ibid., pp. 390–391.) In any case, contemporary continental peoples in both Europe and North Africa were thousands of years more advanced than the peoples of the Canary Islands.

6   Ellen Churchill Semple, *Influences of Geographic Environment*, p. 411.

7   Ibid., p. 434; Bruce G. Trigger, *Understanding Early Civilizations: A Comparative Study* (Cambridge: Cambridge University Press, 2003), p. 338.

8   Judith A. Bazler, *Biology Resources in the Electronic Age* (Westport, Connecticut: Greenwood Press, 2003), p. 105; Alfred W. Crosby, "An Ecohistory of the Canary Islands: A Precursor of European Colonialization in the New World and Australasia," *Environmental Review*, Vol. 8, No. 3 (Autumn 1984), p. 217.

9   Ellen Churchill Semple, *Influences of Geographic Environment*, pp. 19–20, 45, 69, 118, 144–145, 193, 397, 434, 435, 436, 598, 600; J.R. McNeill, *The Mountains of the Mediterranean World: An Environmental History* (New York: Cambridge University Press, 1992), pp. 142–143; Rupert B. Vance, *Human*

Geography of the South: A Study in Regional Resources and Human Adequacy (Chapel Hill: University of North Carolina Press, 1932), pp. 242, 246; Thomas Sowell, *Wealth, Poverty and Politics*, revised and enlarged edition (New York: Basic Books, 2016), pp. 4–5, 20–21, 24, 45, 46, 49, 52, 70, 72–76, 80, 125–126, 209, 211, 228–230, 242–243, 392–393.

10 For documented examples, see Thomas Sowell, *Wealth, Poverty and Politics*, revised and enlarged edition, Part I.

11 Documented examples can be found in Thomas Sowell, *Wealth, Poverty and Politics*, revised and enlarged edition, pp. 4–5, 20–22, 42, 48–54, 59–60, 64–67, 70, 75. See also Ellen Churchill Semple, *Influences of Geographic Environment*, pp. 393, 397, 434, 435.

12 Irving Howe, *World of Our Fathers: The Journey of the East European Jews to America and the Life They Found and Made* (New York: Harcourt Brace Jovanovich, 1976), pp. 369–370; James R. Barrett, *The Irish Way: Becoming American in the Multiethnic City* (New York: Penguin, 2012), pp. 197–198.

13 For documented examples, see Thomas Sowell, *Wealth, Poverty and Politics*, revised and enlarged edition, pp. 396–401.

14 James S. Gardner, et al., "People in the Mountains," *Mountain Geography: Physical and Human Dimensions*, edited by Martin F. Price, et al (Berkeley: University of California Press, 2013), pp. 288–289; J.R. McNeill, *The Mountains of the Mediterranean World*, pp. 223, 225–227; Ellen Churchill Semple, *Influences of Geographic Environment*, pp. 578–579.

15 "Choose Your Parents Wisely," *The Economist*, July 26, 2014, p. 22.

16 See Betty Hart and Todd R. Risley, *Meaningful Differences in the Everyday Experience of Young American Children* (Baltimore: Paul H. Brookes Publishing Co., 1995), pp. 123–124.

17 Ibid., pp. 125–126, 128, 198–199.

18 Ibid., p. 247. Similar social class differences in parent-child interactions were discussed in Edward C. Banfield, *The Unheavenly City: The Nature and Future of Our Urban Crisis* (Boston: Little, Brown, 1970), pp. 224–229.

19 Laurence C. Baker, "Differences in Earnings Between Male and Female Physicians," *The New England Journal of Medicine*, April 11, 1996, p. 962.

20 Hugh Morris, "Why Do Airlines Have Such Large Gender Pay Gaps?" *Daily Telegraph* (London), April 5, 2018 (online).

21 Mandel Sherman and Cora B. Key, "The Intelligence of Isolated Mountain Children," *Child Development*, Vol. 3, No. 4 (December 1932), p. 283; Lester R. Wheeler, "A Comparative Study of the Intelligence of East Tennessee Mountain Children," *Journal of Educational Psychology*, Vol. XXXIII, No. 5 (May 1942), p. 322.

22 Philip E. Vernon, *Intelligence and Cultural Environment* (London: Methuen & Co., Ltd., 1970), p. 155.

23 Hugh Gordon, *Mental and Scholastic Tests Among Retarded Children* (London: His Majesty's Stationery Office, 1923), p. 38.

24　Clifford Kirkpatrick, *Intelligence and Immigration* (Baltimore: The Williams & Wilkins Company, 1926), pp. 24, 31, 34.

25　"In Norfolk, Virginia, women of low socioeconomic status were given vitamin and mineral supplements during pregnancy. These women gave birth to children who, at 4 years of age, averaged 8 points higher in IQ than a control group of children whose mothers had been given placebos during pregnancy." Arthur R. Jensen, *Genetics and Education* (New York: Harper & Row, 1972), p. 152. See Ruth F. Harrell, Ella Woodyard, and Arthur I. Gates, *The Effect of Mothers' Diets on the Intelligence of Offspring* (New York: Teachers College, Columbia University, 1955), pp. 32–33, 60; Ana Amélia Freitas-Vilela, et al., "Maternal Dietary Patterns During Pregnancy and Intelligence Quotients in the Offspring at 8 Years of Age: Findings from the ALSPAC Cohort," *Maternal & Child Nutrition*, Vol. 14, Issue 1 (January 2018), pp. 1–11; Ann P. Streissguth, Helen M. Barr, and Paul D. Sampson, "Moderate Prenatal Alcohol Exposure: Effects on Child IQ and Learning Problems at Age 7 ½ Years," *Alcoholism: Clinical and Experimental Research*, Vol. 14, No. 5 (September/October 1990), pp. 662–669.

26　Thomas Sowell, *Intellectuals and Race*, pp. 23, 31, 32, 33, 38–39, 59, 63–64.

27　See Mitchell Lerner, "Howard Arthur Tibbs 1919–1986: A Tuskegee Airman's Story in Pictures," *Callaloo*, Vol. 26, No. 3 (Summer 2003), pp. 670–690. See also J. Todd Moye, *Freedom Flyers: The Tuskegee Airmen of World War II* (New York: Oxford University Press, 2010); Lawrence P. Scott and William M. Womack, Sr., *Double V: The Civil Rights Struggle of the Tuskegee Airmen* (East Lansing: Michigan State University Press, 1994).

28　"Medical Leaders at Dr. Drew Rites," *New York Times*, April 6, 1950, p. 28.

29　Robin Marantz Henig, "Scientist at Work," *New York Times*, June 8, 1993, p. C1.

30　Arthur R. Jensen, *Genetics and Education*, pp. 196–197. See also Arthur R. Jensen, "Social Class, Race and Genetics: Implications for Education," *American Educational Research Journal*, Vol. 5, No. 1 (January 1968), p. 34; Arthur R. Jensen, "Patterns of Mental Ability and Socioeconomic Status," *Proceedings of the National Academy of Sciences of the United States of America*, Vol. 60, No. 4 (August 15, 1968), pp. 1331–1332; Arthur R. Jensen, "Intelligence, Learning Ability and Socioeconomic Status," *The Journal of Special Education*, Vol. 3, No. 1 (January 1969), p. 33.

31　Arthur R. Jensen, *Genetics and Education*, pp. 43–44.

32　See Chapter 3 of Thomas Sowell, *Economic Facts and Fallacies* (New York: Basic Books, 2008). See also Diana Furchtgott-Roth, *Women's Figures: An Illustrated Guide to the Economic Progress of Women In America* (Washington: AEI Press, 2012).

33　Yuan-li Wu and Chun-hsi Wu, *Economic Development in Southeast Asia: The Chinese Dimension* (Stanford: Hoover Institution Press, 1980), p. 51; Victor Purcell, *The Chinese in Southeast Asia*, second edition (Kuala Lumpur: Oxford University Press, 1965), pp. 7, 68, 83, 180, 245, 248, 540.

34 Ezra Mendelsohn, *The Jews of East Central Europe between the World Wars* (Bloomington: Indiana University Press, 1983), pp. 25–27.

35 Haraprasad Chattopadhyaya, *Indians in Africa: A Socio-Economic Study* (Calcutta: Bookland Private Limited, 1970), p. 394.

36 R. Bayly Winder, "The Lebanese in West Africa," *Comparative Studies in Society and History*, Vol. IV (1961–62), p. 309; H.L. van der Laan, *The Lebanese Traders in Sierra Leone* (The Hague: Mouton & Co., 1975), p. 65.

37 Uğur Ümit Üngör and Mehmet Polatel, *Confiscation and Destruction: The Young Turk Seizure of Armenian Property* (New York: Continuum, 2011), pp. 17–19.

38 Warren C. Scoville, *The Persecution of Huguenots and French Economic Development: 1680–1720* (Berkeley: University of California Press, 1960), pp. 228–229, 242–243, 248.

39 Jean Roche, *La Colonisation Allemande et le Rio Grande do Sul* (Paris: Institut Des Hautes Études de L'Amérique Latine, 1959), pp. 388–389.

40 C. Harvey Gardiner, *The Japanese and Peru: 1873–1973* (Albuquerque: University of New Mexico Press, 1975), p. 64.

41 Medha Kudaisya, "Marwari and Chettiar Merchant's, c. 1850s–1950s: Competitive Trajectories," *Chinese and Indian Business: Historical Antecedents*, edited by Medha Kudaisya and Ng Chin-keong (Boston: Brill, 2009), pp. 97–98.

42 Robert F. Foerster, *The Italian Emigration of Our Times* (New York: Arno Press, 1969), pp. 254–259, 261.

43 Dan Bilefsky, "A New Facet of Diamond Industry: Indians," *Wall Street Journal*, May 27, 2003, p. B1.

44 Steven Pinker, *The Better Angels of Our Nature: Why Violence Has Declined* (New York: Viking, 2011), pp. 85–87, 93–104.

45 The Economist, *Pocket World in Figures: 2017 edition* (London: Profile Books, 2016), p. 18.

46 Bureau of Justice Statistics, *Survey of State Prison Inmates, 1991* (Washington: U.S. Department of Justice, 1993), p. 9.

47 Oliver MacDonagh, "The Irish Famine Emigration to the United States," *Perspectives in American History*, Vol. X (1976), p. 405; Thomas Bartlett, *Ireland: A History* (New York: Cambridge University Press, 2010), p. 284.

48 W.E. Vaughan and A.J. Fitzpatrick, editors, *Irish Historical Statistics: Population, 1821–1971* (Dublin: Royal Irish Academy, 1978), pp. 260–261.

49 Tyler Anbinder, *City of Dreams: The 400-Year Epic History of Immigrant New York* (Boston: Houghton Mifflin Harcourt, 2016), p. 127. See also Catherina Japikse, "The Irish Potato Famine," *EPA Journal*, Vol. 20, Nos. 3–4 (Fall 1994), p. 44; Evan D.G. Fraser and Andrew Rimas, *Empires of Food: Feast, Famine and the Rise and Fall of Civilizations* (New York: Free Press, 2010), pp. 212–214; Evan D.G. Fraser, "Social Vulnerability and Ecological Fragility: Building Bridges Between Social and Natural Sciences Using the Irish Potato Famine as a Case Study," *Conservation Ecology*, Vol. 7, No. 2 (December 2003).

50   Jim Dwyer, "Specialized Schools, Surrounded for Decades by an Admissions Moat," *New York Times*, June 9, 2018, p. A17.

51   Adam Smith, *An Inquiry into the Nature and Causes of the Wealth of Nations* (New York: Modern Library, 1937), p. 729.

52   Thomas D. Snyder, Cristobal de Brey and Sally A. Dillow, *Digest of Education Statistics: 2015*, 51st edition (Washington: U.S. Department of Education, National Center for Education Statistics, 2016), pp. 328, 329. See also Valerie A. Ramey, "Is There a Tiger Mother Effect? Time Use Across Ethnic Groups," *Economics in Action*, Issue 4 (May 3, 2011).

53   Roland G. Fryer and Paul Torelli, "An Empirical Analysis of 'Acting White'," *Journal of Public Economics*, Vol. 94, No. 5–6 (June 2010), p. 381.

54   Eric A. Hanushek, et al., "New Evidence About *Brown v. Board of Education:* The Complex Effects of School Racial Composition on Achievement," National Bureau of Economic Research, Working Paper 8741 (Cambridge, Massachusetts: National Bureau of Economic Research, 2002), Abstract.

55   Ellis B. Page and Timothy Z. Keith, "The Elephant in the Classroom: Ability Grouping and the Gifted," *Intellectual Talent: Psychometric and Social Issues*, edited by Camilla Persson Benbow and David Lubinski (Baltimore: Johns Hopkins University Press, 1996), pp. 203, 204, 208.

56   Roland G. Fryer and Paul Torelli, "An Empirical Analysis of 'Acting White'," *Journal of Public Economics*, Vol. 94, No. 5–6 (June 2010), p. 381.

57   Ibid., p. 380n.

58   Theodore Dalrymple, *Life at the Bottom: The Worldview That Makes the Underclass* (Chicago: Ivan R. Dee, 2001), p. 69. See also pp. 158, 188.

59   Ibid., p. 158.

60   Ibid.

61   Jason L. Riley, *Please Stop Helping Us: How Liberals Make It Harder for Blacks to Succeed* (New York: Encounter Books, 2014), p. 43; John U. Ogbu, *Black American Students in an Affluent Suburb: A Study of Academic Disengagement* (Mahwah, New Jersey: Lawrence Erlbaum Associates, 2003), p. 179; John U. Ogbu and Signithia Fordham, "Black Students' School Success: Coping with the 'Burden of 'Acting White'," *Urban Review*, Vol. 18, No. 3 (September 1986), pp. 176–206.

62   James Bartholomew, *The Welfare of Nations* (Washington: The Cato Institute, 2016), p. 103.

63   See, for example, Katherine Kersten, "No Thug Left Behind," *City Journal*, Winter 2017, pp. 54–61; Teresa Watanabe and Howard Blume, "Disorder in the Classroom," *Los Angeles Times*, November 8, 2015, p. A1; "Classrooms Run by the Unsuspended," *Investor's Business Daily*, July 3, 2014, p. A14; Jason L. Riley, "Upward Mobility: An Obama Decree Continues to Make Public Schools Lawless," *Wall Street Journal*, March 22, 2017, p. A19; Aaron Anthony Benner, "St. Paul Schools: Close the Gap? Yes. But Not Like This," *Saint Paul Pioneer Press*, October 2, 2015; Katherine Kersten, "Mollycoddle No More," *Star Tribune*

(Minneapolis), March 20, 2016, p. OP 1; Paul Sperry, "Obama's Lax Discipline Policies Made Schools Dangerous," *New York Post*, December 23, 2017; Ryan Mackenzie, "Schools Rethink Discipline," *Des Moines Register*, November 27, 2016, p. A9; Mackenzie Mays, "Restorative Justice?" *The Fresno Bee*, December 11, 2016, p. 1B; Claudia Rowe, "Trouble Erupts After Highline Limits School Suspensions," *Seattle Times*, September 11, 2016, p. A1.

64   James Bartholomew, *The Welfare of Nations*, p. 92.

65   See, for example, Katherine Kersten, "No Thug Left Behind," *City Journal*, Winter 2017, pp. 54–61. This article was based on what happened in public schools in St. Paul, Minnesota. However, similar things happened elsewhere across the country—in a Houston public school, for example: "One of the older children walked across the room during class, zipped down his fly, pulled out his penis, and asked a girl for oral sex. Levin sent him to the principal. He was sent back in thirty minutes." Jay Mathews, *Work Hard. Be Nice: How Two Inspired Teachers Created the Most Promising Schools in America* (Chapel Hill: Algonquin Books of Chapel Hill, 2009), pp. 22–23.

66   "The World's Billionaires," *Forbes*, March 28, 2017, pp. 84–85. V.I. Lenin tried to rescue Marxist theory by claiming that rich countries exploited poor countries, and shared some of their "super-profits" with their own working classes, in order to stave off revolution. But in fact most rich countries' international investments are concentrated in other rich countries, with their investments in poor countries being a very small fraction of their foreign investments and their incomes from these investments in poor countries being a very small fraction of their total income from foreign investments. See my *Wealth, Poverty and Politics*, revised and enlarged edition (New York: Basic Books, 2016) pp. 245–247.

67   For documented specifics, see my *Wealth, Poverty and Politics*, revised and enlarged edition, p. 136.

68   See, for example, hostile responses to empirical data from Daniel Patrick Moynihan, James S. Coleman, Jay Belsky and Heather Mac Donald in Jean M. White, "Moynihan Report Criticized as 'Racist,'" *Washington Post*, November 22, 1965, p. A3; William Ryan, "Savage Discovery: The Moynihan Report," *The Nation*, November 22, 1965, pp. 380–384; Diane Ravitch, "The Coleman Reports and American Education," *Social Theory and Social Policy: Essays in Honor of James S. Coleman*, edited by Aage B. Sorenson and Seymour Spilerman (Westport, Connecticut: Praeger, 1993), pp. 129–141; James Bartholomew, *The Welfare of Nations*, pp. 174–175; Tim Lynch, "There Is No War on Cops," *Reason*, August/September 2016, pp. 58–61; William McGurn, "The Silencing of Heather Mac Donald," *Wall Street Journal*, April 11, 2017, p. A15.

69   "Bicker Warning," *The Economist*, April 1, 2017, p. 23.

70   Theodore Dalrymple, *Life at the Bottom*, p. 6.

71   Barry Latzer, *The Rise and Fall of Violent Crime in America* (New York: Encounter Books, 2016), p. 19; *Today's VD Control Problem: Joint Statement by The American Public Health Association, The American Social Health Association,*

The American Venereal Disease Association, The Association of State and Territorial Health Officers in co-operation with The American Medical Association, February 1966, p. 20; Hearings Before the Select Committee on Population, Ninety-Fifth Congress, Second Session, *Fertility and Contraception in America: Adolescent and Pre-Adolescent Pregnancy* (Washington: U.S. Government Printing Office, 1978), Volume II, p. 625; Jacqueline R. Kasun, *The War Against Population: The Economics and Ideology of World Population Control* (San Francisco: Ignatius Press, 1988), pp. 142, 143, 144; Sally Curtin, et al., "2010 Pregnancy Rates Among U.S. Women," *National Center for Health Statistics*, December 2015, p. 6.

72   U.S. Bureau of the Census, *Historical Statistics of the United States: Colonial Times to 1970* (Washington: Government Printing Office, 1975), Part I, p. 414.

73   Stephan Thernstrom and Abigail Thernstrom, *America in Black and White: One Nation, Indivisible* (New York: Simon & Schuster, 1997), p. 262.

74   Steven Pinker, *The Better Angels of Our Nature*, pp. 106–107.

75   John Kenneth Galbraith, *The Selected Letters of John Kenneth Galbraith*, edited by Richard P.F. Holt (Cambridge: Cambridge University Press, 2017), p. 47. "The English urban crowd, in particular, may justly be said to have developed, from its own experience and its own good sense, a species of self-discipline and a tactic of 'fitting in' neatly on a little space. You seldom feel unsafe in a London crowd: you know in your heart that it is experienced— experienced in situations." Earnest Barker, "An Attempt at Perspective," *The Character of England*, edited by Ernest Barker (Oxford: Clarendon Press, 1947), p. 562.

76   George Orwell, *The Complete Works of George Orwell*, Vol. 16: *I Have Tried to Tell the Truth, 1943–1944*, edited by Peter Davison, et al (London: Secker & Warburg, 1998), p. 201.

77   David Fraser, *A Land Fit for Criminals: An Insider's View of Crime, Punishment and Justice in England and Wales* (Sussex: Book Guild Publishing, 2006), p. 13.

78   Lee Kuan Yew, *The Singapore Story* (Singapore: Times Editions, 1998), p. 126.

79   James Bartholomew, *The Welfare of Nations*, pp. 187–189.

80   "Britain: Fight Club," *The Economist*, June 10, 2000, p. 61. See also James Bartholomew, *The Welfare State We're In* (London: Politico's, 2006), p. 19.

81   Fay Wiley, et al., "Traveling Hooligans," *Newsweek*, June 27, 1988, p. 37.

82   Steve Lohr, "The British (Fans) are Coming!" *New York Times*, June 10, 1988, p. D22.

83   George Orwell, *The Complete Works of George Orwell*, Vol. 16: *I Have Tried to Tell the Truth, 1943–1944*, edited by Peter Davison, et al., p. 201.

84   Joyce Lee Malcolm, *Guns and Violence: The English Experience* (Cambridge, Massachusetts: Harvard University Press, 2002), p. 168.

85   Peter Hitchens, *The Abolition of Britain: From Winston Churchill to Princess Diana* (San Francisco: Encounter Books, 2000), p. 32.

86   James Bartholomew, *The Welfare State We're In*, Politico's edition published in 2006, pp. 15–19.

87   George Orwell, *The Complete Works of George Orwell*, Vol. 16: *I Have Tried to Tell the Truth, 1943–1944*, edited by Peter Davison, et al., p. 201.

88   See, for example, Sean O'Neill and Fiona Hamilton, "Mobs Rule as Police Surrender Streets," *The Times* (London), August 9, 2011, pp. 1, 5; Martin Beckford, et al., "Carry On Looting," *The Daily Telegraph* (London), August 8, 2011, pp. 1, 2; Philip Johnston, "The Long Retreat of Order," *The Daily Telegraph* (London), August 10, 2011, p. 19; Alistair MacDonald and Guy Chazan, "World News: Britain Tallies Damage and Sets Out Anti-Riot Steps," *Wall Street Journal*, August 12, 2011, p. A6.

89   Theodore Dalrymple, *Life at the Bottom*, p. 136.

90   Ibid.; James Bartholomew, *The Welfare of Nations*, p. 203.

91   Andrew F. Smith, "Cafeterias," *Savoring Gotham: A Food Lover's Companion to New York City* (New York: Oxford Press, 2015), p. 92.

92   John P. Shanley, "Cafeterias Built on Honesty Fail," *New York Times*, November 9, 1963, p. 22.

93   Theodore Dalrymple, *Life at the Bottom*, pp. 149, 150; James Bartholomew, *The Welfare of Nations*, pp. 125–136; Robyn Minter Smyers, "High Noon in Public Housing: The Showdown Between Due Process Rights and Good Management Practices in the War on Drugs and Crime," *The Urban Lawyer*, Summer 1998, pp. 573–574; William Julius Wilson, "The Urban Underclass in Advanced Industrial Society," *The New Urban Reality*, edited by Paul E. Peterson (Washington: The Brookings Institution, 1985), p. 137.

94   Lizette Alvarez, "Out, and Up," *New York Times*, Metropolitan section, May 31, 2009, p. 1.

95   Ibid., p. 6.

96   Walter E. Williams, *Up from The Projects: An Autobiography* (Stanford: Hoover Institution Press, 2010), pp. 6–7.

97   Ibid., p. 7.

98   Theodore Dalrymple, *Life at the Bottom*, p. 150.

99   Luis Ferre-Sadurni, "The Rise and Fall of Good Intentions," *New York Times*, July 9, 2018, p. A19.

100   Ibid., p. A20.

101   David E. Nye, *When the Lights Went Out: A History of Blackouts in America* (Cambridge, Massachusetts: MIT Press 2010), pp. 84–91.

102   Ibid., p. 94; "The Longest Night," *Newsweek*, November 22, 1965, pp. 27–33; Robert J.H. Johnston, "Bright Side to Blackout," *New York Times*, November 10, 1965, p. 4; Emanuel Perlmutter, "Crime Rate Off Despite the Dark," *New York Times*, November 11, 1965, p. 41; Saul Pett, "New York Took It Largely in Stride," *Boston Globe*, November 10, 1965, p. 5.

103   Peter Goldman, et al., "Heart of Darkness," *Newsweek*, July 25, 1977, pp. 18, 19.

104   Ibid., p. 18; Richard Severo, "Two Blackouts and a World of Difference," *New York Times*, July 16, 1977, p. 8.

105 "Power Blackouts Then and Now. . ." *Washington Post*, July 15, 1977, p. A9; David E. Nye, *When the Lights Went Out*, pp. 101, 123–128.

106 Stephan Thernstrom and Abigail Thernstrom, *America in Black and White*, p. 238.

107 Ibid., p. 237.

108 Charles Murray, *Coming Apart: The State of White America 1960–2010* (New York: Crown Forum, 2012), pp. 160, 161.

109 James Bartholomew, *The Welfare State We're In*, Politico's edition published in 2006, p. 251.

110 James Bartholomew, *The Welfare of Nations*, p. 164.

111 Ibid., p. 165.

112 *PISA 2015: Results in Focus* (Paris: OECD, 2018), p. 5.

113 See, for example, J. Martin Rochester, *Class Warfare: Besieged Schools, Bewildered Parents, Betrayed Kids and the Attack on Excellence* (San Francisco: Encounter Books, 2002), pp. 16–18; Thomas Sowell, *Inside American Education: The Decline, the Deception, the Dogmas* (New York: Free Press, 1993), Chapter 1; The National Commission on Excellence in Education, *A Nation at Risk: The Full Account* (Cambridge, Massachusetts: USA Research, 1984).

114 E.W. Kenworthy, "Action by Senate: Revised Measure Now Goes Back to House for Concurrence," *New York Times*, June 20, 1964, p. 1; "House Civil Rights Vote," *New York Times*, July 3, 1964, p. 9; E.W. Kenworthy, "Voting Measure Passed by House," *New York Times*, August 4, 1965, pp. 1, 17; "Vote Rights Bill: Senate Sends Measure to LBJ," *Los Angeles Times*, August 5, 1965, p. 1.

115 Stephan Thernstrom and Abigail Thernstrom, *America in Black and White*, pp. 233–234.

116 Ibid. See also U.S. Census Bureau, *Statistical Abstract of the United States: 1970* (Washington: U.S. Department of Commerce, Bureau of the Census, 1970), p. 328. For information on national trends in poverty during these decades, see Richard J. Herrnstein and Charles Murray, *The Bell Curve: Intelligence and Class Structure in American Life* (New York: The Free Press, 1994), p. 128.

117 See, for example, Barry Hugill and David Rose, "No Hope in No-Go Land," *The Guardian and the Obersver*, September 15, 1991, p. 23; Larry Martz and Daniel Pedersen, "Yob Politics in Britain," *Newsweek*, April 16, 1990, pp. 34–35; Sheila Rule, "2 Die, 600 Seized in Britain in Riots Over Soccer Defeat," *New York Times*, July 6, 1990, p. A3. See also Theodore Dalrymple, *Life at the Bottom*, pp. x, xi, 45, 67, 72, 139, 153, 166, 181, 188, 223–225.

118 Steven Pinker, *The Better Angels of Our Nature*, pp. 106–116.

119 Shelby Steele, *White Guilt: How Blacks and Whites Together Destroyed the Promise of the Civil Rights Era* (New York: HarperCollins Publishers, 2006), p. 123.

120 Ibid., p. 124.

121 Stephan Thernstrom and Abigail Thernstrom, *America in Black and White*, pp. 233–234.

122 See, for example, Charles Murray, *In Our Hands: A Plan to Replace the Welfare State* (Washington: American Enterprise Institute, 2006); Stephen Moore, *Who's The Fairest of Them All? The Truth about Opportunity, Taxes, and Wealth in America* (New York: Encounter Books, 2012), p. 2. For counter-arguments, see Edward C. Banfield, *The Unheavenly City: The Nature and Future of Our Urban Crisis* (Boston: Little, Brown, 1970), pp. 123ff.

123 Seattle provides one of many examples: "Over the past five years, the Emerald City has seen an explosion of homelessness, crime, and addiction. In its 2017 point-in-time count of the homeless, King County social-services agency All Home found 11,643 people sleeping in tents, cars, and emergency shelters. Property crime has risen to a rate two and a half times higher than Los Angeles's and four times higher than New York City's. Cleanup crews pick up tens of thousands of dirty needles from city streets and parks every year. At the same time, according to the *Puget Sound Business Journal*, the Seattle metro area spends more than $1 billon fighting homelessness every year. That's nearly $100,000 for every homeless man, woman, and child in King County, yet the crisis seems only to have deepened, with more addiction, more crime, and more tent encampments in residential neighborhoods." Christopher F. Rufo, "Seattle Under Siege," *City Journal*, Autumn 2018, p. 20.

124 James Bartholomew, *The Welfare of Nations*, p. 204.

125 Ibid., p. 127.

126 James Bartholomew, *The Welfare State We're In*, Politico's edition published in 2006, pp. 189, 190, 203–209; James Bartholomew, *The Welfare of Nations*, p. 103; Theodore Dalrymple, *Life at the Bottom*, pp. 69, 158, 188; Katherine Kersten, "No Thug Left Behind," *City Journal*, Winter 2017, pp. 54–61; Teresa Watanabe and Howard Blume, "Disorder in the Classroom," *Los Angeles Times*, November 8, 2015, p. A1; "Classrooms Run by the Unsuspended," *Investor's Business Daily*, July 3, 2014, p. A14; Jason L. Riley, "Upward Mobility: An Obama Decree Continues to Make Public Schools Lawless," *Wall Street Journal*, March 22, 2017, p. A19; Aaron Anthony Benner, "St. Paul Schools: Close the Gap? Yes. But Not Like This," *Saint Paul Pioneer Press*, October 2, 2015; Katherine Kersten, "Mollycoddle No More," *Star Tribune* (Minneapolis), March 20, 2016, p. OP 1; Paul Sperry, "Obama's Lax Discipline Policies Made Schools Dangerous," *New York Post*, December 23, 2017; Ryan Mackenzie, "Schools Rethink Discipline," *Des Moines Register*, November 27, 2016, p. A9; Mackenzie Mays, "Restorative Justice?" *The Fresno Bee*, December 11, 2016, p. 1B; Claudia Rowe, "Trouble Erupts After Highline Limits School Suspensions," *Seattle Times*, September 11, 2016, p. A1.

127 James Bartholomew, *The Welfare of Nations*, p. 202. The instrumental use of babies takes a more sophisticated form in a *New York Times* essay by a 38-year-old unmarried woman who celebrates her own defiance of convention by choosing to have a baby— and urging other women to do the same, without even a mention

of the consequences for the child. Emma Brockes, "Single at 38? Have That Baby," *New York Times*, June 24, 2018, Sunday review, p. 3.

128   James Bartholomew, *The Welfare of Nations*, p. 134. The mother of one of the rapists seemed to take a similar view, pointing out that she herself had been raped when she was 7 years old and again when she was 12.

129   Steven Pinker, *The Better Angels of Our Nature*, pp. 106–107.

Chapter 7: FACTS, ASSUMPTIONS AND GOALS

Epigraph

Winston Churchill, *Churchill Speaks 1897–1963: Collected Speeches in Peace & War*, edited by Robert Rhodes James (New York: Chelsea House, 1980), p. 418.

1   Ulrich Bonnell Phillips, *The Slave Economy of the Old South: Selected Essays in Economic and Social History* (Baton Rouge: Louisiana State University Press, 1968), p. 269.

2   See, for example, Daniel Boorstin, *The Americans: The Colonial Experience* (New York: Random House, 1958), Chapters 12–16; Joshua Muravchik, *Heaven on Earth: The Rise and Fall of Socialism* (San Francisco: Encounter Books, 2002).

3   David Gelles, "Millions at Top, A Pittance Below," *New York Times*, May 27, 2018, Sunday Business section, pp. B1ff.

4   Bernard Shaw, *The Intelligent Woman's Guide to Socialism and Capitalism* (New York: Brentano's Publishers, 1928), p. 22.

5   See, for example, "The Celebrity 100 Turns 20," *Forbes*, August 31, 2018, pp. 26–27. See also "The World's Highest-Paid Entertainers," Ibid., pp. 106–107.

6   Derek Sayer, *The Coasts of Bohemia: A Czech History* (Princeton: Princeton University Press, 1998), p. 90.

7   See, for example, Donald L. Horowitz, *Ethnic Groups in Conflict* (Berkeley: University of California Press, 1985), pp. 219–224; Myron Weiner and Mary Fainsod Katzenstein, *India's Preferential Policies: Migrants, the Middle Classes, and Ethnic Equality* (Chicago: University of Chicago Press, 1981), p. 98; Robert N. Kearney, *Communalism and Language in the Politics of Ceylon* (Durham: Duke University Press, 1967), Chapter III; Donald L. Horowitz, *The Deadly Ethnic Riot* (Berkeley: University of California Press, 2001), pp. 278–282.

8   See, for example, Derek Sayer, *The Coasts of Bohemia*, pp. 50, 115–116; Gary B. Cohen, *The Politics of Ethnic Survival: Germans in Prague, 1861–1914* (Princeton: Princeton University Press, 1981), pp. 42, 239–241; Paul Vysny, *Neo-Slavism and the Czechs, 1898–1914* (Cambridge: Cambridge University Press, 1977), pp. 15, 16.

9   Eve Haque, *Multiculturalism Within a Bilingual Framework: Language, Race, and Belonging in Canada* (Toronto: University of Toronto Press, 2012), pp. 47–49.

10   Donald L. Horowitz, *The Deadly Ethnic Riot*, pp. 279–280.

11   Ibid., pp. 280–282; Stephen May, "Language Rights and Language Repression," *The Oxford Handbook of Language Policy and Planning*, edited by James W. Tollefson and Miguel Pérez-Milans (Oxford: Oxford University Press, 2018), p. 245.

12   John McWhorter, *Talking Back, Talking Black: Truths About America's Lingua Franca* (New York: Bellevue Literary Press, 2017), pp. 12, 13.

13   Melanie Kirkpatrick, "Business in a Common Tongue," *Wall Street Journal*, August 28, 2017, p. A15.

14   David Deterding, *Singapore English* (Edinburgh: Edinburgh University Press, 2007), pp. 4–5; Sandra L. Suárez, "Does English Rule? Language Instruction and Economic Strategies in Singapore, Ireland, and Puerto Rico," *Comparative Politics*, Vol. 37, No. 4 (July 2005), pp. 465, 467–468.

15   Malcolm Gladwell, *Outliers: The Story of Success* (New York: Little, Brown and Company, 2008), pp. 89–90. See also Joel N. Shurkin, *Terman's Kids: The Groundbreaking Study of How the Gifted Grow Up* (Boston: Little, Brown & Company, 1992), p. 35; Wolfgang Saxon, "William B. Shockley, 79, Creator of Transistor and Theory on Race," *New York Times*, August 14, 1989, p. D9; J.Y. Smith, "Luis Alvarez, Nobel-Winning Atomic Physicist, Dies," *Washington Post*, September 3, 1988, p. B6.

16   William S. Maltby, *The Rise and Fall of the Spanish Empire* (New York: Palgrave Macmillan, 2009), p. 18; Peter Pierson, *The History of Spain* (Westport, Connecticut: Greenwood Press, 1999), pp. 7–8.

17   John H. Chambers, *A Traveller's History of Australia* (New York: Interlink Books, 1999), p. 35.

18   Leon Volovici, *Nationalist Ideology and Antisemitism: The Case of Romanian Intellectuals in the 1930s*, translated by Charles Kormos (Oxford: Pergamon Press, 1991), p. 60.

19   "Not One But Two New Malay Dilemmas," *Straits Times* (Singapore), August 1, 2002.

20   Joseph Rothschild, *East Central Europe between the Two World Wars* (Seattle: University of Washington Press, 1992), p. 385.

21   Irina Livezeanu, *Cultural Politics in Greater Romania: Regionalism, Nation Building, & Ethnic Struggle, 1918–1930* (Ithaca: Cornell University Press, 1995), pp. 30–31, 235–236, 241.

22   John M. Richardson, "Violent Conflict and the First Half Decade of Open Economy Policies in Sri Lanka: A Revisionist View," *Economy, Culture, and Civil War in Sri Lanka*, edited by Deborah Winslow and Michael D. Woost (Bloomington: Indiana University Press, 2004), pp. 63–65.

23   Carl K. Fisher, "Facing up to Africa's Food Crisis," *Foreign Affairs*, Fall 1982, pp. 166, 170.

24   W. E. B. Du Bois, *The Philadelphia Negro: A Social Study* (Philadelphia: University of Pennsylvania Press, 1996), p. 395. Generations later, Professor Edward C.

Banfield posed essentially the same question by asking what the outcome would be if all blacks suddenly turned white. His answer was very similar to the answer given earlier by Du Bois. Edward C. Banfield, *The Unheavenly City Revisited* (Prospect Heights, Illinois: Waveland Press, 1990), pp. 85–86.

25 Victor Purcell, *The Chinese in Southeast Asia*, second edition (Kuala Lumpur: Oxford University Press, 1965), p. 184; U. S. Bureau of the Census, *Historical Statistics of the United States: Colonial Times to 1970* (Washington: Government Printing Office, 1975), Part 1, p. 422.

26 Henry Morgenthau, *Ambassador Morgenthau's Story* (Garden City, New York: Doubleday, Page & Company, 1919), pp. 301, 322.

27 See, for example, Paul Johnson, *A History of the Jews* (New York: Harper & Row Publishers, 1987), pp. 216–217; Michael Miller, "The Ukraine Commission of the Joint Distribution Committee, 1920, with Insight from the Judge Harry Fisher Papers," *Jewish Social Studies*, Vol. 49, No. 1 (Winter 1987), pp. 53–60.

28 Empirical studies have demonstrated the negative consequences of admitting students under group quotas to academic institutions whose standards they do not meet, whether in the United States or elsewhere. See, for example, Richard Sander and Stuart Taylor, Jr., *Mismatch: How Affirmative Action Hurts Students It's Intended to Help, and Why Universities Won't Admit It* (New York: Basic Books, 2012), and my own *Affirmative Action Around the World: An Empirical Study* (New Haven: Yale University Press, 2004). An attempt to vindicate such group preferences— *The Shape of the River: Long-Term Consequences of Considering Race in College and University Admissions* (Princeton: Princeton University Press, 1998), by William G. Bowen and Derek Bok— was widely acclaimed in the media but, among its major flaws was that its authors refused to reveal the raw data on which its statistical conclusions were based.

29 Thomas Sowell, *Wealth, Poverty and Politics*, revised and enlarged edition (New York: Basic Books, 2016), pp. 396–399.

30 Alison Stewart, *First Class: The Legacy of Dunbar, America's First Black Public High School* (Chicago: Lawrence Hill Books, 2013), pp. 91–93.

31 Ibid., p. 90.

32 See "Success Academy: #1 in New York," downloaded from the website of Success Academy Charter Schools: http://www.successacademies.org/app/uploads/2017/08/sa_1_in_new_york.pdf.

33 "The NAACP's Disgrace," *Wall Street Journal*, October 17, 2016, p. A14; "A Misguided Attack on Charter Schools," *New York Times*, October 13, 2016, p. A24; "The NAACP vs. Minority Children," *Wall Street Journal*, August 27, 2016, p. A10; Emma Brown, "School Choice Is Not the Answer, NAACP Asserts," *Washington Post*, July 27, 2017, p. A14.

34 Jervis Anderson, "A Very Special Monument," *The New Yorker*, March 20, 1978, pp. 93, 113, 114.

35 Mats Hammarstedt, "Assimilation and Participation in Social Assistance Among Immigrants," *International Journal of Social Welfare*, Vol. 18, Issue 1 (January 2009), pp. 86, 87.

36 Silje Vatne Pettersen and Lars Ostby, "Immigrants in Norway, Sweden and Denmark," *Samfunnsspeilet*, May 2013, p. 79.

37 Mats Hammarstedt, "Assimilation and Participation in Social Assistance Among Immigrants," *International Journal of Social Welfare*, Vol. 18, Issue 1 (January 2009), pp. 87, 89.

38 Tino Sanandaji, "Open Hearts, Open Borders," *National Review*, January 26, 2015, p. 25.

39 Richard Milne, "Swedish Prime Minister Baffled by Public Gloom," *Financial Times* (London), April 12, 2016, p. 10.

40 Tino Sanandaji, "Open Hearts, Open Borders," *National Review*, January 26, 2015, p. 25.

41 Hugh Eakin, "Scandinavians Split Over Syrian Influx," *New York Times*, September 21, 2014, Sunday Review, page 4.

42 Peter Nannestad, "Immigration as a Challenge to the Danish Welfare State?" *European Journal of Political Economy*, Vol. 20, Issue 3 (September 2004), p. 760.

43 Christopher Caldwell, "A Swedish Dilemma," *Weekly Standard*, February 28, 2005, p. 21.

44 Ibid., p. 22.

45 Ruud Koopmans, "Trade-Offs Between Equality and Difference: Immigration Integration, Multiculturalism and the Welfare State in Cross-National Perspective," *Journal of Ethnic and Migration Studies*, Vol. 36, No. 1 (January 2010), p. 19.

46 Christopher Caldwell, "Islam on the Outskirts of the Welfare State," *New York Times Magazine*, February 5, 2006, p. 58.

47 Thomas Sowell, *Wealth, Poverty and Politics*, revised and enlarged edition, pp. 110–115.

48 Victor Purcell, *The Chinese in Southeast Asia*, second edition, pp. 128, 268–269, 540.

49 Carlo M. Cipolla, *Clocks and Culture: 1300–1700* (New York: Walker and Company, 1967), pp. 66–69.

50 Lucy Forney Bittinger, *The Germans in Colonial Times* (Philadelphia: J.B. Lippincott Company, 1901), p. 233.

51 Pyong Gap Min, *Caught in the Middle: Korean Communities in New York and Los Angeles* (Berkeley: University of California Press, 1996), p. 1.

52 Oli Smith, "Migrants at War," *Express.UK* (Online), January 28, 2017.

53 John Stuart Mill, *Principles of Political Economy*, edited by W.J. Ashley (New York: Longmans, Green and Company, 1909), p. 947.

54 John Larkin, "Newspaper Nirvana? 300 Dailies Court India's Avid Readers," *Wall Street Journal*, May 5, 2006, pp. B1, B3; "Poverty," *The Economist*, April 21, 2007, p. 110; "Unlocking the Potential," *The Economist*, June 2, 2001,

p. 13; Charles Adams, "China—Growth and Economic Reforms," *World Economic Outlook*, October 1997, pp. 119–127.

55   Daniel Yergin and Joseph Stanislaw, *The Commanding Heights: The Battle Between Government and the Marketplace That Is Remaking the Modern World* (New York: Simon & Schuster, 1998), pp. 35–38, 140, 167, 171–172; Surjit S. Bhalla and Paul Glewwe, "Growth and Equity in Developing Countries: A Reinterpretation of the Sri Lankan Experience," *World Bank Economic Review*, Vol. 1, No. 1 (September 1986), pp. 35, 36, 51–52, 53, 61.

56   Thomas C. Leonard, *Illiberal Reformers: Race, Eugenics & American Economics in the Progressive Era* (Princeton: Princeton University Press, 2016), pp. 158–164.

57   Thomas Nagel, "The Meaning of Equality," *Washington University Law Review* Volume 1979, Issue 1 (January 1979), p. 28.

58   On July 13, 2012, President Barack Obama made a speech in which he stated: "If you were successful, somebody along the line gave you some help. There was a great teacher somewhere in your life. Somebody helped to create this unbelievable American system that we have that allowed you to thrive. Somebody invested in roads and bridges. If you've got a business— you didn't build that. Somebody else made that happen." "You Didn't Build That," *Wall Street Journal*, July 18, 2012, p. A14. Elizabeth Warren had made similar remarks in August 2011 during her campaign for the U.S. Senate: "There is nobody in this country who got rich on his own. Nobody! You built a factory out there— good for you! But I want to be clear: You moved your goods to market on the roads the rest of us paid for. You hired workers the rest of us paid to educate. You were safe in your factory because of police forces and fire forces that the rest of us paid for. You didn't have to worry that marauding bands would come and seize everything at your factory . . . because of work the rest of us did." Jeff Jacoby, "Entrepreneurs Don't Deserve the Professor's Ire," *Boston Globe*, September 28, 2011, p. A13.

59   See, for example, John Katzman and Steve Cohen, "Let's Agree: Racial Affirmative Action Failed," *Wall Street Journal*, October 27, 2017, p. A15.

60   There is much evidence that the ostensible beneficiaries of affirmative action in college admissions have been negatively affected in many ways. See, for example, Richard Sander and Stuart Taylor, Jr. *Mismatch*, Chapters 3, 4, 6. A brief summary of some of their key findings can be found in Thomas Sowell, "The Perversity of Diversity," *Claremont Review of Books*, Fall 2012, pp. 76–78. For documented examples of the social backlash, both in the United States, and in India, see Thomas Sowell, *Inside American Education: The Decline, the Deception, the Dogmas* (New York: Free Press, 1993), Chapter 6; Thomas Sowell, *Affirmative Action Around the World*, pp. 17–18, 50, 148–149.

61   Stephan Thernstrom and Abigail Thernstrom, "Reflections on *The Shape of the River*," *UCLA Law Review*, Vol. 46, No. 5 (June 1999), p. 1589.

62   "Going Global," *The Economist*, December 19, 2015, p. 107. See also M.A. Tribe, "Economic Aspects of The Expulsion of Asians from Uganda," *Expulsion of a Minority: Essays on Ugandan Asians*, edited by Michael Twaddle (London:

281

The Athlone Press for the Institute of Commonwealth Studies, 1975), pp. 140–176.

63 Amy Chua and Jed Rubenfeld, *The Triple Package: How Three Unlikely Traits Explain the Rise and Fall of Cultural Groups in America* (New York: The Penguin Press, 2014), pp. 36–39.

64 Nathan Glazer, *American Judaism* (Chicago: University of Chicago Press, 1957), p. 13.

65 David S. Landes, *Revolution in Time: Clocks and the Making of the Modern World* (Cambridge, Massachusetts: Harvard University Press, 1983), pp. 237–238; Warren C. Scoville, "The Huguenots and the Diffusion of Technology II," *Journal of Political Economy*, Vol. 60, No. 5 (October 1952), p. 408.

66 Cacilie Rohwedder, "Germans, Czechs Are Hobbled by History as Europe Moves Toward United Future," *Wall Street Journal*, November 25, 1996, p. A15; Ulla Dahlerup, "Sojourn in Sudetenland," *Sudeten Bulletin/Central European Review*, December 1965, pp. 395–403.

67 "Your Mine Is Mine," *The Economist*, September 3, 2011, p. 64.

68 See, for example, Orlando Patterson, *Slavery and Social Death: A Comparative Study* (Cambridge, Massachusetts: Harvard University Press, 1982), p. 176; Stanley L. Engerman, *Slavery, Emancipation & Freedom: Comparative Perspectives* (Baton Rouge: Louisiana State University Press, 2007), pp. 3, 4; William D. Phillips, Jr., *Slavery from Roman Times to the Early Transatlantic Trade* (Minneapolis: University of Minnesota Press, 1985), pp. 46, 47; Ellen Churchill Semple, *Influences of Geographic Environment* (New York: Henry Holt and Company, 1911), p. 90; R.W. Beachey, *The Slave Trade of Eastern Africa* (New York: Barnes & Noble Books, 1976), p. 182; Harold D. Nelson, et al., *Nigeria: A Country Study* (Washington: U.S. Government Printing Office, 1982), p. 16; Christina Snyder, *Slavery in Indian Country: The Changing Face of Captivity in Early America* (Cambridge, Massachusetts: Harvard University Press, 2010), pp. 4, 5; T'ung-tsu Ch'ü, *Han Social Structure*, edited by Jack L. Dull (Seattle: University of Washington Press, 1972), pp. 140–141.

69 William D. Phillips, Jr., *Slavery from Roman Times to the Early Transatlantic Trade*, pp. 34, 59; Martin A. Klein, "Introduction: Modern European Expansion and Traditional Servitude in Africa and Asia," *Breaking the Chains: Slavery, Bondage, and Emancipation in Modern Africa and Asia*, edited by Martin A. Klein (Madison: University of Wisconsin Press, 1993), p. 15.

70 See, for example, Andrew Cockburn, "21st Century Slaves," *National Geographic*, September 2003, pp. 2–25; "Slaves to Its Past," *The Economist*, July 21, 2018, p. 36; Simon Robinson and Nancy Palus, "An Awful Human Trade," *Time*, April 30, 2001, pp. 40–41; "Slave Trade in Africa Highlighted by Arrests," *New York Times*, August 10, 1997, Foreign Desk, p. 9.

71 Paul Krugman, *The Conscience of a Liberal* (New York: W.W. Norton & Company, 2007), p. 11.

72   Adam Smith, *An Inquiry into the Nature and Causes of the Wealth of Nations* (New York: Modern Library, 1937), p. 365.

73   Robert C. Davis, *Christian Slaves, Muslim Masters: White Slavery in the Mediterranean, the Barbary Coast, and Italy, 1500–1800* (New York: Palgrave Macmillan, 2003), p. 23; Philip D. Curtin, *The Atlantic Slave Trade: A Census* (Madison: University of Wisconsin Press, 1969), pp. 72, 75, 87.

74   Monique O'Connell and Eric R. Dursteler, *The Mediterranean World: From the Fall of Rome to the Rise of Napoleon* (Baltimore: Johns Hopkins University, 2016), p. 252. See also Robert C. Davis, *Holy War and Human Bondage: Tales of Christian-Muslim Slavery in the Early-Modern Mediterranean* (Santa Barbara: Praeger, 2009), pp. 87–89; Fernand Braudel, *The Mediterranean and the Mediterranean World in the Age of Philip II*, translated by Siân Reynolds (New York: Harper & Row, 1972), Vol. I, p. 130; Fernand Braudel, *The Mediterranean and the Mediterranean World in the Age of Philip II*, translated by Siân Reynolds (New York: Harper & Row, 1973), Vol. 2, pp. 845–849.

75   Edmund Burke, *Reflections on the Revolution in France and Other Writings*, edited by Jesse Norman (New York: Alfred A. Knopf, 2015), p. 549.

ACKNOWLEDGEMENTS

1   "The whole science of anthropo-geography is as yet too young for hard-and-fast rules, and its subject matter too complex for formulas." Ellen Churchill Semple, *Influences of Geographic Environment* (New York: Henry Holt and Company, 1911), p. 125.

2   Ibid., p. 7.

3   Despite Professor Semple's many examples of how geographic isolation can leave a people lagging far behind the progress of the rest of the world, she also pointed out situations in which a certain amount of geographic isolation could be protective during "the early development of a people." Ellen Churchill Semple, *American History and Its Geographic Conditions* (Boston: Houghton, Mifflin and Company, 1903), p. 36.

4   N.J.G. Pounds, *An Historical Geography of Europe 1800–1914* (Cambridge: Cambridge University Press, 1985), p. 1.

5   Ibid., p. 43.

Index

INDEX